W9-BTP-499

JOSEPHUS AND THE NEW TESTAMENT

JOSEPHUS
and the New Testament

● ●

STEVE MASON

HENDRICKSON
PUBLISHERS
PEABODY, MASSACHUSETTS 01961-3473

ISBN 0–943575–99–0

Second printing — November 1993

Library of Congress Cataloging-in-Publication Data

Mason, Steve, 1957–
    Josephus and the New Testament   /   Steve Mason
        p.   cm.
    Includes bibliographical references and indexes.
    ISBN 0–943575–99–0 (pbk.)
    1. Josephus, Flavius.   2. Jewish historians—Biography.
3. Bible.   N.T.—Biography.   4. Bible.   N.T.—Criticism, interpretation, etc.   I. Title
DS115.9.J6M38   1992
933′.05′092—dc20   92-33067
                                                                              CIP

For Glenna, Cara, and Ian,
the joys of my life

Table of Contents

Introduction: The Purpose of This Book

When I first became interested in Josephus a dozen years ago, I was discussing my new passion with a lawyer friend who also had a strong, though not professional, interest in the New Testament world. He said, "I must sit down some time and read Josephus right through, from cover to cover." We have since lost touch and I don't know whether his ambition was ever fulfilled, but I doubt it. "Reading Josephus through" is a daunting task and probably not the most efficient way to come to terms with the ancient author. When visiting a new city, we first buy a map of the place in order to orient ourselves, so that we get some idea of the "big picture." This book is intended as a kind of map to the world of Josephus—his life, thought, and writings—for readers of the New Testament. I offer it to all those who have bought or borrowed the works of Josephus, out of a keen interest in the New Testament world, only to feel frustrated at the obscurity of his writings.

Every student of the Bible realizes that Josephus is extremely significant for New Testament study. He was born in AD 37, just a few years after Jesus' death and not much later than Paul's conversion to Christianity. He grew up in Jerusalem and was intimately acquainted with the religion of Israel, its temple and its feasts, at one of which Jesus was arrested. He knew a lot about the important background figures in the Gospels—King Herod and his sons, Roman governors like Pontius Pilate, the Pharisees and Sadducees—and he was a priest himself. Having worked for a time in Jesus' home region of Galilee, he wrote in detail about its fertile landscape and social conditions. Josephus was reaching maturity at about the time that the apostle Paul was imprisoned and sent to Rome; he even moved to Rome within a decade of Paul's execution there, though under circumstances very different from Paul's. Finally, Josephus did not write solely about events of his own day but reached back to begin his story where the "Old Testament"[1] had ended, so his writings provide abundant examples of how the Old Testament was interpreted by Jewish contemporaries of Jesus and Paul.

Thus Josephus' works offer us a potential gold mine for understanding the world of the New Testament as well as being a resource that is not even remotely paralleled in another ancient writer. If his writings had not survived, Bible dictionaries would all be pocketbook size, and textbooks on the background of the New Testament would have little to tell us. We would still have the considerable archaeological work of the last twenty-five years, to be sure, but physical remains do not speak for themselves; even here, Josephus has been the archaeologist's constant companion, suggesting where to look and how to interpret what is found.

Here is where the problems begin. Although everyone realizes the *value* of Josephus' writings, not many are able to sit down and read through them with profit. I confess to having fallen asleep a few times while working through some lengthy digression—and Josephus likes to digress. So I suspect that, in spite of the fact that his collected works continue to sell in the tens of thousands every year, they mainly gather dust on the shelves of the ministers, rabbis, seminarians, and interested lay people who purchase them.

The reasons for this neglect are clear enough. First, his writings are extensive—somewhat longer than the Old Testament and more than four times the size of the New. Second, they often seem to ramble endlessly, especially the lethargic *Antiquities,* which paraphrases the entire Old Testament story in its first half and then continues with subsequent Jewish history. Readers looking for immediate enlightenment on the background of early Christianity are apt to find much in Josephus that is annoyingly trivial or irrelevant. Third, the most popular English text of Josephus today was translated in 1737 by William Whiston. Although Whiston's translation and accompanying essays were a tremendous achievement in the early eighteenth century, today's reader gets the feeling that they are themselves "period pieces" from the remote past. To make matters worse, Whiston's Josephus is usually printed in double columns, and with the books arranged out of order (*Life* first, *Antiquities* second, *War* third, *Against Apion* last). Even the twentieth-century translation made for the Loeb Classical Library is quickly becoming dated. And no matter how good the translation, the substance of Josephus remains a challenge to the most curious investigator. The result is that Josephus' works often suffer the same fate as the King James Version of the Bible: a perennial bestseller, much loved, occasionally quoted, hardly ever read.

Professional analysts of Josephus are aware of these problems and, in the past few years, have taken some important steps to provide students with the necessary "maps." Some have reissued portions of his works in attractive formats which include scholarly commentaries, such as the Penguin edition of the *Jewish War* (translated by G. A. Williamson, 1981) and the beautifully illustrated edition by Gaalya Cornfeld and others (1982).

Two authors have written very useful introductions to Josephus. Tessa Rajak, a classical historian, published *Josephus: The Historian and His Society* in 1983. And Per Bilde's *Josephus Between Jerusalem and Rome: His Life, His Works, and Their Importance* appeared in 1988. We would not be academics if we did not disagree on minor points, but these two books are exemplary introductions. Both are quite readable, and I recommend them to interested students. (Though Bilde leaves some French and German quotations untranslated, these are not extensive enough to prevent the English speaker from understanding.) They serve to update a series of lectures given by H. St. John Thackeray in the 1920s, published as *Josephus: The Man and The Historian* (1927), which are themselves still worth reading.

More adventurous readers might also want to tackle two recent collections of essays on Josephus edited by Louis H. Feldman and Gohei Hata. Entitled *Josephus, Judaism, and Christianity* (1987) and *Josephus, the Bible, and History* (1988), respectively, these two volumes provide an outstanding survey of current research by the world's leading scholars. The project was commissioned by a Tokyo press to accompany Professor Hata's translation of Josephus' writings into Japanese, to apprise Japanese readers of the "state of the art" in Josephan studies. These English originals of the translated essays are sometimes heavy going for the general reader, with sprinklings of untranslated Latin, Greek, and Hebrew, but they will reward the patient student. When I refer to particular essays from these volumes I shall cite them as *JJC* and *JBH*, to avoid repeating the full titles of each book.

Louis Feldman has also compiled a series of annotated bibliographies to Josephus which are categorized by subject. These are superb reference works, since they give not only the title of the book or article in question, but also in most cases a summary of its contents. Most important are Feldman's thousand-page *Josephus and Modern Scholarship (1937–1980)*, published in 1984, and his more recent article, "A Selective Critical Bibliography of Josephus," in *JBH*, pp. 330–448.

The book in your hands was not written because of any deficiency in the materials just mentioned. It simply has a different focus. This book was written explicitly for students of the New Testament and its world who want to know how to approach Josephus so that he will shed light on the New Testament texts. It will draw heavily from recent research on Josephus' life and writings, especially in chapters 2 and 3. But whereas that research forms the core of the studies mentioned above, we shall focus our attention on matters of direct relevance to New Testament interpretation.

Chapter 1, "The Use and Abuse of Josephus," sets the stage by sketching out how Christian readers have usually read Josephus, arguing that this method is inappropriate. Scholars, too, come under some criticism in their use of the ancient writer. I argue that the best approach is to try to meet Josephus as a person from the first century, to enter his world of thought and language, and to deal with the issues that were of importance to him. Only then can we understand him.

This does not mean that we cannot ask him about things that interest us as readers of the New Testament, but only that we should read his answers in the context of his own thought-world, and not manipulate his statements for our purposes. So chapters 2 and 3, while discussing his life and writings, outline some major features of his thought-world, especially his assumptions about writing history and his view of religion. We shall look also at key words in his vocabulary to get a feeling for his "world view."

Chapter 4 applies our stated approach to some prominent groups in the background of the New Testament: the family of King Herod, the Roman governors, the Jewish high priesthood, and the Pharisees and Sadducees. Our goal is not, in the first instance, to learn the historical truth about these issues; rather, we need first to ask how Josephus, a real person with his own biases, understood them. Chapter 5 continues in the same direction, but now with the major figures of the early Christian world who are mentioned by Josephus, namely: John the Baptist, Jesus, and Jesus' brother James.

In chapter 6, I take up the fascinating question of the relationship between Josephus' works and the two NT volumes known as "The Gospel of Luke" and the "Acts of the Apostles." I demonstrate there some striking parallels of structure, aim, and vocabulary between Josephus and Luke–Acts, and then ask how those parallels are best explained.

A concluding chapter draws together the main lines of the book and reflects on the "Significance of Josephus for New Testament Study." It is my contention that, if we try to understand him as a real person from the first-century Jewish world, our reading of the Christian scriptures will at least be greatly enriched, if not radically changed.

To avoid the appearance of making false promises, academics often like to state in advance what they are *not* intending to do. The ritual is meant primarily for the eyes of specialist readers (and reviewers!). First, this book does not seek to provide an objective summary of the current state of scholarship on the issues it touches, much less a history of scholarship. Since every account is also an interpretation, such objectivity is neither possible nor desirable. In any case, my goal is to help the beginning student encounter Josephus. I shall certainly draw upon those scholarly insights that seem helpful in this project, but I make no attempt at either systematic presentation or rebuttal of others' arguments. Interested readers will find that sort of thing in the journal articles and monographs mentioned.

Likewise, I have tried to use the footnote sparingly, so that the reader is not faced with reading two books at the same time—the one in the text and the one in the notes. My goal has been to reserve the notes for essential explanations of unusual terms and for crediting scholars with absolutely peculiar ideas.

Otherwise, the scholarly works will be cited *en bloc* at the end of each chapter (under "For Further Reading"). Although a vast amount of modern scholarship on Josephus is in languages other than English, I have usually referred only to English titles. The few exceptions are some truly seminal works written in other languages, which informed readers should know about even if they cannot consult them at the moment.

In short, the book before you is not the "last word" on Josephus; it is intended to be more of a *first* word. It will be a success, in this writer's view, if it provides some shape and contour to what might otherwise seem like bewildering terrain, and thereby stimulates the reader to explore more fully the writings of Josephus.

NOTES

1. I use quotation marks because for Josephus, as for Jesus and the early Christians, there was no "old" testament. What we call the Old Testament was, of course, their Bible. The Christian writings that would later come to be collectively called the "new testament" were being written about the time of Josephus, but he seems not to have known of them. In any case, even for Christians they were not considered "scripture" until at least a century after their time of writing.

I have assumed that the reader has a copy of both the NT and Josephus' writings alongside this text. That assumption excuses me from quoting extensively from either collection, which would have made the book a considerable burden to carry. References to classical authors, including Josephus, follow the "Loeb Classical Library" (LCL) scheme wherever possible. Readers using the Hendrickson Publishers edition of Josephus will find these section numbers in parentheses, supplementing Whiston's chapter divisions. In those places where I have quoted from the NT, the translations are mine. In the case of Josephus, I have often translated shorter segments—to bring out some particular nuance; otherwise, I have deferred to the LCL standard, as the references indicate.

1

The Use and Abuse of Josephus

In modern English, when we speak of "using" people, we often mean abusing them—exploiting them for some selfish benefit while disregarding their personal integrity. I believe this is precisely what has happened to the legacy of Flavius Josephus in the nineteen hundred years since he lived: he has been widely *used* but little understood and seldom appreciated as an intelligent author. And this exploitation has come at the hands of both religious and scholarly communities. The last two decades have brought some welcome changes, however, and a major goal of this book is to convey the significance of those changes to the NT reader. Let me explain.

Most of the thousands of books that were written in the ancient world did not survive into the Middle Ages, let alone into the modern world. In the absence of paper, printing presses, and photocopiers, it was not a foregone conclusion that any given book would live beyond its author's own generation. The stationery of the period, usually papyrus but also parchment,[1] was susceptible to rapid deterioration in humid weather. This meant that a work had regularly to be recopied by hand if it were to endure. Therefore, only those texts that enjoyed a lively readership or some sort of official sponsorship could remain "in print." Only such committed readers would invest the necessary effort to copy lengthy documents by hand.

Initially, Josephus owed his literary survival to government sponsorship. His account of the Jewish revolt against Rome (AD 66–74) was officially sanctioned by the Roman emperors Vespasian and Titus, who ordered that it be deposited in the imperial library in Rome. His subsequent writings seem to have enjoyed the same treatment (*Life* 428–29). These rulers, from the "Flavian" dynasty, even honored the Jewish historian with a prominent statue in Rome.[2] And their endorsement was enough to ensure that his writings were maintained in Roman libraries and recopied in public *scriptoria,*[3] until the decline of the empire.

What, then, enabled Josephus' works to persevere beyond the collapse of the empire? The decisive factor was the Christian church's appropriation of the Jewish historian's writings. Two famous church leaders in particular, Origen (d. 254) and Eusebius (d. 340), cited Josephus extensively in their writings and thus popularized his works in Christian circles. By the time that the central power of the Roman empire began to falter, in the late fourth century, the world had officially embraced Christianity. It was the church, with its own infrastructure, that would rise from the ashes of the empire to preserve the Greco-Roman heritage. So the church's attachment to Josephus assured him an ongoing role in Western tradition.

WHY JOSEPHUS' WRITINGS WERE PRESERVED

But why were Christian authors so attached to Josephus? Already by the late second century AD, some Christian writers had become interested in the famous Jewish author for several reasons. First, his writings provided extraordinary background information for the reader of early Christian writings, especially the Gospels. Many of the characters and places mentioned in those works in passing are elaborately discussed by Josephus, for example: the wicked King Herod and his sons Archelaus and Antipas; the Roman prefect Pontius Pilate; the high priests Ananus (or Annas) and Caiaphas; the temple in Jerusalem, which provided the scene for Jesus' arrest; the region of Galilee, where Jesus lived and taught; the Samaritans; and the Pharisees and Sadducees who opposed Jesus. For second-century Christians far removed from tiny Judea and its politics, Josephus' writings had much the same fascination as they have held for every subsequent generation of Christian readers. They filled in a vast amount of history between the close of the Old Testament and the birth of Christianity.

Especially valuable for Christian readers were Josephus' discussions, brief though they were, of John the Baptist, Jesus' brother James, and Jesus' own career. As we shall see, it is almost certain that Josephus' paragraph on Jesus has been edited by Christian copyists, but the editing was done early on, by about AD 300. Consequently, subsequent Christian readers thought that the glowing account of Jesus in our versions of Josephus had been written by the Jewish historian himself. Josephus' descriptions of the Baptist and of James' death seem to have remained intact. Naturally, these short passages were highly valued. Since Christianity had not made a major impression on either the Jewish or larger Greco-Roman worlds in the first century, and since no other writers from that period mention the Christians,[4] these few references were seen as crucial independent testimony to the historical foundations of the church.

It is one of history's paradoxes that Josephus enjoyed a surge of popularity at the time of the Christian "crusades" in the twelfth century, because of his detailed information about Palestinian geography. Beginning in 1096, Christian soldiers marched from all over Europe to wrest Jerusalem from the Muslims, who had administered the city since the seventh century. (The crusaders were ultimately unsuccessful.) Many crusaders took copies of Josephus' writings with them as a kind of tour guide to the holy land. But these same Josephus-toting crusaders thought nothing of stopping off along the way to Jerusalem to butcher Josephus' coreligionists—the men, women, and children in the Jewish communities of several European cities—for being "Christ-killers." This contradiction between a high valuation of Josephus (for historical and geographical detail) and an utter inattention to what he was saying (an explanation and defense of Judaism) is a consistent feature of the Christian misuse of Josephus.

A second reason for the early church's interest in Josephus was that he seemed to offer help with the Christians' pressing social-political predicament. That predicament stemmed from the novelty of Christianity: in a culture that respected what was old and established, Christianity seemed to be a new religion—a contradiction in terms for Roman thinking!—for it worshiped as Lord someone who had been quite recently executed by the Roman authorities, in the humiliating way reserved for trouble-making provincials (crucifixion), and in a backwater province no less. Strangest of all, this new faith had neither a national center nor an ethnic character, unlike the familiar religions of Greece, Egypt, Phrygia, Persia, and Syria. In what seemed to be a most antisocial stance, it even prohibited its members from participating in local festivals on the grounds that those celebrations inevitably involved sacrifice to the traditional gods. And because Christians met in private homes, at night, where men and women greeted each other with kisses and then partook of "body and blood," all sorts of lurid rumors circulated about their behavior. Just as medieval Christians would later accuse the Jews of sacrificing children at Passover, so the early Christians were charged with promiscuity and cannibalism.[5]

Josephus was indirectly helpful to the young church on this score because he had faced something of the same animosity toward his nation and religion. Although Judaism did have a national and ethnic base, and though most Greco-Roman authors seem to have recognized the antiquity of the Jews, there was still a fair amount of misinformation about Jewish origins and customs. A large part of Josephus' concern had been to defend Judaism against charges that it was merely a corrupt derivation of Egyptian religion and that it practiced immorality, including human sacrifice. Especially in his *Jewish Antiquities* and *Against Apion*, he had sought to demonstrate his nation's long and noble history, to show that its "constitution" espoused the highest standards of morality, and to explain the Jewish belief in "one God only" (monotheism) in a way that would both deflect charges of anti-social propensities and appeal to philosophically minded readers.

All of this apologetic effort was extremely useful to Christian spokesmen. Most early Christians tended to see themselves as the "true Israel," as heirs to the biblical tradition. The church's apologists, therefore, were quick to see the value of Josephus' *Against Apion*, which gently chided Greco-Roman morality and religion while eloquently arguing the superiority of biblical ethics. This work became something of a model for Christian self-representation to the Greco-Roman world, especially with Origen, who wrote a book called *Against Celsus* that drew extensively from Josephus' *Against Apion*.[6]

Without question, however, the most compelling source of Josephus' appeal to early Christians was his detailed description of the Roman siege and destruction of Jerusalem in AD 68–70. Of all the Christian references to Josephus that have survived from the ancient world and Middle Ages, the passage most commonly cited from his works, next to his reference to Jesus, is one that describes a horrible act of cannibalism during the Roman siege.[7] A formerly wealthy woman named Mary, he claims, took refuge with her infant son in Jerusalem during its final days. Faced with starvation because of the scarcity of food within the besieged city, this aristocratic woman took her son and ate him (*War* 6.201–213). It may seem peculiar to modern Christians that this grisly detail should have so awakened the church's interest, but it did. Christian authors cited it even more often than Josephus' important references to John the Baptist or to Jesus' brother James. This little story was chosen for illustration in medieval editions of Josephus' works and was reenacted in Christian plays.[8] Largely because of this brief episode and a few others, Josephus' book on the unsuccessful Jewish revolt, the *Jewish War*, was much more interesting to early Christians than his *Jewish Antiquities*, which contains the references to Jesus, John the Baptist, and James. Some explanation is necessary.

It has been a standard feature of Christian preaching through the ages that the Roman destruction of Jerusalem in 70 was really God's decisive punishment of the Jewish people for their rejection of Jesus, who had died around the year 30. The earliest Christian sermon that we possess, outside of the NT, is largely a tirade against the Jews for their treatment of Jesus. Melito, bishop of Sardis in the late 100s, declares that the Jewish people and its scripture became an "empty thing" with the arrival of Christianity and the gospel (*Passover Sermon* 43); only those Jews who believe in Jesus have any ongoing religious validity. Melito accuses the Jews as a nation of having "murdered" Jesus and asserts that their current suffering (after 70 and a further failed revolt in 132–135) is a consequence: "You cast the Lord down, you were cast down to earth. And you, you lie dead, while he went up to the heights of heaven" (*Passover Sermon* 99–100).

Not long after the year 200, Bishop Hippolytus of Rome reflected in the same vein:

Why was the temple made desolate? Was it on account of the ancient fabrication of the calf? Or was it on account of the ancient idolatry of the people? Was it for the blood of the prophets? .... By no means, for in all these transgressions, they always found pardon open to them. But it was because they killed the Son of their Benefactor, for He is coeternal with the Father (*Against the Jews* 7).

Origen, who taught in the early 200s, pointedly restated the theme:

I challenge anyone to prove my statement untrue if I say that the entire Jewish nation was destroyed less than one whole generation later on account of these sufferings which they inflicted on Jesus. For it was, I believe, forty-two years from the time when they crucified Jesus to the destruction of Jerusalem. . . . For they committed the most impious crime of all, when they conspired against the Savior of mankind, in the city where they performed the customary rites which were symbols of profound mysteries. Therefore, that city where Jesus suffered these indignities had to be utterly destroyed. The Jewish nation had to be overthrown, and God's invitation to blessedness transferred to others, I mean to the Christians, to whom came the teaching about the simple and pure worship of God.[9]

Eusebius, a Christian author of the early 300s, made the same sort of claims in his *Ecclesiastical History,* which became an extremely influential document for subsequent generations of Christians; his history fixed many aspects of the Christian understanding of history until the modern period. Speaking of the fall of Jerusalem in 70, he asserts that Christians fled the city so that "the judgement of God might at last overtake them for all their crimes against the Christ and his Apostles, and all that generation of the wicked be utterly blotted out from among men" (*Eccl hist* 3.5.3, trans. K. Lake, LCL). Similar sentiments are found in such notable authorities as Minucius Felix, John Chrysostom, and Augustine, not to mention many lesser figures.

Obviously, Christian fascination with the destruction of the temple and the fate of the Jews was not a matter of merely antiquarian interest. As we have seen, Christians saw the "death" of the Jews as the necessary condition for the birth of Christianity. These authors leave no doubt that the church took over the heritage of God's covenant from the Jews, who then more or less disappear from the scene. This theological interpretation of Jerusalem's fate explains why the Christian authors tended to view the events of 70 as a total or near-total destruction of the Jews, when, in reality, most Jews lived outside of the Jerusalem region by the first century.[10] The large Jewish communities of Rome, Alexandria, Greece, Asia Minor, and Babylonia were not physically affected by the events of 70. In those places, and even in Palestine itself after the war, Judaism continued to thrive; hence its vigorous existence today. But the church fathers spoke of the death or destruction of the Jews for symbolic reasons: to support their contention that God's grace had passed from Judaism to the church. Far from being an incidental event in history, the fall of Jerusalem to the Romans provided a critical foundation for Christian self-understanding.

The common interpretation of Jerusalem's fall as God's punishment of the Jews continued to flourish throughout the Middle Ages. By then it was part of popular Christian culture and not just the property of theologians. From the ninth to the fifteenth centuries, a recurring theme of plays and novels was "The Revenge of our Lord," in which the Roman conquest was triumphantly reenacted. Several French communities produced such plays on a regular basis, to complement their "passion" plays, in which the Jews were charged with Jesus' death. By the time of Martin Luther, the great reformer who initiated what would become "Protestant" Christianity, the Christian interpretation of Jerusalem's capture had long been fixed. His tract on "The Jews and their Lies" reflects the common view: the Romans were God's instruments, punishing the Jews for their "delusions regarding their false Christ and their persecution of the true Christ."[11] (In that same tract, Luther advocates that Jews be deprived of normal civil rights, that their property and books be burned, and that they be herded together in forced labor camps.)

This brief sketch of traditional Christian attitudes toward the Jews and the destruction of Jerusalem in 70, which could easily be expanded, helps to explain why Josephus' writings, and especially his *Jewish War*, were so popular among Christian theologians. Although the Jewish historian did not make any connection between Jesus' death and the fall of Jerusalem, his writings provided detailed corroboration of the horrors that the Jews suffered forty years after Jesus' death. The episode of Mary's cannibalism was so popular because it showed (for Christian apologists) the depths to which the Jews had sunk, allegedly as a result of their rejection of Jesus.

It was perhaps inevitable that, once Josephus' works were known, his *Jewish War* would be exploited for details of the Jewish catastrophe. Melito of Sardis probably already knew something of Josephus, for he includes a reference to the cannibalism episode to illustrate the depravity of non-Christian humanity (*Passover Sermon* 52). But the pivotal figures in the Christian adoption of Josephus were Origen and Eusebius. Both of these men had traveled extensively throughout the Roman world; both had visited the city of Rome itself, where Josephus' works were maintained in the libraries; and both lived for some time in Caesarea, the coastal city of Josephus' native Palestine. Because of these unusual opportunities, both men were able to read Josephus at first hand, so they both saw the potential in his works for Christian adaptation.

In addition to his borrowing from Josephus for the *Against Celsus*, Origen cites him in his Bible studies on Lamentations, in which he discusses among other things the fall of the Jewish temple. In that discussion, he claims that Josephus had researched the cause of the debacle and had attributed it to the Jews' execution of Jesus' brother James around the year AD 62. This is a considerable distortion. In reality, Josephus' writings are peppered with various reasons for the city's fall; any conspicuous violation of the Mosaic law or Jewish custom is a candidate. He does express horror at the unlawful treatment of James (*Ant.* 20.200–201) but does not isolate this episode as a reason for the destruction. Rather, it is one of a number of infractions, including the bestowal of unprecedented privileges on the Levites (!), that he lists as causes of the later punishment. So Origen significantly misleads his readers in claiming that Josephus attributed the fall of Jerusalem to James' mistreatment.

In any case, Origen himself pointedly disagrees with Josephus. He criticizes the Jewish historian for not realizing that it was the Jew's part in Jesus' death, not James', that brought about the "annihilation" (as he says) of the Jewish people: "If, therefore, he says that the destruction of Jerusalem happened because of James, would it not be more reasonable to say that this happened on account of Jesus the Christ?" (*Ag. Celsus* 1.47). Evidently Origen distorted Josephus' account because Josephus' real explanation of Jerusalem's fall would not have served his purpose (see below). By pretending that Josephus had cited James' death as the cause, he pulls the Jewish historian into the Christian orbit, where he appears to be at least "close to the truth."

It is in support of his claim that Jerusalem fell in retribution for Jesus' death that Origen cites Josephus' account of the horrors suffered by the Jews during the war. He dwells in particular on the cannibalism episode, which he sees as fulfilling Lam 4:10 (*Fragmenta in Lamentationes* 105). But he also mentions Josephus' claim that, some months before the destruction, strange voices were heard in the temple, saying "We are departing from here" (Josephus, *War* 6.299–230). Origen interprets these voices as those of the angels who supervised the temple activities. He sees their departure as the definitive moment of collapse for the whole temple regime and Judaism itself (*Lam* 109).

In a similar way Eusebius, a student of Origen's writings, uses Josephus to bolster his theological interpretation of the fall of Jerusalem. He sets down his thesis in his *Ecclesiastical History* 3.5, first by alleging that the Jews compounded their guilt after Jesus' death: "After the Ascension of our Saviour in addition to their crime against him the Jews at once contrived numerous plots against his disciples" (3.5.2). Having established a litany of Jewish sins, including the stoning of Stephen and the execution of James (son of Zebedee), he argues that the Jews suffered increasing calamities as punishment. He concludes: "Those who wish can retrace accurately from the history written by Josephus how many evils at that time overwhelmed the whole nation, . . . how many thousands of youths, women, and children perished by the sword" (3.5.4).

Significantly, Eusebius decides to focus his account on the starvation faced by the Jews who were trapped in Jerusalem during the siege, "in order that those who study this work may have some partial knowledge of how the punishments of God followed close after them for their crime against the Christ of God" (3.5.7). Thus he proceeds to quote verbatim several pages from Josephus concerning the misery faced by the Jews during the Roman siege. His concentration on the starvation of the Jews allows him to bring up Josephus' heart-rending story of Mary's cannibalism (3.6.20–28). Immediately after this climactic episode (for Eusebius), he concludes: "Such was the reward of the iniquity of the Jews for their crime against the Christ of God" (3.7.1).

But if the destruction of Jerusalem was punishment for the Jews' treatment of Jesus, why did it not occur until forty years after the crucifixion? Aware of the problem, Eusebius responds that God suspended his justice for forty years both because of the presence of the apostles, who protected the city by their presence, and in order to provide the Jews with a suitable opportunity for repentance (3.7.8–9). God even sent warnings of the coming catastrophe if the Jews did not repent. These warnings are the omens mentioned by Josephus, and Eusebius confidently refers the reader to the Jewish author as an external witness. But Josephus himself does not connect the omens with Jesus in any way.

Eusebius takes over Origen's distortion about Josephus' attributing the destruction of Jerusalem to the death of James, but he is bold enough to manufacture the missing passage. We have seen that Josephus did not link the fall of Jerusalem specifically to James' death, although Origen implied that he did. Eusebius, however, actually quotes Josephus: "Of course Josephus did not shrink from giving written testimony to this, as follows: 'These things happened to the Jews to avenge James the Just, who was the brother of Jesus' " (*Eccl hist* 2.23.20). We see here how easily traditions can corrupt the truth, as in the child's game of "broken telephone."

Two other significant distortions on Eusebius' part deserve mention. First, when speaking of Philo's accounts of anti-Jewish activities in Alexandria, he remarks, "Josephus confirms him [Philo], showing in the same way that the universal misfortunes of the nation began with the time of Pilate and the crimes against the Saviour" (*Eccl hist* 2.6.3, LCL). This is a serious misrepresentation, for it implies that Josephus himself cited crimes against Jesus as a cause of punishment, or at least that troubles began at the death of Jesus. Josephus in fact traces the beginnings of the Jews' problems to the rise of the freedom party, or "fourth philosophy," in AD 6 (*War* 2:118; *Ant.* 18:3–10).

Eusebius' other noteworthy distortion is his implication that the fall of Jerusalem occurred at Passover. He finds this significant because he wants to draw a parallel with Jesus' death, which had also occurred at Passover:

> It was indeed right that on the same day on which they had perpetrated the passion of the Saviour and Benefactor of all men and the Christ of God they should be, as it were, shut up in prison and receive the destruction which pursued them from the sentence of God (3.5.6).

The problem with this neat scheme is that Josephus carefully dates the various stages of the war and makes it plain that the temple finally fell in late September (by our calendar, *War* 6.392, 407), whereas the Passover feast was in the spring. Josephus does note that those who had come for Passover in the spring were trapped in the city when war broke out in earnest, and some had to stay for the duration. But several months went by before the end came. Eusebius has evidently collapsed the dates in order to strengthen the symbolic connection that he wants to make between Jesus' death and the destruction of the temple. In his hands, we see Josephus already well on the way to becoming a kind of quasi-Christian because of the support he seemed to offer for Christian claims.

The need to domesticate or "Christianize" Josephus is most obvious in a Latin paraphrase of his *Jewish War* that was written around 370. By this time, Latin had become the common language of the Western empire (not only for Roman governmental use as it had been in the first century), and so a translation of Josephus was deemed necessary. The author of this adaptation takes over much of Josephus' work bodily, but, like Origen and Eusebius, the writer criticizes Josephus for failing to see that the real cause of Jerusalem's destruction was the Jewish role in Jesus' death. So this author, usually known as Hegesippus, takes the opportunity to rewrite Josephus from a Christian perspective, so that his writings will suit the church's position even more exactly. In his preface, he acknowledges Josephus' usefulness but claims that he was too Jewish in his outlook. He was:

> an outstanding historian, if only he had paid as much attention to religion and truth as he did to the investigation of facts and moderation in writing. For he shows himself to be sympathetic to Jewish faithlessness even in the very things he sets forth about their punishment (1.1).[12]

In other words, although Josephus wrote the *Jewish War* to explain the causes of the temple's destruction, he failed to see the true (i.e., Christian) interpretation. The author of Hegesippus will not make such a mistake:

> And so that no one will think I have undertaken a useless task, or one of no value to the Christian faith, let us consider the whole race of the Hebrews embodied in its leaders . . . (1.3).

The Jewish race, he wants to demonstrate, is "depraved" and has lost its place in the story of salvation. He intends to use Josephus' account to show what Josephus had not shown, namely, that in the fall of Jerusalem the Jews "paid the penalty for their crimes, because after they had crucified Jesus they persecuted his disciples" (2.12).

A telling example of the way in which Hegesippus' Christian outlook determines his subsequent narrative is his rendering of a scene in which Cestius Gallus, the Roman governor of Syria, withdraws his troops from the attack on Jerusalem in the autumn of 66, after the very first Roman attempt to quell the revolt.[13] Josephus had expressed wonder at this withdrawal because (a) if Cestius had pressed the attack, the whole war could have been won then and there, and (b) the Jewish rebels' victory over the withdrawing Roman troops (whom they successfully ambushed and massacred) gave them a false sense of strength, which emboldened them to prosecute the war more vigorously. As to why Cestius decided to retreat when he was not in peril, Josephus hints that the Syrian commander had been bribed by the governor of Judea, who wanted to see the Jews utterly annihilated (*War* 2.531). His more religious explanation is that "God, I suppose, because of those miscreants [i.e., the relatively few rebels, whom Josephus despises], had already turned away even from His sanctuary and ordained that that day should not see the end of the war" (*War* 2.539).

When Hegesippus took over this story, however, he reworked it significantly by offering a Christian theological explanation for Cestius' withdrawal:

> The will of God delayed the imminent end of the war until the ruin could involve much—almost all—of the Jewish race. God expected, I think, that the enormity of their [the Jews'] crimes would increase until, by the heaping up of impropriety, it would equal the measure of his supreme punishment (2.15).

We find here once again the erroneous claim that virtually all of the "Jewish race" was in Jerusalem during the siege. This assertion can only be explained on theological grounds, for it permits the Christian writer to dispense with Judaism as an ongoing reality. God wiped out the heart and soul of Judaism in 70; the few that remain witness to the truth of Christianity by their homeless suffering. Whereas Josephus himself had spoken from within Judaism, as its passionate spokesman and defender *after 70,* Hegesippus took that portrayal and used it to depict the Jews as a destroyed nation.

To summarize thus far: Josephus' writings were preserved from antiquity by the Christian church for several reasons. They provided a lot of useful background information, a paraphrase of the Old Testament, a valuable model for apologetics, and even some brief references to key figures in the birth of Christianity. But the single most important factor was their detailed description of the atrocities that accompanied the Jewish revolt against Rome and the destruction of the temple. Josephus' vivid account of the war seemed ample proof of the Christian belief that the Jews had become God's enemies by rejecting Christ and persecuting his followers. Eusebius' role in the preservation of Josephus was thus pivotal, for he made him the key "outside" witness for his Christian interpretation of history. We know that other accounts of Jewish history and Palestinian geography survived the first century and that some even lasted to the ninth century. But when decisions were made about which ancient texts should continue to be copied, the respected authority Eusebius' glowing endorsement of Josephus secured him a privileged position.[14] Other major works, like those by Josephus' rival Justus of Tiberius or the massive history by Nicolaus of Damascus, lacked such impressive endorsement; consequently, they have survived only in fragments.

PROBLEMS WITH THE TRADITIONAL USE OF JOSEPHUS

I hope that the foregoing survey of how and why Josephus' works were preserved will explain what I mean when I say that the ancient author has usually been abused. He wrote, as we shall see, in order to explain Judaism to outsiders and to demonstrate its virtues in a world that was often hostile. But Christian authors took over his most self-critical work, in which he castigates a small number of Jews for their failure to live up to the standards of Judaism, and turned that work against the Jewish people as a whole, thus exactly reversing Josephus' intention. His writings were treated not as the production of an intelligent human mind but as a mine of data that could be excerpted willy-nilly to produce a new document such as that of Hegesippus. His elaborate treatment of the causes of the Jewish revolt was entirely ignored by his Christian interpreters; most neglected of all was his impassioned defense of Judaism. In Josephus we have an example of vigorous post-70 Judaism; yet his Christian adapters used him, with scant regard for his own purposes, to argue that Judaism had been overthrown in 70. By putting in his mouth statements that were contrary to his intention, they grotesquely distorted the very source that they prized for its witness to the truth of Christianity.

An obvious problem is that the Christian interpretation of Jerusalem's fall is diametrically opposed to Josephus' own view. In effect, the Christian claim was that the Jews suffered for being so stubbornly "Jewish," that is, for clinging to their ancestral traditions and not responding to the gospel concerning Jesus. Josephus argued, however, that Jerusalem fell because some Jews were not Jewish enough: they did not act in accord with their tradition, but rebelled against the power that God had ordained for that era (the Romans), permitted the sacred temple to be polluted with murder, and caused the interruption of the sacrificial regimen. Josephus, a priest, expressed repeated concern for scrupulous, punctilious observance of the divine laws. Accordingly, he attributed the fall of Jerusalem to the people's failure to keep the laws, whereas the Christians charged the Jews with failing to abandon the laws of Moses in favor of Christ.

In making his case, Josephus considers himself to stand in the long line of prophets (though he would not call himself a "prophet") who had threatened Israel with punishment, back in biblical times, for its laxity in keeping the divine teaching or "torah." [15] Notice how the Old Testament accounts for the fall of the first temple, which was built by Solomon. Jeremiah repeatedly warned of disaster because the people had disobeyed God's commands. Their crimes included worship of other nations' gods (Jer 17:1–4) but also, and equally grievous, carrying water jugs and lighting fires for warmth and cooking on Saturday, the sabbath (17:21–27). In short, the people had not scrupulously maintained the terms of the covenant; these terms occupy the greater part of Exodus through Deuteronomy and include much more than the "ten commandments." When the disaster finally came in 586 BC, and Solomon's temple was destroyed, the prophets inferred that it was God's means of punishing the people for having departed from the worship of the one God of Israel. Ezekiel, Nehemiah, and Daniel all confess that ever since the divine teachings were given to Moses, the people have lapsed from their observance, and that is why Jerusalem and its great temple have been destroyed (Ezek 20:4–44; Neh 9:12–37; Dan 9:4–14). When the Jews were permitted by the Persians to return to their land and rebuild their temple in the late sixth century BC, they naturally took this opportunity as a second chance from God. So they begged forgiveness for past errors and resolved scrupulously to adhere to the divine teachings. They took "an oath with sanctions to follow the Teaching of God, given through Moses the servant of God, and to observe carefully all of the commandments of the LORD our Lord, His rules and laws" (Neh 10:30, JPS).

In explaining the fall of the "second temple," Josephus has largely taken over the model provided by the Old Testament prophets. He wants to portray himself as a latter-day Jeremiah, lamenting the fall of the city and the sins that caused it. Needless to say, the prophets had not mentioned faith in Jesus as a criterion of righteousness, and neither does Josephus. It is the Christian interpretation that introduces a new claim: the Jews were punished for having killed Jesus and for not being his followers. They did not accept Jesus as their Lord.

This variance in explaining the fall of Jerusalem shows how difficult it is to infer cause from sequence—to say: "Y came after X; therefore, Y was caused by X." There is simply no way to prove such claims to be either true or false. They will be convincing only to those who already believe the proposition being advanced. That is because any number of X's (here, pre-70 events) might be cited as potential causes. For example, some Romans said that the temple fell because of the wrath of *their* gods, who were angry at the Jews because of their rebellion against Rome. The second-century philosopher Celsus asserted that the destruction of Jerusalem decisively proved the weakness of the God worshiped by both Jews and Christians; the Roman victory, by implication, proved that the traditional Greco-Roman gods were more powerful and worthy of worship. Significantly, Celsus also adduced the miserable plight of second-century Christians (who were under regular threat of discovery and execution) as evidence of the futility of Christian worship.[16] So it was somewhat inconsistent for Christian authors, when the church had finally won imperial recognition and security in the fourth century, to cite the destruction of Jerusalem and the plight of the Jews (which was deliberately worsened by the legislation of Christian rulers) as proof of Jewish guilt and Christian truth.

Before leaving this matter of the early church's misuse of Josephus to bolster its interpretation of the fall of Jerusalem, we need to admit that such an interpretation also suffers from serious moral objections. It ought to be given up, lock, stock, and barrel. What I mean is that the traditional Christian view rests on the principle of "collective responsibility," thus: all Jews of all times and places share the guilt of a very few, who acted two thousand years ago. In the first place, the standard is unevenly applied. For if the Jewish Sanhedrin was involved in Jesus' crucifixion, it had somewhere between twenty-three and seventy-one members—a group small enough, apparently, to fit in the high priest's home (Mark 14:53; 15:1).[17] But the Roman governor Pilate and his entourage, according to the Gospels, also had a crucial share in Jesus' death. Crucifixion was a Roman (not Jewish) punishment, and Pilate was the one who passed and executed the sentence. His soldiers beat and mocked Jesus, and it was they who hung him on the cross. How then is it that no one has ever accused *any* Italians, of *any* generation, of being "Christ-killers," while the charge has been *relentlessly* leveled against the Jews? Where are the church fathers' sermons denouncing Romans? On the contrary, Pilate became "in his secret heart already a Christian," who had allegedly written a glowing account of Jesus to the emperor.[18]

Second, the whole concept of collective responsibility is repugnant because it involves indiscriminate revenge: anybody with certain religious or genetic characteristics becomes morally responsible for the actions of all others with those features. In view of normal life expectancy in the first century, it is unlikely that many of the sages who were involved in Jesus' death, about the year 30, were still active or even alive when the temple was destroyed in 70. If hundreds of thousands of men, women, and children died in that catastrophe to punish their fathers and grandfathers, how is that just? It is extremely unlikely that any of the magistrates involved in Jesus' death were still alive when Melito preached in the late second century, yet he addresses Israel in the second person as if it had a single corporate personality: "You, on the contrary, voted against your Lord. The nations worshiped him. The uncircumcised [i.e., non-Jews] marveled at him. . . . Even Pilate washed his hands in this case. This one you did to death on the great feast" (*Passover Sermon* 92). Evidently Melito and the later Fathers had forgotten the words of Ezekiel seven centuries before:

> The person that sins, he alone shall die. A child shall not share the burden of a parent's guilt, nor shall a parent share the burden of a child's guilt; the righteousness of the righteous shall be accounted to him alone, and the wickedness of the wicked shall be accounted to him alone (Ezek 18:20, cf. 2–4, JPS).

The tenacity of the claim that Jerusalem fell as punishment for "the Jews' " treatment of Jesus, the incredible energy devoted to this matter over the centuries, and the Christian lack of interest in the Roman involvement in Jesus' death call for an explanation. But that would take us too far afield. It is enough for now if we recognize the problem and resolve not to engage in the same sort of polemics.

So far we have seen that the customary use of Josephus by Christian authors has been doubly abusive: first, his material has been wrenched out of its narrative setting, so that his own story has been lost. Second, that material has been used to tell another story—one that he did not espouse. My contention is that readers of the NT need not resort to these traditional devices, which are really cheap tricks, in order to make Josephus' writings useful. They do not need to rewrite him or baptize him as a Christian. It is a sign of maturity when we stop trying to make everyone into clones of ourselves (whether they be our students, children, or employees) and begin to appreciate them for who they are. We are invariably rewarded when we make the effort to encounter another person in his or her integrity. We need to do the same sort of thing with Josephus. If we will read him as a genuine, first-century, Jewish author, with his own concerns and interests, our reading of the NT will be greatly enriched.

JOSEPHUS AND JUDAISM

One would think that, if Christian transmitters of Josephus had completely ignored his Jewish identity, Jewish readers at least would have noticed and appreciated it. But strangely enough, this did not happen. Jewish responses to Josephus have always been ambivalent at best, because of his personal history.

The key point is that Josephus seems to have abandoned his own people in their fateful hour, in a conflict that would spell the end of the temple and, ultimately (in AD 135), the disbarment of Jews from Jerusalem.[19] Sent to Galilee as a regional commander in the revolt, he capitulated to the Romans when they besieged his base at Jotapata. He not only surrendered, but went so far as to become a friend of the Romans, speaking on their behalf during the remainder of the war. After the war, he was granted Roman citizenship and a generous pension by the emperor, and it was in these circumstances that he wrote his account of the revolt, which includes lavish praise of the imperial family and relentless castigation of the Jewish rebels (though not of the Jews as a whole). Consequently, Jews have traditionally tended to see him as a traitor to the Jewish people.

In the next chapter, we shall look more closely at how Josephus saw the revolt and at some possibly mitigating factors in his actions. But even from his own writings it is clear that he surrendered under highly questionable conditions. He was keenly aware of a principle that Jewish commanders ought to fight to the death (*War* 3.400; *Life* 137), and some of his attempts to justify himself are patently phony. In his own account, he seems to confess his deceitfulness in trying to flee the besieged Jotapata (*War* 3.193–201).

In any event, from the moment of his surrender until his death, he faced relentless hatred from his compatriots. Some tried to have him executed, while others wrote accounts of his wartime behavior that challenged his own self-vindicating portrayal (*War* 3.438; 7.447–450; *Life* 425; cf. 40, 336). Understandably, the cozier he became with the Romans—the military conquerors of the Jews—the more detestable he became to his people. And when this Jewish historian was posthumously adopted by the church, which claimed that he had even declared Jesus to be the Messiah—the same church that immediately passed laws restricting Jewish civil rights, relegating Jews to second-class status as "Christ-killers," and using Josephus to support their claims—his fate was sealed. His name does not appear in either version of the voluminous Talmud, which was finally edited in the fifth and sixth centuries, or in any other early Jewish writing.[20]

Josephus' perceived cowardice would also prevent him from achieving respect in modern Jewish circles, particularly in view of the Zionist movement, which took root in the late nineteenth century and culminated in the creation of Israel in 1948. A nation built on the determination to survive against all odds had no place for someone who could so easily surrender, accept luxurious privileges from enemies, and then serve those enemies' propaganda aims. So Jewish writers of the modern period, and more than a few Gentiles, have routinely denounced him as a traitor.[21]

On the other hand, the sheer wealth of historical information offered by Josephus has necessarily commanded at least grudging respect among all those who are interested in either biblical interpretation or post-biblical history. Already in the middle of the tenth century, when Jewish scholarship was flourishing in southern Italy, someone from the region was motivated to translate Josephus' writings into Hebrew. This version of his *War* and *Antiquities* 1–16 proved extremely popular and was itself recopied and translated into several languages. Known as "Josippon," from a corruption of Josephus' name, this text was used extensively by medieval Jewish commentators to illuminate their interpretation of the Bible and Talmud.[22]

In modern times too, especially since the capture of East Jerusalem in 1967 and the resultant flourishing of Israeli archaeology, Josephus has become an indispensable guide to first-century Palestinian geography. He has proven particularly helpful on the matter of King Herod's building projects, which once covered the land and now provide a major focus of modern archaeology. Since this archaeological effort is in part a function of the nationalist agenda (to demonstrate Jewish roots in the land), Josephus has paradoxically become an ally of the Zionist cause. While his personal history is deplored in some Jewish literature, his writings are still valued as unparalleled sources of history.[23]

Josephus' perceived betrayal of the Jewish people has loomed so large that his obvious devotion to Judaism and enthusiastic defense of Jews against common slanders in the Greco-Roman world have received relatively little attention in Jewish scholarship until recently. Whereas traditional Christian readers had disregarded his Jewish perspective because they found it distasteful, Jewish readers often dismissed it as an artificial ploy meant to deflect the hostility that he faced from his own people. In both cases, his fundamental viewpoint was lost to the world.

SCHOLARS' MISTREATMENT OF JOSEPHUS

Before we discuss Josephus' writings and outlook, fairness demands a quick word about the *scholarly* mistreatment of Josephus, for the academic community, too, has until recently tended to wrench Josephus' statements out of their original context and exploit them for its own purposes.

The intensive historical study of Josephus, as of the NT and early Judaism, took flight in the middle of the nineteenth century. These branches of study were based in Germany, where there was a remarkable awakening of scholarly interest in the ancient world. Professors began to produce massive reference works in their efforts to recover as much information as possible about ancient life and language. Numerous manuals, encyclopedias, lexicons, atlases, and dictionaries appeared, and serious archaeological work was begun in the

Mediterranean countries. Although scholars of preceding centuries had already tried to reconstruct the original Greek texts of the NT and Josephus, by comparing the many manuscripts that had survived, scholars of the nineteenth century saw a renewed and much more painstaking effort along those lines, based in part on recent discoveries of new manuscripts.

It was in this atmosphere that Emil Schürer wrote his magisterial text, *A Manual of New Testament Background History* (1874), which later became *The History of the Jewish People in the Age of Jesus Christ* (1886–90). This manual was so influential that it has been updated, translated into English, and reissued in recent years. For Schürer, naturally, Josephus' writings were a major source of information. Yet his method of treating the ancient author was sometimes alarming. He regularly cited Josephus' isolated statements as if they were "facts," which could be combined with other facts (i.e., statements of other writers or archaeological evidence) to produce a whole picture. For example, Schürer opens his discussion of the Pharisees with a collection of passages from Josephus, combined with fragments from other sources, and then proceeds to weld these together into a coherent whole. He fails to take into account, however, that Josephus' remarks can be understood only in the context that Josephus gave them, for words have meaning only in context. Josephus wrote lengthy stories, not digests. If we want to know what he meant to say about the Pharisees, we must read his remarks about them as part of his story, paying careful attention to his use of language. We cannot simply pull them out and combine them with statements from other people who had entirely different stories to tell and who used language in different ways.

Schürer's method is often called the "scissors-and-paste" style of history. Although everyone today realizes that it doesn't work, in principle, we all find ourselves drifting into it from time to time. We still see authors, some of whom would insist on interpreting passages from, say, the Gospels, within their narrative contexts, ripping chunks out of Josephus and citing them as "raw data" or facts—as if they were the product of a robot and not a real human mind with a story to tell.

Examples abound. (a) One commentator has argued that, since Josephus mentions "fate" in his discussions of the Jewish groups, and since fate was generally understood in antiquity in astrological terms, as an inescapable and oppressive power, Josephus must be implying that Judaism offers deliverance from fate (as some other religions claimed for themselves).[24] A careful reading of Josephus, however, would show that he speaks positively of fate and considers the recognition of it a religious duty. (b) Several scholars in recent years have tried to distill from Josephus' narratives, which claim to deal with Jewish history up to the war with Rome, some insight into *post-war* Jewish history.[25] They propose that when Josephus speaks well of some group in the past (e.g., high priests, Herodians, Pharisees), he really means to advance the interests of the group's post-war heirs. Although he does not say so, he is an advocate in the internal Jewish politics of his own day. But this kind of analysis is somewhat arbitrary: it cannot account for most of the praise and blame that Josephus assigns, since most of his characters have no obvious post-war representatives (e.g., the kings of ancient Israel and the Hasmoneans). In general, such proposals pay scant regard to his own theses. Scholarly impatience can even lead to the misinterpretation of his intended blame as praise.[26] In effect, then, modern scholars have shared to some degree in the traditional failure to listen carefully enough to Josephus' own story.

Another approach to Josephus that has effectively denied his personality is "source-critical" analysis. This method was extremely popular from about 1880 to 1920, when much of the fundamental work on Josephus was accomplished. Now source analysis is an essential part of historical study because it asks the important question: Where did this author acquire his or her information? Since most of the events Josephus discusses occurred either before his lifetime or outside of his personal experience, it is crucial for us to know where he obtained his information if we are to determine its value. But what tended to happen in the heyday of source criticism was that *everything* in Josephus was attributed to some source, with the result that scholars lost interest in Josephus himself.[27] For example, scholars claimed that Josephus took his paraphrase of the Old Testament (in *Ant.* 1–11) from someone else, ready-made, so they had no interest in trying to see what that paraphrase revealed about Josephus' own thought. If he wrote differently about such figures as Herod the Great in *War* and *Antiquities*, that must have been because he used different sources in the two works, not because he changed his mind or had different purposes in writing the two books. Or if he sometimes expressed great admiration for the Hasmoneans, he must have found those passages in a "pro-Hasmonean source," even though he claimed in his autobiography to be a proud descendant of the Hasmoneans (*Ant.* 16:187; *Life* 2). This kind of criticism was taken to such an extreme that even Josephus' reports about things that he certainly knew first-hand—e.g., his discussions of groups like the Sadducees, Essenes, and Pharisees—were attributed to his sources.

Once again, most scholars today would repudiate such a thoroughgoing source criticism, one that ignored Josephus' own intelligence as an author; but those early treatments still wield a considerable influence, and we occasionally find modern scholars falling into the same way of thinking.

Since the late 1960s, a new and much more realistic approach to Josephus has taken root, and it seems to be reinforced with almost every new study that appears. What unifies this newer scholarship is the realization that Josephus was, more or less, the author of his own literary productions. He wrote with a purpose and accommodated his material (extensively borrowed from other sources, to be sure) to his own agenda. He used words, as we all do, in a distinctive way. A team of scholars has now produced *A Complete Concordance to Flavius Josephus*, which enables us to trace his characteristic vocabulary. His writings can also be searched electronically, by computer. It turns out that he had pet phrases and themes that he liked to emphasize. Recent studies of his paraphrase of the Old Testament have shown that he carefully worked over the biblical story to serve his larger purposes. From his earliest to his latest writings, his "world view" remains remarkably consistent.

This is not to deny that he was sloppy at times, that he sometimes went off on tangents, that he contradicted himself in some places and dissembled in others. All of these things are to be expected with an ancient author of such extensive writings, who had such a controversial past. In my view, they make Josephus particularly intriguing. But none of this excuses us from taking him seriously as a person from another time and place who had something to say about his world.

CONCLUSION

We find ourselves in the peculiar position of being grateful that Josephus' works did survive, while at the same time regretting the primary reason for their survival—as a rod with which to beat the Jews. Josephus himself was a Jew and, to borrow from Sinatra, "not in a shy way." Paradoxically, although he was probably the most influential (non-biblical) Jewish writer of all time, his intended meaning was not influential at all, with either Jews or Christians. On the contrary, it was completely inverted. Even when the religious maltreatment of Josephus subsided, the poor fellow was largely abused by the academic world, which also tended to fragment his writings into little bits of data. As a result it has taken us the better part of two thousand years to begin reading what Josephus actually wrote.

The new willingness to listen to Josephus' own voice has been greatly facilitated by a new academic atmosphere. Since World War II, Jewish, Christian, and other scholars have begun an unprecedented adventure in cooperative scholarship within university departments of religious studies. This cooperation has meant that we can no longer use as proof things that would only convince our own constituencies, but must discuss history in a public way—with proof that is universally compelling. If we cannot appeal to our own traditions for our interpretations of Josephus, we must finally read what he had to say for himself. When we do that, remarkably enough, we can agree to a large extent about what he was up to.

I hope that the following chapters will begin to show how truly useful Josephus can be for readers of the NT, when we try to engage him as an authentic person with something to say. The next chapter will introduce his life, writings, and world of thought. After that we shall explore particular issues in Josephus' works that are of interest to NT readers, attempting in each case to relate the passage or theme to his larger concerns.

FOR FURTHER READING

On the earliest Roman impressions of Christianity, see:

- Molly Whittaker, *Jews and Christians: Graeco-Roman Views* (Cambridge University Press, 1984).

- Robert Wilken, *The Christians as the Romans Saw Them* (New Haven: Yale University Press, 1984).

- Stephen Benko, *Pagan Roman and the Early Christians* (Bloomington: Indiana University Press, 1986).

On the position of the Jews in Western (Christian) history, see:

- Marcel Simon, *Verus Israel: A Study of the Relations between Christians and Jews in the Roman Empire (135–425)* (Littman Library of Jewish Civilization; Oxford: Oxford University, 1986).

- Wayne A. Meeks and Robert L. Wilken, *Jews and Christians in Antioch in the First Four Centuries of the Common Era* (SBL Sources for Biblical Study 13; Missoula: Scholars, 1978).

- Jacob R. Marcus, *The Jew in the Medieval World: A Source Book: 315–1791* (New York: Atheneum, 1975).

- Rosemary Ruether, *Faith and Fratricide: The Theological Roots of Anti-Semitism* (New York: Seabury, 1974).

On the transmission of Josephus' writings, the most complete studies are in German, by Heinz Schreckenberg of Münster. But *JJC* includes a brief summary essay by Schreckenberg in English translation, called "The Works of Josephus and the Early Christian Church," pp. 315–24. It also contains several important essays on the Christian use of Josephus, pp. 325–426. They deal with Origen, Josephus' passage on Jesus, Hegesippus, Josephus in Byzantium, the illustration of Josephus' manuscripts through the Middle Ages, and Martin Luther. An accessible essay on the Hebrew Josippon is:

- D. Flusser, "*Josippon*, a Medieval Hebrew Version of Josephus," *JJC*, 386–97.

NOTES

1. Paper made from wood pulp was not introduced into the Western world until the late Middle Ages. Papyrus, its ancient precursor, was made from strips of the papyrus reed, laid side by side and pressed together in double thickness.

2. This statue was known still to the fourth-century historian Eusebius (*Eccl hist* 3.9.2). Cf. Bilde, *Flavius Josephus*, 60.

3. A scriptorium was an ancient copying room for the mass production of books. A reader would stand in front of a group of scribes and read aloud, slowly, from the master text. The scribes would listen carefully and copy what they heard. Needless to say, this method, which remained in effect until the invention of the printing press in 1454, could result in all sorts of errors, because of sound-alike words or sleepy scribes. That is why the first stage in the scholarly study of any ancient work—Josephus, the New Testament, or Plato—is the "reconstruction" of what the author really wrote, based on a careful comparison of the various scribal copies that have come down to us.

4. The first Roman authors to mention the Christians were Pliny the Younger, Tacitus, and Suetonius, all of whom wrote in the second decade of the second century.

5. The earliest surviving reference to Christianity by a Roman comes in Pliny's letter to Trajan concerning the Christians (10.96). Writing in about AD 111, Pliny assumes that Christians practice cannibalism and other crimes. A full description of the vices attributed to Christians is given by the character Caecilius in the *Octavius* of Minucius Felix, 8–10 (early third century). See the first three items under "For Further Reading."

6. Cf. Wataru Mizugaki, "Origen and Josephus," *JJC*, 334.

7. In Heinz Schreckenberg, *Die Flavius-Josephus-Tradition in Antike und Mittelalter* (Leiden: E. J. Brill, 1972), 186–203, there is a list of known references to Josephus through the Middle Ages.

8. Cf. Guy N. Deutsch, "The Illustration of Josephus' Manuscripts," *JJC*, 408–9.

9. Origen, *Contra Celsum* (trans. and ed. H. Chadwick; Cambridge: Cambridge University Press, 1965), 198–99.

10. Cf. Albert A. Bell, Jr., "Josephus and Pseudo-Hegesippus," *JJC*, 354.

11. *Luther's Works* (ed. Helmut T. Lehmann and Jaroslav Pelikan; St. Louis: Concordia, 1955–1986, 56 vols., 47:233; cited in Betsy Halpern Amaru, "Martin Luther and Flavius Josephus," *JJC*, 418. Compare also Luther's "Lectures on the Psalms," ibid., vol. 13, 258.

12. From Albert A. Bell, "Josephus and Pseudo-Hegesippus," *JJC*, 352–53.

13. I owe this example to the essay by Albert Bell, ibid., p. 354.

14. Cf. Stephen Bowman, "Josephus in Byzantium," *JJC*, 365–68.

15. The Hebrew word *torah* means "instruction" or "teaching." It is the expression used in the Old Testament for the terms of the covenant received from God by (especially) Moses. Although often rendered "law," in English translation, the word conveys a much more comprehensive scope and positive nuance than we tend to associate with "laws." See, for example, the psalmist's exultation over the "laws" in Ps 119, which may seem strange to English readers.

16. For obvious reasons, Celsus' writings were not thought worthy of preservation during the Christian Middle Ages. They are known to us only in fragments quoted by Origen in his tract *Against Celsus*. These are conveniently accessible in Molly Whittaker, *Jews and Christians*, 185.

17. See the Mishnah (a compendium of Jewish law compiled in about AD 200), tractate Sanhedrin 1:4–5.

18. See Tertullian, *Apology* 21.24 (and 5.2); compare the second-century *Gospel of Peter* 1–24, 46; Eusebius, *Eccl hist* 2.2.1; and the apocryphal *Acts of Pilate*.

19. A second major Jewish revolt against Rome, from 132 to 135, resulted in the total destruction of Jerusalem and its rebuilding as a Roman colony called Aelia Capitolina, with a temple to the God Jupiter on the site of the demolished Jewish temple. The Roman emperor Hadrian forbade Jews to enter this city on pain of death.

20. A possible exception is a reference in a (fifth-century?) text called Derek Ereṣ Rabba, to a wealthy Jew in Rome, at the end of the first century, identified as "FLSOFOS," which some have taken as a corruption of "Flavius Josephus." See Heinz Schreckenberg, *Rezeptionsgeschichtliche und Textkritische Untersuchungen zu Flavius Josephus* (Leiden: E. J. Brill, 1977), 49. Other Greek-speaking Jewish authors, like Philo, likewise receive no mention in rabbinic literature; other factors, therefore, may have contributed to the neglect of Josephus.

21. Cf. Norman Bentwich, *Josephus* (Philadelphia: Jewish Publication Society, 1914); A. Schalit, "Josephus Flavius," *EncJud* (1971), vol. 10, 251–65; and, in general, Louis H. Feldman, *JMS*, 75–98.

22. See David Flusser, "*Josippon*, a Medieval Hebrew Version of Josephus," *JJC*, 386–97.

23. For a concise statement of Josephus' importance to the archaeologist, see Louis Feldman, *JBH*, 434–40.

24. So Luther H. Martin, "Josephus' Use of *Heimarmene* in the *Jewish Antiquities* XIII, 171–73," *Numen* 28 (1981), 127–37.

25. See most recently Seth Schwartz, *Josephus and Judaean Politics* (Leiden: E. J. Brill, 1990). Schwartz follows a direction begun by Richard Laqueur and Hans Rasp in the 1920s, taken up in English by Morton Smith (1956), Jacob Neusner (1972), and S. J. D. Cohen (1979) among others. Full references may be found in Feldman's or Schwartz's bibliographies.

26. See for example Steve Mason, "Josephus on the Pharisees Reconsidered: A Critique of Smith/Neusner," *SR* 17 (1988), 455–69.

27. See Gustav Hölscher, "Josephus," *PWRE* 18 (1916), 1934–2000.

The Career of Josephus and Its New Testament Context

	Career of Josephus	Early Christian Writings and Figures	Significant Events
6 BC		Birth of Jesus of Nazareth	
AD 6			Census in Syria/Judea
30		Death of Jesus of Nazareth	
37	Birth of Josephus	Conversion of Paul	
38			Gaius Caligulas' Statue Ordered in Temple
40		1 Thessalonians	
		d. James brother of John	
		1 Corinthians	
		Philippians, 2 Corinthians	
	Advanced	Philemon	
	Education	Galatians, Romans	
		"Q" Sayings Source	
		Gospel of Thomas?	
	Trip to Rome	d. James brother of Jesus	
	Galilean Commander, d.	Jewish Revolt	
	Paul, Peter		
70	prisoner	Gospel of Mark	Fall of Jerusalem
			Fall of Masada
	Aramaic *War*,		
	Greek *War*	Hebrews	
	(1st edn)		
		Gospel of Matthew	
		Gospel of John	
	Antiquities	Johannine letters	
	Life		
	Against Apion	Luke and Acts	
100	d. ca. 100?		

2 The Career of Josephus

In the preceding chapter we have seen how *not* to use Josephus for the study of the NT. That leaves me with the obligation of proving, in the remainder of this book, that there is a better way. I have argued that we need to read him on his own terms, to allow him his integrity. This is a bit of an over-simplification because, once scholars have accepted that point, they must still define what his "own terms" are. In many minor respects, specialists do not yet agree about what Josephus was up to. That is inevitable, but it should not hinder us from making some fundamental observations. Once again, I make no pretense of objectivity here, since every account is an interpretation, but I can promise to introduce Josephus in a way that reflects the current insights of scholarship.

Before we get down to specific examples of how Josephus can shed light on the NT, we must get to know him a little better. This chapter and the next will take a broad view of his life and writings within their social contexts. The resulting overview will provide us with an indispensable basis for interpreting specific passages as they come up in the following chapters.

Unlike the vast majority of ancient authors whose works have survived, Josephus tells us a good deal about himself. At first this seems like a rare treat. None of the Gospel authors even divulges his or her name, let alone the circumstances of their writing. Even such a prolific author as Philo of Alexandria betrays little about his own life. Those who wrote the Dead Sea Scrolls, the apocalyptic literature, and most of the "apocryphal" material, if they did not falsely attribute their work to some great figure from the past, were content with anonymity. That is why scholars must spend a good deal of their time weaving careful hypotheses about who wrote these texts, where, when, and why.

Josephus, however, writes what may be the first auto-biography in Western history (the *Life of Josephus*). It offers plenty of information about his life.[1] And his *Jewish War* also recounts many details of his career. The problem is that a fair bit of this proffered data makes no sense. Ancient writing was so completely given over to persuasion, or "rhetoric," that no author from that time should be taken at face value. (Nor should a modern author, but for different reasons.) By Josephus' time, Greek and Latin writers had developed a vast arsenal of conventions, called *topoi* (singular is *topos*), to assist them in writing persuasively. Manuals on rhetoric abounded, and someone like Josephus, who studied Greek at a moderately advanced level, would have had ample exposure to these texts (*Ant.* 20.263). Even those who lacked such educational opportunities (Paul?) were bound to have absorbed rhetorical conventions from their environment, much as we absorb a lot of "pop psychology" even if we lack formal psychological training. So, entering Josephus' world of thought means first of all being wise to the kinds of conventions that he used. And in assessing the function of rhetoric in Josephus we must note up front that one of the most common rhetorical devices was a repudiation of rhetoric and an insistence that one was writing the plain truth! Let me illustrate.

THE EARLY YEARS

Josephus opens his *Life* with a pedigree of his aristocratic heritage (1–6). This genealogy is perfectly in order for an ancient "life," though it may seem strange to us. We tend to believe in individual freedom and so care little about the parents of our famous athletes, musicians, and actors. Indeed, we often expect to hear that a famous industrialist or other celebrity came from ignominious roots, that he or she escaped from a web of poverty. But this is a modern Western bias. Most of the world, most of the time, has functioned under more rigidly defined class lines. In Josephus' world, social mobility—the freedom to "rise up the ladder"—was minimal. One was born into a particular social class and, unless truly extraordinary circumstances occurred, one could expect to remain within its confines. Therefore, the indispensable condition of real prestige was a noble parentage. Although a few philosophers challenged this assumption, the traditional prejudice could recognize nobility only in the "well born." The Bible of the Greco-Roman world, comprising Homer's epics *The Iliad* and *The Odyssey*, plainly reflects this identification of status with lineage: Odysseus' son Telemachus, for example, is treated with great respect because of his father's prestige. In the Jewish world, the apocryphal book of Tobit presents young Tobias in much the same light; even the archangel Raphael, who is sent to help him, must concoct a genealogy in order to be accepted by Tobias' father![2] So the provision of a genealogy was a rhetorical convention, especially necessary if there was some doubt about the subject's pedigree.

Josephus provides his genealogy because he has no choice. According to him, it has come under attack from some of his adversaries (*Life* 6). Against these unnamed opponents he insists that the public archives confirm his issue from both priestly and royal roots. Although he claims merely to transmit that public record, his genealogy does not inspire confidence. (a) In *Life* 2, he asserts that his royal heritage comes from his mother, who descended from the Hasmoneans (=Maccabees), who "for a very considerable period were kings, as well as high-priests, of our nation." But the genealogy that follows in support of this claim goes through his father, not his mother. He now says that it was his great-great-grandfather on his *father's* side who married into the Hasmonean line (*Life* 4); no further mention is made of his mother. (b) According to Josephus (*Ant.* 13.301), the Hasmoneans did *not* assume the title of "king" until Aristobulus (104 BC)—well after Josephus' ancestor's marriage. (c) The dates that he gives for his ancestors do not compute. Josephus puts his great-grandfather Matthias' birth at 135 BC, his son Joseph's at 70 BC, and his son Matthias' at 6 BC. That his forebears should have sired children at 65 and 76 years of age, respectively, is not impossible; but it would be a back-to-back feat of Abrahamic proportions. It is especially problematic in view of the short life expectancy in

Greco-Roman antiquity. (We may leave aside such additional problems as why Simon's son Matthias was "known as the son of Ephaeus," *Life* 4)

Most scholars would agree on the futility of undertaking heroic measures to salvage Josephus' genealogy. It seems clear enough that he was, as he claimed, both a priest and a descendant of the Hasmoneans. We know this because priestly and pro-Hasmonean biases creep into his writings in many places where he is not trying to make a case about his heritage. For example, his narrative history treats the Hasmonean John Hyrcanus as a hero, and he even named his oldest son after this ruler (*Life* 5). For historical purposes, this *unintentional* evidence is much more convincing than Josephus' formal attempt, in the genealogy, to prove his ancestry. As for the genealogy itself, it is easiest to believe that Josephus was unclear about the details of his parentage beyond two or three generations, but that he was forced by rhetorical convention to provide an impressive pedigree. He knew very well that his Roman readers had no access to (and probably no interest in) the public archives of Jerusalem.[3]

Even more obviously conditioned by rhetorical convention is Josephus' account of his youth and education (*Life* 7–12). He was such a precocious youngster, he claims, that the leading dignitaries of the city used to seek out his advice when he was but fourteen years of age (*Life* 8). At the age of sixteen, he embarked on advanced philosophical training in the major Jewish schools—those of the Pharisees, the Sadducees, and the Essenes. Not content with that experience, though it required painstaking discipline and effort, he attached himself to a teacher named Bannus. This monk practiced a rigorous lifestyle in the Judean desert, wearing clothes made from bark and leaves and eating only wild vegetation. Josephus was deeply committed to Bannus' way and remained with him three years, but at the appropriate age (eighteen or nineteen) he returned to the city and began his public career (*Life* 10–12). One of his major diplomatic efforts was a trip to Rome to secure the release of some fellow priests who had been summoned by Nero (*Life* 13–16).

What are we to make of this account? To begin with, it is brimming with rhetorical commonplaces. The image of the child prodigy, both brilliant and wise beyond his years, appears in many other famous lives. The philosopher Pythagoras, while still a youth, was a model of virtue and wisdom; Apollonius of Tyana, as a child, miraculously spoke with perfect grammar; Moses did not engage in childish pursuits but quickly surpassed his teachers in wisdom; and Jesus, according to the apocryphal Infancy Gospel of Thomas, confounded his teachers with mysterious understanding.[4]

Equally common is the *topos* of broad, preferably exotic, philosophical training such as Josephus claims. Upper-class Romans were ambivalent toward philosophy. Their ideal was for a man to be engaged primarily in public affairs—first military service, to prove his mettle, and then in more prestigious government posts. Such a career left no room for protracted philosophical pursuits, which were often considered inimical to public life. Philosophical fanaticism was as abhorrent then as religious fanaticism is today. Nevertheless, since a statesman must be wise and inwardly noble, he must be well acquainted with the teachings of philosophy. Further, many Romans admired the simplicity of life associated with such philosophers as the Pythagoreans and enjoyed reading about the exploits of Eastern philosophers. The usual compromise was for a man to study philosophy in his late teens, as the core of his upper-level (gymnasium) education; he might even be forgiven for a little fanaticism arising from adolescent idealism. But the completion of one's education required a decisive transition to the serious affairs of the real world. Nero's advisor, Seneca, for example, had been a vegetarian for a while, until his father, a famous Roman orator, forbade him to continue. And Tacitus writes that his father-in-law Agricola, as a youth, "was inclined to drink more deeply of philosophy than is permitted to a Roman and a Senator, had not his mother's discretion imposed a check upon his enkindled and glowing imagination."[5] Though a broad acquaintance with philosophical issues was commendable, one had to stop short of out-and-out "conversion" to philosophy.[6]

Josephus' account of his education deftly engages these Roman sensibilities. In accord with his social status, at the appropriate age he studied intensively the major schools of Jewish philosophy. But he also had an admirable, youthful passion for something deeper than the ordinary school teachings could offer. Finding a guru who would expose him to the most rigorous lifestyle imaginable, he became this man's zealous disciple (*Life* 10–11). Still he was sensible enough to put these youthful adventures behind him (at a suitable age) and begin his diplomatic career (*Life* 12). Although designed to impress Roman readers, Josephus' account of his youth also manages to blend in the biblical-Jewish theme of desert-sojourn as preparation for divine service.

We cannot take this whole rhetorical construction as a plain statement of what really happened. For one thing, the numbers are a problem. Josephus claims to have begun his advanced education at about age sixteen and to have completed it in his nineteenth year. We should naturally interpret this as a three-year period corresponding to the final phase of a Roman aristocrat's training. But he then says that his life with Bannus alone lasted three years (*Life* 12). This would leave little time for his "laborious exercises" in the Pharisaic, Sadducean, and Essene schools, even if we stretched the three years to four. In another context, Josephus asserts that it took three years just to become a full member of the Essene community (*War* 2.137–142), and it is likely that the Pharisees also had degrees of initiation. So once again we run afoul of Josephus' arithmetic. Such obvious inconsistencies mean that either our text of Josephus is flawed (as some think) or he was rather careless in these matters.

Plainly, Josephus' presentation of his youth and education owes much to the rhetorical conventions of his day. We can assume that he did come from an aristocratic family, that he was well educated, and that he knew a good deal about the Pharisees, Sadducees, and Essenes. But these points come to light elsewhere in his narratives where he is not trying to prove them. His deliberate statements in the *Life* seem contrived and should, therefore, be taken with a grain of salt.

JOSEPHUS AND THE JEWISH REVOLT

The same problems face us when we turn to consider the most controversial period of Josephus' career, his six months of service in Galilee at the outbreak of the Jewish revolt. This period was already a matter of contention during Josephus' lifetime. He had briefly described it in the *War*, but was forced to write the *Life* in response to writers who challenged that portrayal. So we have two accounts, each with its own rhetorical constraints, which do not entirely agree.

In *War* 2.562–582, Josephus claims that the Jewish rebels' early victories over the Romans brought over those who had initially opposed the revolt (presumably including Josephus) to the rebel cause. The Jewish leaders, he says, met at the temple and appointed "generals" to prosecute the war in the various regions of Palestine. Given command of Galilee, Josephus set about his duties with zeal. He appointed a council of seventy men to assist him in administering the region, as well as seven men in each town to handle smaller matters. He fortified all of the major cities under his command, in preparation for the Roman attack; Gischala and Sepphoris were fortified by others, but at Josephus' command (*War* 2.575). Moreover, he created a professional standing army of about 65,000, which he organized and trained along Roman lines.[7] Josephus allows that he faced some opposition while in the Galilee, especially from one John of Gischala, but he dismisses this fellow as a thoroughly evil man, "the most unscrupulous and crafty of all who have ever gained notoriety" (*War* 2.585). John was a mischief-maker and a robber, who (because of his evil nature) challenged Josephus' duly constituted authority.

In the *Life*, we get a radically different picture. Here, Josephus portrays the Jewish leadership (including himself) as consistently favoring peace, even after the rebels' initial success. They send Josephus to the Galilee along with two other priests, not as a general but as part of a committee. This delegation's task was to persuade the Galileans to lay down their arms, which were to be reserved for the professional soldiery. The delegates were not to prepare for war, but to wait and see what the Romans did (*Life* 29). Their "chief concern was the preservation of peace in Galilee" (*Life* 78). Josephus was not free to act independently, but had to submit when the other two voted against him (*Life* 73).[8]

Far from having military control of the Galilee, according to the *Life*, Josephus faced significant opposition from numerous quarters and often feared for his life (*Life* 141–144). Most important, his arch-rival John of Gischala now appears as having originally opposed the revolt, as Josephus did; he was not thoroughly evil, but originally shared Josephus' aristo-

cratic outlook (*Life* 43). John fortified his native town of Gischala in opposition to Josephus, not at his command (*Life* 45,
189). And John, it now turns out, was a close friend of the
Jewish leaders in Jerusalem, including the high priest and the
eminent Pharisee, Simon son of Gamaliel. These respected
leaders sponsored his effort to remove Josephus (*Life* 189–
198). Further, John's cause was supported by aristocrats such
as Justus of Tiberias. So the opposition to Josephus looks much
more respectable than it had in *War*. Moreover, we are shocked
by Josephus' new admission that he cut off the hands of his
opponents (*Life* 169–173) and recruited the Galilean "brig-
ands" as a mercenary force (*Life* 77). In addition, we now
learn the substance of published accusations against Josephus: he and his mercenaries incited the city of Tiberias to
revolt against Rome (*Life* 340); he was a greedy tyrant who
sought to extend his own power through deceit (*Life* 302).

It is not easy to reconstruct a coherent picture from these
conflicting reports. Many scholars suspect that Josephus has
something to hide. That a credible opposition produced alter-
nate accounts of his tenure in the Galilee and that he was
forced to defend his conduct in the *Life* indicate that the *War*
was something of a whitewash. One critic has argued that
Josephus began as an independent warlord in Galilee in competition with other freelance rebel leaders. He was not an
appointed general but a successful tyrant.[9] Others suggest
that he went to Galilee with a mandate for peace but, once he
arrived, saw the opportunities for personal gain and became
a tyrant.[10]

Still other scholars are inclined to give Josephus the benefit of the doubt, emphasizing the ambiguities that must have
confronted someone in his position. He was an aristocrat with
a Greek education, but also a Jewish priest committed to his
national tradition. We need only look at Western-educated
leaders of non-Western countries today to understand something of the tensions that result from such culture conflicts.
These scholars also point out the different contexts and purposes of *War* and *Life* (see further below) as a partial explanation of the disparities. In my view, the problem of ambivalent
loyalties must be taken seriously, but it does not account for
the outright contradictions. These indicate that Josephus is
lying about his past, presumably because he has something to

hide. Yet because the writings of his opponents were not considered worthy of preservation, and because of the fog that he has thrown over his actions in Galilee, that past may no longer be recoverable. At least we still await a satisfying reconstruction.

SURRENDER TO THE ROMANS

Josephus' surrender to the Romans is one of the most famous episodes of his life. Once the Roman general Vespasian had arrived in Galilee, the outcome of the war was a foregone conclusion. Josephus' men deserted him immediately, and he fled to Tiberias, as far away as possible from the conflict (*War* 3.127–131). When Vespasian moved against the fortress town of Jotapata (yo-TA-pa-ta), Josephus paid a visit to help strengthen it. With disarming honesty, however, he plainly states that once he knew that the city was going to fall, he planned to leave. The citizens got wind of this and implored him to stay, fearing for their lives. He responded, with apparently conscious duplicity, that if he escaped he could distract the Romans as well as send help (*War* 3.200). The townspeople were not convinced, but preferred to believe that "with Josephus on the spot, . . . no disaster could befall them" (*War* 3.202). They forced him to stay.

Their trust in his presence turned out to be unfounded. The Roman siege concluded, inevitably, with an attack on the city. Just before the capture, Josephus claims, "some divine providence" inspired him to run and hide in an underground cavern (perhaps a water reservoir, *War* 3.341). When his hiding spot was betrayed by a captured woman, Vespasian sent messengers to offer him safety if he would surrender. Again, he frankly admits that he was afraid to surrender because of the hardship that he had caused the Romans; he thought that he would be killed (*War* 3.346). Vespasian then sent an old acquaintance of Josephus to persuade him that he would be safe and, once again, divine intervention came to his aid. Just as he was considering the offer of safety, "suddenly there came back into his mind those nightly dreams, in which God had foretold to him the impending fate of the Jews and the destinies of the Roman sovereigns" (*War* 3.351). Only then did Josephus resolve to surrender to the Romans, now that his motives were unmistakable. He was keenly aware of the Jewish law that a general must die with his men (*War* 3.400), but in this special case the law was preempted by a divine mission. Extremely sensitive to charges of cowardice and betrayal, Josephus repeatedly insists that he would have been happy to die there in the cave had not God chosen him for his divine mission, to announce to the world the coming fortunes of his Roman captors (*War* 3.137–138, 354). So he decided to surrender.

But it was not that easy. His fellow captives, unimpressed by his divine mission, drew their swords to prevent his surrender. He could die as a hero or as a traitor, but die he must. Unfazed, Josephus proceeded to reason with them on the evils of suicide (*War* 3.362–386). But this too failed to move them. Ever resourceful, he devised a plan that would satisfy everyone. He proposed that they go ahead and kill themselves, but not in suicide. They should draw lots (straws?); the one chosen first should present himself for death to the second, the second to the third, and so on. They must solemnly agree that the ones left to the end would also take their lives, for it would be unconscionable, he notes, for the last ones to spare their own lives. In the end, remarkably, Josephus and one other were left. He persuaded the other not to kill him, and they both surrendered. On the one hand, given Josephus' confidence in proposing this stratagem, and given his own admissions of telling barefaced lies to save himself, it seems that here too he simply outsmarted his colleagues.

On the other hand, we must remember that we are dealing with ancient literary conventions. In Homer's *Odyssey*, mentioned earlier, the hero of the story routinely fabricates stories about his past to save himself from danger. That kind of deception, when practiced by a hero in the service of his just cause, was considered scandalous only by the more severe philosophers. Within the beloved epic itself, Odysseus' ploys evoke the admiration of the goddess Athena, who compares his wily resourcefulness to her own (*Odyssey* 13.250–301). In Jewish literature there was a famous precedent in the apocryphal novel about Judith, who had told a fabulous lie to the Assyrian general in order to save her people. Both of these stories use the theme of deception to show the triumph of the resourceful hero(ine) over insurmountable odds. That is the kind of situation in which Josephus also found himself while defending Jewish territory against the Romans.

Josephus' frankness about his many deceptions is probably best explained as a literary device intended to prove his heroic craftiness. Since his ruses may have been invented out of whole cloth, as a rhetorical artifice, it makes no sense for us to turn them against him on the basis of our own moral criteria. He will later declare against his adversaries: "nor was it in your power to ascertain the part which I played in the siege [of Jotapata], since all possible informants perished in that conflict" (*Life* 357). Although directed against others' accounts, this notice serves to remind us of the latitude that Josephus had in telling about his past.

PREDICTION OF VESPASIAN'S RISE

After Josephus surrendered to the Romans, the course of his career seems easier to follow. Even here we find plenty of posturing, but since much of his subsequent life was lived before the eyes of his Roman patrons, he would have less occasion to dissemble about the past.

Once in chains, Josephus was due to be sent to the emperor Nero because he was an important prisoner. To prevent this inconvenience, he decided that this was the time to tell Vespasian about the prophecies he had earlier received concerning the general's future; it was this prophetic mission, after all, that had justified his surrender in the first place. Granted an audience with Vespasian, he addressed his conqueror as follows:

> I come to you as a messenger of greater destinies. . . . To Nero do you send me? Why then? Think you that [Nero and] those who before your accession succeed him will continue? You will be Caesar, Vespasian, you will be emperor, you and your son [Titus] here (*War* 3.400–401, LCL).

This prediction was made in July or August, 67. Just a few months later, some of the legions in Europe revolted against Nero's rule; then, facing a conspiracy by his own elite troops, the emperor committed suicide on June 9, 68. The following

tumultuous year saw three Roman generals—Galba, Otho, and
Vitellius—seize power in rapid succession. But in December
of 69, in keeping with Josephus' prediction, the people of
Rome finally acclaimed Vespasian emperor, ratifying the acclamation by his own troops (*War* 4.655). As soon as Vespasian
saw that he was going to become emperor, he released Josephus from his chains and bestowed many privileges on him.

How should we evaluate this amazing prediction? Josephus' use of it to preclude questions about his behavior positively invites the suspicion that he is covering something up.
A similar prediction would later be attributed to the rabbi
Yohanan ben Zakkai, who fled Jerusalem during the revolt and
worked out a deal with the Roman authorities to establish a
school at Yavneh/Jamnia (b. Gittin 56a–b; *'Abot R. Nat* 4.5). In
that case, too, the spectacular prophecy seems to mask some
less noble pleading for survival. We might be inclined, therefore, to think that Josephus invented the episode in the interest of self-justification, and that rabbinic tradition borrowed
the device to exonerate Rabbi Yohanan.

But Josephus' prediction quickly became famous in Rome,
probably as a result of the new ruler's propaganda effort. Tessa
Rajak has pointed out that Vespasian had no hereditary claim
to rule and thus was in serious need of legitimation in his bid
for power during the last months of 69. In a superstitious
world that valued signs and wonders, it was natural that the
general's supporters would pay careful attention to tales of
good omens that had appeared at the time of his accession. We
find lists of these marvels in several Roman authors of the
period, and Josephus' prediction is included among them (Suetonius, *Vespasian* 4–5; Dio Cassius 65.1.4). Since the writers in
question do not seem to have read Josephus, the omens concerning Vespasian must have been widely known. This political need was more than sufficient motive for the Flavian
emperors (Vespasian, Titus, and Domitian) to publicize and
dramatize whatever Josephus had said about their dynasty.[11]

This does not yet require that Josephus actually made the
prediction, any more than it requires the veracity of the other
omens collected in support of the Flavians. It is conceivable
that Vespasian conspired with Josephus to fabricate the story
in return for his life: this Jewish priest could be retained as
living proof of a mysterious Eástern oracle confirming Ves-

pasian's right to rule. But there are more likely explanations, based on clues in Josephus' own writings.

Josephus links his revelations with scriptural prophecy. Back in the cave at Jotapata, he was enabled to understand his dreams because he was "not ignorant of the prophecies in the sacred books" (*War* 3.352). What prophetic statements might have been associated with Vespasian? (a) Josephus himself says that they are "ambiguous utterances" (*War* 3.352), which require special insight to be understood. (b) We know that Josephus was especially fond of the book of Daniel. Although traditional Judaism did not ultimately include Daniel among the prophets, Josephus considered him "one of the greatest of the prophets" (*Ant.* 10.266). Josephus confirms the evidence of the NT that Daniel was widely read by first-century Jews, because that book was thought to have revealed events of their own time. That is, the four-kingdom scenario envisioned by Daniel (2:31–45), which seems to end with the reign of Antiochus Epiphanes (d. 164 BC), was understood by later Jews to present the Roman empire as the last world power (*Ant.* 10.276). This interpretation was doubtless enhanced by Dan 9:24–27, which counts seventy weeks of years (= 490) from the rebuilding of the temple to its final desecration and the appearance of an "anointed ruler." Since the temple had been rebuilt in about 500 BC (no one knew the exact dates), speculation was ripe throughout the first century that the end was near. Thus, although many biblical statements were interpreted by Jewish groups to refer to the awaited deliverer, we have good reason to suppose that Josephus was thinking of Daniel when he spoke of such prophecies.

(c) We have one further key insight into Josephus' thinking in this matter. In *War* 6.312, he notes that the Jewish rebels had been provoked to war in part by their misunderstanding of an "ambiguous oracle in their sacred scriptures, to the effect that at that time one from their country would become king of the world." Josephus comments that, though most Jewish teachers believed this prophecy to refer to a *Jewish* leader, in reality it "signified the sovereignty of Vespasian, who was proclaimed emperor on Jewish soil" (6.313). The Roman historian Tacitus makes a similar comment on the Jews' misunderstanding of their own prophecy, which led them to oppose rather than support Vespasian (*Histories* 5.13).

If we put all of these clues together, Josephus' prediction does not seem nearly as remarkable. He was well aware of current Jewish interpretations of Daniel, which looked for an anointed leader to appear in his own time. Although this hope was usually interpreted in opposition to Roman power, it was natural for someone with Josephus' sympathies to transfer the prediction to a Roman leader. Since Roman rule seemed inevitable anyway, such a reading would be more intrinsically probable to him than the Jewish, nationalistic one. And it had a precedent in the Bible itself, for Isaiah calls the Persian leader Cyrus, benefactor of the Jews, God's "anointed" ruler (Isa 45:1). It seems plausible, at least, that such an interpretation of Daniel was current among Josephus' social circles, which opposed the revolt. He might well have had this gem in his hip pocket to be produced at an appropriate moment. Or perhaps, the link with the Romans was his own innovation.

That still leaves his personal application of the prophecy to Vespasian. There seem to be four possibilities. (a) He possessed supernatural or paranormal insight. (b) He made a lucky guess, based on his knowledge of political realities at the time. It was widely known that Nero, who had ruled for fourteen years, faced substantial opposition; and Josephus might well have judged that Vespasian was the most likely of the generals to succeed him. In any case, this general was on Jewish soil and showed every intention of attacking Jerusalem in fulfillment of the prophecy (Dan 9:26). If Josephus took the prophecy seriously, there was good reason for him to associate it with Vespasian.[12] (c) He did not in fact *predict* Vespasian's rise but only brought up this "oracle" after Vespasian's soldiers had acclaimed the new emperor. We note that Josephus was not released from his bonds until after the acclamation of Vespasian (*War* 4.623–629). Given the new emperor's need for legitimation discussed above, we can imagine that a timely word from his prisoner, even now, about this very old Eastern oracle would be seized upon and promoted vigorously. Josephus too had every reason to read his declaration back to the time of his surrender, to cover up his otherwise cowardly behavior. (d) Josephus had two encounters with Vespasian. In the first, soon after his capture, he divulged his understanding of the prophecy that *the Romans* would rule the world by God's favor. That might explain why he was not sent to Nero (if indeed Vespasian ever intended such a thing; that he remained in Judea is as easily explained by his usefulness to Vespasian as a willing informant). Then, after Vespasian's acclamation, he pointed out that the prophecy must have concerned the Flavian general personally.

The one factor that seems slightly to favor (b) is that Josephus continues to regard himself as endowed with predictive abilities. Although this notion might have been either self-delusion or deceit, it is perhaps easier to understand as the result of an important "prediction" that came true. Yet Josephus concedes that others considered his prediction "a nonsensical invention of the prisoner to avert the storm which he has raised" (*War* 3.406). Although this was said in story time before the prediction came true, we may suppose that it remained the view of Josephus' opponents: he somehow manufactured a prediction to serve Vespasian's public relations needs.[13]

CAPTIVITY AND LITERARY CAREER

The sequel may be presented briefly. Josephus makes much of his involvement in the war, but it turns out that he spent most of the war in captivity. The war began in earnest only in March or April of 67, when Vespasian and his son Titus gathered their legions in Ptolemais. By July of the same year, Jotapata had fallen and Josephus was in chains. Jerusalem would not fall until September of 70, and the war would not end completely until the fall of Masada in 74. In all of this, Josephus was an onlooker.

For most of the period he was imprisoned in the Roman headquarters at Caesarea. There, he was permitted to marry a captive, presumably Jewish, from Caesarea (*Life* 414)—his second marriage (cf. *War* 5.419). He would later insist that priests were not permitted to marry captive women, who were assumed to be impure (*Ag. Ap.* 1.35); that is probably why he mentions that this woman was a virgin. With the legions' acclamation of Vespasian in the autumn of 69, Josephus accompanied the new ruler to Alexandria, leaving his captive wife and finding another there. He then returned to the siege of

Jerusalem with Titus, who was now in charge, to help bring the revolt to a swift end. Upon its successful conclusion with the fall of Jerusalem, he traveled with the triumphant Titus to Rome and married yet again. His third wife, who bore him three sons, he divorced because he was "displeased at her behaviour" (*Life* 426). Two of his sons by the previous marriage died prematurely. His fourth wife bore him two more.

The remainder of Josephus' life was both highly privileged and tormented. Everywhere in his writings, we see him under attack from fellow Jews for being a coward and a traitor. Describing the scene when Vespasian first arrived in Galilee, Josephus writes:

> As for himself [Josephus], although he might look for pardon from the Romans, he would have preferred to suffer a thousand deaths rather than betray his country and disgracefully abandon the command which had been entrusted to him, in order to seek his fortune among those whom he had been commissioned to fight (*War* 3.137, LCL).

Here, as in the description of his divine mission considered above, he takes some trouble to head off the accusation of cowardice. In another telling passage, he writes that when the Jews of Jerusalem thought that he had died at Jotapata, they mourned him as a hero with thirty days of lamentation. But when they then learned of his survival and comfortable circumstances, "some abused him as a coward, others as a traitor, and throughout the city there was general indignation, and curses were heaped upon his devoted head" (*War* 3.439). This hostility would pursue him to the grave. After the war, one Jew accused him of having financed a revolt in Cyrene (*Life* 424). Others wrote accounts of his role in the war against Rome that pointedly challenged his accuracy and charged him with having been a petty tyrant. Josephus attributes all of this to envy of his good fortune, but obviously his adversaries had deeper motives. Fortunately for him, he had the support of his imperial patrons, who silenced many of his accusers by execution (*Life* 425, 429).

The Flavian emperors permitted Josephus to live in Vespasian's private residence, granted him prized Roman citizenship, gave him large tracts of land in Judea, and ultimately exempted him from taxation. As his name "Flavius" suggests, they also brought him under the protection of their family and became his literary patrons (see chapter 6). It was under imperial and other patronage in Rome that Josephus wrote his four surviving works: the *Jewish War, Jewish Antiquities, Life of Josephus,* and *Against Apion.* To the analysis of those works we now turn.

The exact year of Josephus' death is unknown. His writings require that he lived at least to about AD 100, or age 64, but he may have survived well into the second century.

FOR FURTHER READING

The fullest study in English of the problems surrounding Josephus' biography is:

- Shaye J. D. Cohen, *Josephus in Galilee and Rome: His Vita and His Development as a Historian* (Leiden: E. J. Brill, 1979). He includes a fine survey of previous scholarship in this area (pp. 8–23), the bulk of which was in German.

For a recent synopsis of the issues, see:

- Per Bilde, *Flavius Josephus Between Jerusalem and Rome* (Sheffield: Sheffield Academic Press, 1988), 27–60.

- H. St. John Thackeray, *Josephus: The Man and the Historian* (New York: Jewish Institute of Religion, 1929), esp. 15–22.

A sympathetic effort to understand Josephus' outlook from within his social context is:

- Tessa Rajak, *Josephus: The Historian and His Society* (London: Duckworth, 1983).

NOTES

1. Some reserve that honor to the *Confessions* of St. Augustine, 350 years later, on the grounds that Josephus' is not a true portrait of his inner self.
2. Cf. Tacitus, *Agricola* 4.1; Matt 1:2–17; Luke 3:23–38.

3. Josephus elsewhere claims that the Jerusalem archives had been utterly destroyed during the revolt of 66–70, first by the rebels and then by the victorious Romans (*War* 2.427; 6.354). A less certain tradition reported by Eusebius held that King Herod (reigned 37–4 BC) had already burned the genealogical registers so as to eliminate anyone else's claims to royal ancestry (*Eccl hist* 1.7.13).

4. A convenient selection of such commonplaces is in David R. Cartlidge and David L. Dungan, *Documents for the Study of the Gospels* (Philadelphia: Fortress, 1980), 129–36, 261.

5. *Agricola* 4.3.

6. See Arthur Darby Nock, *Conversion: The Old and the New in Religion from Alexander the Great to Augustine* (Oxford: Oxford University Press, 1933); Ramsay MacMullen, *Enemies of the Roman Order* (Cambridge, Mass.: Harvard University Press, 1966), 46–94.

7. So *War* 2.583. But in 2.576 he had put the size at upwards of 100,000 men. For purposes of comparison, Canada's armed forces today number about 80,000.

8. In *Life* 341, Josephus does claim to have been elected to the command of the Galilee, a datum that does not fit well with the preceding narrative. In the context, it should refer to Josephus' final and grudging confirmation (*Life* 310), which came only at the end of his long struggles with adversaries. It could be that in *War* he has telescoped all of this conflict and final confirmation as if it were a single commission.

9. Richard Laqueur, *Der jüdische Historiker Flavius Josephus* (Darmstadt: Wissenschaftliche Buckgesellschaft, 1970 [1928]).

10. Hans Rasp, "Flavius Josephus und die jüdischen Religionsparteien, *ZNW* 23 (1924), 27–47.

11. See Rajak, *Josephus*, 185–95.

12. Notice that Daniel 7:7 presents the fourth beast as ten-horned. Since many people seem to have counted "emperors"from Julius Caesar, Vespasian would have been the tenth horn in such a scheme.

13. See J. Blenkinsopp, "Prophecy and Priesthood in Josephus," *JJS* 25 (1974), 239–62.

3

The Writings of Josephus

As a writer, Josephus was much more sophisticated than his behavior might suggest. The beneficiary of a first-rate aristocratic education, he was not only intimately familiar with his native Hebrew and Aramaic traditions, but he also had achieved some basic facility in Greek language, literature, and thought even before he left Judea. These influences had pervaded the Mediterranean world since Alexander the Great. Because of his obviously stormy relationship with his fellow Jews after the revolt, it is important to ask: In writing about the recent war and earlier Jewish history, what is Josephus trying to tell his Roman readers about the Jews? Has he become hostile to Jews or Judaism? Does he speak as a traitor? What is his message?

To understand how his writings would have been interpreted by Roman readers, we first need to have some picture of how they perceived Jews and Judaism before Josephus came along. That will set the stage for our interpretation of each of his compositions in turn.

GRECO-ROMAN PERCEPTIONS OF THE JEWS

Quite a bit of research has been done recently into Greco-Roman attitudes toward the Jews. Here we can do little more than summarize the main points.

In traditional Christian writing, the Roman empire receives a lot of bad and misleading press. Because of their persecution of the young church, these "pagans" are often thought to have lived in evil darkness, motivated by a desire to extinguish the light of the gospel. In fact, however, Roman officials were extremely tolerant of non-Roman religions. They saw themselves as the champions of piety and morality. It was understood that every nation had its own ancestral traditions, its own temples and gods, and these were inviolable to the Romans. They expected that all nations, like theirs, treated worship as an integral part of daily life. For both theoretical and practical reasons, they had no desire to convert the nations within their empire to traditional Roman religion. Most intellectuals had come to believe that there was ultimately only one God or ground of being anyway, and that the "gods" of Rome, Egypt, Persia, Greece, or Judea were symbolic or local representatives of this ultimate truth. It would have been foolish for the Romans to risk alienating any of these regional deities; far better to promote the local religions and even sacrifice to the various gods.

To be sure, Roman aristocrats often looked down their noses at the "superstitions" of the Eastern masses—much, perhaps, as modern North Americans often fail to comprehend what motivates Shi'ite Muslims or Buddhists. They especially complained when the foreigners started arriving in Rome and began building temples to their native gods. But the government allowed all of these religions to flourish. In one famous case, the Romans even deliberately imported a shrine of the "Great Mother" goddess (Cybele) from the Middle East, in gratitude for her help in war. The only time that Roman officials became upset with foreign religious groups was when they seemed to threaten the worldwide "peace and security" that had been established so carefully. The senate did move to shut down some groups, for gross immorality (cannibalism, human sacrifice, or orgiastic behavior), for plotting against the empire, or for drawing people away from normal civic loyalty. Further, they took a dim view of new political or religious groups, on the assumption that "new truth" was a contradiction, and on the suspicion that such groups were up to no good. But established national traditions usually had little to fear.

Judaism benefited from this tolerance. The Greek and Latin words for "Jew" simply mean "Judean." Romans thought of the Jews as the people from Judea who, naturally enough, had their own traditions of worship, their own God, and their own temple where their God lived. They knew that the nation was quite old and most had heard of Moses, its founder. More than that, some educated Greeks and Romans admired the Jews for their "philosophical" view of God. Unlike other nations, whose masses worshiped symbolic representations of the true God, the Jewish tradition prohibited even its humblest members from making images of the divine. Jewish ethics, which, for example, forbade the abandonment of unwanted children (common in the empire), were also respected. There is abundant evidence that many in the Greco-Roman world were so attracted to Judaism that they either became Jews or associated themselves with Jewish places of worship (synagogues). Finally, the Jews as a nation had established political ties with the Romans long before the empire had extended to Judea; once the Romans arrived, the Judean King Herod had been a faithful Roman ally. This long history of cooperation assured the "Judeans" a secure place in the empire's kaleidoscope of religions and cultures.

Yet the Jews were a unique group in the empire, and their uniqueness led inevitably to social conflict. The theoretical problem was their traditional commitment to "only one God," or monotheism. Whereas Roman intellectuals could be philosophical monotheists while still respecting the symbolic gods of the nations, most Jews could not. Their sacred texts demanded exclusive devotion to the God of Israel and forbade any recognition of other gods on pain of death.

The real problem, however, was not abstract but painfully concrete. Because religion was so closely woven into the fabric of life, Jews living in the cities of the Greco-Roman world could not participate fully in normal civic affairs. They could not join their neighbors in celebrations of local holidays, which necessarily involved sacrifice to the local god. They could not eat their neighbors' food, for it did not meet the requirements spelled out by their God in the scriptures. They could not engage in normal business on Friday evenings or Saturdays, because their God had commanded rest. Jewish men could not attend the public baths without exposing their circumcision, which was derided by Greeks and Romans as "mutilation" of the body. And they could not run for civic offices that would involve, as most did, some reverence for the

gods of the region. All of this created the impression that they
were social misfits. A Sicilian author claims that the Jews "made
the hatred of humanity into a tradition" (Diodorus Siculus
34.1.2). The Roman historian Tacitus, when describing Jerusalem's fortifications, asserts that the city's founders anticipated many wars "because the ways of their people differed so
from those of the neighbours" (*Histories* 5.12; cf. Cicero, *For
Flaccus* 28.69).

So the Jewish position in the Greco-Roman world was
ambiguous, and probably differed from region to region, depending on local personalities. But the dominant literary image,
at least, was negative. Jews were routinely accused of "atheism," for not respecting the traditional Greco-Roman gods,
and of "misanthropy," for withdrawing from normal social life.
We know of several incidents in which these hostile attitudes
led to actual conflict between Jews and Gentiles living in the
same cities. In some of those cases (Alexandria, Sardis), the
central Roman government had to step in and insist on the
protection of Jewish rights. We do not know how fully such
decrees were observed, but we can be sure that hostilities
smoldered in some locales.

Needless to say, when the Jews revolted against Roman
rule in Judea, in AD 66–74, this was seen by the rest of the world
as but a glaring example of their stubbornness and hatred of
humanity. Tens of thousands of Jews living in Egypt and Syria,
at least, were massacred in retaliation (*War* 2.559; 7.367–368).
That revolt was only the final explosion of a simmering anti-
Romanism among Judean Jews that had already expressed
itself in several smaller rebellions. From the Jewish side, the
revolt came because they could take no more of the insensitive
and corrupt procurators who had been sent to govern them.
But the Romans saw the revolt as an impudent challenge to
their cherished world order. Sitting near the eastern edge of
the empire's frontier, the Jewish nation had proven an irritat-
ing thorn in their side.

Once Rome had quashed the revolt, anti-Jewish sentiments erupted throughout the world. Romans saw their victory as a triumph of their gods and traditions. The land of
Judea was confiscated as the emperor's personal property. Special coins were issued with the triumphal slogan "Judea captive!"
A commemorative arch, which still stands today, was built

Coin from the First Jewish Revolt. Photo courtesy of the British Museum.

on a conspicuous Roman hill. In a highly symbolic gesture, the annual contribution that Jews around the world had formerly sent to Jerusalem for the upkeep of their temple was now redirected to support the temple of Jupiter in Rome. This tax was often collected in a ruthless and vindictive manner. Cicero's sentiments about the original surrender of Jerusalem to the Romans in 63 BC were doubtless repeated after AD 70:

> Each state has its own religion, . . . we have ours. Even while Jerusalem was still standing and the Jews were at peace, their religious rites were alien to the splendor of this Empire, the weight of our name, the institutions of our ancestors. Now this is even more so, because that nation has disclosed under arms what it thought of our rule. How dear it was to the immortal gods it has shown by being vanquished, let out for taxes, enslaved.[1]

Tacitus notes that the timing of the Jewish revolt, since it continued after other domestic and foreign threats had been removed, fueled Roman hostility: "the fact that the Jews alone had failed to surrender increased our resentment" (*Histories* 5.10).

It was in this situation that "Flavius Josephus"—the Jewish priest, Galilean commander in the revolt, Roman sympathizer turned informant, now pensioned and housed in the emperor's own villa—wrote his four works about the Jews. What did he mean to say?

THE *JEWISH WAR*

His first work, the *Jewish War*, appeared very soon after his arrival in Rome. The Greek version, which describes events up to the year 75, was finished in large measure before the death of Vespasian in 79. But in the preface to the Greek *War*, Josephus claims that it is a re-edition of an earlier version that he wrote in his native language (Hebrew or Aramaic), for the benefit of Parthians and Babylonians—nations to the east of the Roman empire (*War* 1.3, 6). We no longer possess this earlier, Semitic version of *War*. Nevertheless, modern scholars have usually seen the lost original as the key to understanding Josephus' purpose in writing the book.

Their argument goes like this. Here is Josephus, a proven collaborator with the Romans, who provided them with much information during the war, now dashing off an account of the conflict, from Rome, to the nations beyond the borders of the empire. The book contains numerous passages that declare the invincibility of Rome and Rome's divine favor. The emperors Vespasian and Titus receive lavish praise for their heroic and virtuous conduct throughout the campaign. Especially telling is Josephus' enthusiastic description of Roman military procedures, which is intended, he says, to offer "consolation to those who have been conquered and *dissuasion to those contemplating revolt*" (3.108; emphasis added). If we recall that the Parthians, at least, came close to war with Rome a couple of times during the first century, we might easily conclude that "Josephus was commissioned by the conquerors to write the official history of the war for propagandistic purposes."[2] That he wrote *War* as a lackey of the Romans, retained by them to help quell any further revolutionary hopes in the East, is the standard scholarly view.

In recent years, however, several commentators have raised serious objections to this theory. The main one is that our Greek *War* is not merely a translation of the Semitic account that was sent to the East. On the contrary, the Greek version is written in an original, highly literary style—not "translation Greek." It is filled with themes and vocabulary (e.g., for fate, free will, providence, and historical accuracy) that were native to Greek and Hellenistic literature. It uses Greek dramatic forms in its involved portrayal of Herod the Great, as in numerous other scenes. In the fashion of Hellenistic history-writing, Josephus creates suitable speeches for several of the important characters. And he often pauses to reflect on current issues of Hellenistic philosophy or historiography. In short, the Greek *War* fits perfectly within the Greco-Roman literary context. We need not doubt that Josephus wrote an earlier account of the revolt in a Semitic language, and that it may have been a piece of imperial propaganda, but we do not possess that version of *War*. The one that we do have contains a great deal that is not well explained by the usual view of the book's purpose.

Take, for example, the preface to *War*. It was required of history books in the first century that they have a compelling beginning. These "books" were actually scrolls. Because readers could not flip the pages to skim the chapter titles, or to check an index at the back, the preface was critical to the book's success. It had to give the prospective reader a fair idea of the book's contents in advance, and it also had to serve as a "hook" to stimulate interest. After unrolling this first section, the reader would decide whether to purchase the work or not. So the preface of any ancient text is a basic guide for the interpreter. That is where we too should begin to understand an ancient author's most important purpose and themes. Remarkably, this elementary principle of interpretation has often eluded interpreters of Josephus' *War*, because of their preoccupation with the earlier Semitic version.

But Josephus' lengthy preface to the Greek *War* is quite revealing. Admittedly, it contains a lot of the stock features of an ancient preface. Its first line, predictably, declares that the Jewish revolt was the greatest conflict of all time! The crucial point for an author to establish, naturally, was that his (female writers were a rarity) account of the event in question was far superior to all others. (Why would a reader pick it up if it merely rehashed what others had already said?) Josephus does not fail to drive this point home from the start (1.3). But he has a good case. Although several other accounts of the Jewish war had appeared, what other author could claim to know *both* sides of the conflict as well as he? He was not only an eyewitness but was actively engaged as both a Jewish commander *and* a Roman informant. After the war, he had privileged access to all official documents concerning the campaign. These are impressive credentials for describing "what really happened," and Josephus flaunts them.

Most important, however (and seldom noted), is the thoroughly Jewish tone of the preface. The problem with previous accounts of the war, Josephus asserts, is that they were all written with either a pro-Roman or an anti-Jewish bias. In other words, it was a heads-I-win, tails-you-lose prospect for Jews. As we might have anticipated, after the Roman victory the Jews had become the butt of Roman ridicule. (Compare triumphant Western ridicule of defeated enemies, especially in the little-understood Middle East.) Josephus complains of the war's earlier chroniclers:

> They desire to represent the Romans as a great nation, and yet they continually depreciate and disparage the actions of the Jews. But I fail to see how the conquerors of a puny people deserve to be accounted great (*War* 1.8, LCL).

In contrast to these authors, Josephus writes as a proud Jewish priest (1.3). He gives due regard to the courage of the Jews but doesl not exaggerate, as the Roman authors have done (1.9). He wants to provide what everyone claimed to be looking for in history: the precise, unvarnished truth. But in effect, as he makes clear, this balanced portrayal will be a huge step up for the much-maligned Jewish side.

These bold statements in the preface do not fit the usual view of *War* as a piece of imperial propaganda. On the contrary, they introduce a note of tension into the work that might have caused a Roman reader some uneasiness: "Here is a Jewish writer who had the good sense to surrender to us while he could (sniveling coward) and now he's going to stick up for the Jews! And from the emperor's own house!" We can see immediately that Josephus was confronted with potentially conflicting loyalties.

He resolves the problem deftly, by developing an interpretation of the Jewish war that allows him both to remain loyal to his patrons and to speak as a committed Jew. His essential thesis (*War* 1.9–12) is that the revolt was caused by only a few troublemakers among the Jews—power-hungry tyrants and marauders who drove the people to rebel against their will. The vast majority of Jews, he contends, have always been peace-loving, devoted to the Roman virtues of order and harmony. Those who fomented revolt were aberrations from true Judaism. They introduced innovations in the ancestral customs and polluted God's temple by their actions. So in destroying Jerusalem and its temple the Romans were acting as God's agents, bringing divine punishment for the outrageous actions of a few rebels.

Such a thesis is impressively elegant. Against the prevailing Roman denigration of "the Jews" as a nation, Josephus wants to make a sharp distinction between the few rebels, who met their deserved fate, and the many who survive. These latter Jews are committed to order and are therefore spiritual allies of the Romans. This approach allows Josephus to weld together his Jewish and Roman sympathies into a coherent whole, for he implies that the two nations have the same kind of traditions and aspirations.

The whole narrative of *War*, seven books in all, is devoted to proving Josephus' thesis. He begins by describing another Jewish revolt, more than 200 years earlier, in order to demonstrate that the Jews *could* fight nobly in the face of real evil. He praises the Maccabees, who opposed the wicked King Antiochus IV Epiphanes in his bid to wipe out their nation and its traditions (*War* 1.34–69). But Antiochus and his family had also been the Romans' enemy, so this is a fairly safe example to demonstrate that the Jews could fight courageously if attacked. Yet the bulk of the book shows that the Romans did not try to stamp out the Jews, so the Jews had no reason to oppose the central government. Indeed, King Herod and his whole family had been great allies of the Romans, supporting them in their conflicts against others.

Even Josephus' description of the various Jewish religious groups (2.118–166) serves his larger purposes. He introduces this account while describing a rebel named Judas of Galilee, who had counseled revolt as early as AD 6. Josephus insists that this man's philosophy of freedom from all earthly masters had nothing to do with traditional Judaism (2.118). This leads him to a description of the three recognized "schools" of Jewish philosophy—those of the Pharisees, Sadducees, and Essenes. Of these, he presents the Essenes as the most purely Jewish of the schools. He speaks at great length about their humility, order, and simplicity of life. "In their dress and deportment they resemble children under rigorous discipline" (2.126). Most important, new members must swear an oath to "keep faith with all men, especially with the powers that be, since no ruler attains his office save by the will of God" (2.140; cf. Paul, Rom 13:1). All of this is plainly calculated to mitigate the widespread hostility toward Jews throughout the empire.

Likewise, Josephus carefully composes the speeches for his leading characters. His own speeches and those of King Agrippa II, who also counseled submission to Rome, recognize that God grants world power now to one nation, now to another (2.390; 6.110). The proper course is to cooperate with God's choices. If revolt ever were necessary, God himself would bring it about. Even the stirring speech of the last rebel leader at Masada, Eleazar ben Yair, grudgingly acknowledges that God has been on the Roman side all along, so that the rebels must pay the price for the "many wrongs which we madly dared to inflict upon our countrymen" (7.332). Throughout his narrative Josephus repeatedly claims that, while the Jewish nation as a whole was disposed to harmony, the monstrous rebels introduced a radical innovation into Jewish tradition.

The rebels' chief crime was not, in Josephus' view, rebellion against Rome; it was their sin against the Jewish God and his sacred dwelling, the temple. *War* is replete with accusations that the revolutionaries defiled God's shrine and so drove his presence from them. The revolt begins when rebel priests break with hallowed tradition by refusing to offer sacrifice on behalf of the Romans (2.409). The high priestly guardians of the shrine are murdered, and rebels kill each other within the temple precincts. Josephus remarks that the holy city was "polluted by such a stain of guilt as could not but arouse a dread of some visitation from heaven" (2.455). As the situation deteriorated, with further assassinations, the rebels "transferred their insolence to the Deity and with polluted feet invaded the sanctuary" (4.150); the blood of their victims stained the sacred ground (4.201).

As a result of these offenses against the sanctuary, God himself flees the temple to stand on the Roman side (5.412). His departure is signified by terrifying omens: a sacrificial cow gives birth to a lamb; the massive eastern gate of the temple opens of its own accord; and the priests serving in the holy place hear mysterious voices declare: "We are departing from here" (6.292–300). Although this kind of temple apologetic would have been intelligible to Josephus' Roman readers (cf. Horace), it reflects a Jewish priestly, not Roman, interpretation of history. The Jewish God, Josephus implies, remains entirely in control of events; he merely uses the Romans to purge his temple of its pollution (6.110).

All ancient history writing was supposed to teach a lesson, and the intended lesson of Josephus' *War* is unmistakable: those few Jews who recklessly led the nation into revolt were entirely idiosyncratic. Their mad squabbling among themselves and ruthless behavior in Jerusalem proves that they were only out for personal gain. They had nothing of the characteristic Jewish virtue of harmony. As for the Roman leaders, Josephus infers from their obvious supremacy that God is on their side, but he does not buy into their ideology of world dominion. He does not, like other non-Roman writers, commit himself to the historic destiny of Rome.[3] He writes throughout from a Jewish and priestly perspective.

Given the social context in which Josephus composed *War*, we are forced to interpret it as a fairly bold plea on his part for the cessation of anti-Jewish writing and behavior. The obvious energy that he has devoted to sustaining his thesis throughout a detailed narrative should leave no doubt as to his sincerity. He was engaged in serious business, perhaps in trying to save lives. Even though his attempt to isolate anti-Roman feeling among the Jews may be implausible (cf. *Ant.* 20.257), he made a valiant effort to reduce the post-war hostility of Roman readers. His careful work is gravely misunderstood if it is viewed as Roman propaganda. The earlier *War* may have been; we do not know what was in it. But the Greek *War* is directed to a Greco-Roman readership, to influence them to perceive the Jews in a positive light.

This is not to deny that Josephus takes every opportunity to flatter his masters. Ancient writers knew that this was the cost of writing about contemporary events: one had to white-wash those in power. And Josephus' *War* was endorsed by the imperial family, after the fact, as the standard account of the conflict. But it is not *their* version of the conflict. On the contrary, it takes the ground away from any macho equation between "Roman victory" and "victory of the Roman gods," for it was the Jews' own God who punished them for the rebels' impious actions.

Josephus' *War* served the emperors' goals well because they had no intention of trying to stamp out the Jewish race, which was old and had been officially protected by all of their predecessors. Their goal was merely to pacify Jews around the world. It was extremely useful for them to have some credible witness who could make internal distinctions between the few aberrant troublemakers and the nation as a whole. Yet Josephus wrote the book from his own perspective, to reflect his own point of view.

THE *JEWISH ANTIQUITIES*

If we have picked up the right sense of the *War,* then that account is well complemented by the much longer *Jewish Antiquities,* which Josephus completed almost twenty years later (AD 93/94). Both were written "to refute those who in their writings were doing outrage to the truth" (*Ant.* 1.4, speaking of *War*). Scholars have universally recognized the apologetic purpose of *Antiquities.* Believing that *War* had been a Roman propaganda vehicle, however, they have often supposed that Josephus had a massive change of heart between the composition of the two works, and that *Antiquities* is a work of repentance for his earlier subservience to Rome. Such a theory is precluded by the interpretation of *War* offered above. We should rather understand both works as apologies (in the sense of "defenses") for Judaism. One deals with the recent revolt, the other with ancient Jewish traditions. Josephus himself always speaks of the two works as if they were distinguished only by their subject matter, not by their purposes (*Ant.* 1.1–6; *Ag. Ap.* 1.54–55).

One can understand why it was necessary to defend the Jews after their revolt against Rome, but why recount their ancient history? We have already noted the common slander about their alleged "hatred of humanity." This was accompanied by wild tales about Jewish origins. Just as an individual's genealogy determined his nobility, so a nation's greatness was thought to be conditioned by its origins and history. The Romans believed, for example, that their own city had been established by the gods; so Rome's greatness was to be expected. As far as they knew, the Jewish nation had been founded by Moses, who was somehow negatively associated with Egypt, a country revered for its ancient and sophisticated culture. It was perhaps inevitable that, knowing nothing of the Bible's account of the Exodus, they would try to trace the Jews' perceived antisocial tendencies back to Moses.

Several unkind versions of the Moses story circulated. Most originated in Egypt, where there was an old antagonism between the Jewish and Gentile residents of Alexandria. One of the earliest stories (mentioned about 300 BC) held that the Jews had been expelled because of a famine in Egypt resulting from the Egyptian gods' displeasure over the presence of these aliens. After leading these outcasts to Palestine, Moses "introduced a way of life that was unsociable and hostile to strangers."[4] Another legend held that the Jews were originally a nation of shepherds that had invaded Egypt and behaved murderously for 500 years until they were driven out (see Josephus, *Ag. Ap.* 1.228). Perhaps the most common version claimed that they were Egyptian lepers, whom the gods had ordered to be banished for the sake of purity. These lepers were naturally antisocial because of the pathetic physical condition that had caused them to be banished. According to one Egyptian writer, the Jewish Sabbath had no more lofty origin than a groin infection that had forced the Israelites to stop their wandering on the seventh day out from Egypt (Apion, cited in *Ag. Ap.* 2.21). And the Jews' abstinence from pork was commonly explained on the ground that this animal was subject to scabies, which reminded them of their former leprous condition.[5]

So we can see that, in a world fascinated by the origins (or "etiologies") of contemporary things, Greco-Roman perceptions of Jewish peculiarity in the present were tied up with all sorts of rumors about the nation's past. No matter which story they embraced, most authors would have agreed with Tacitus' remark that it was Moses who "gave [the Jews] new rites, contrary to those of the rest of mankind."[6] The lawgiver was variously seen as a war-lord, a con-man, a leper, or a renegade Egyptian priest, but little good was said about him.

It was to combat all of this misinformation concerning Jewish history that Josephus wrote *Jewish Antiquities*. In the preface to this work he lays out its aim and scope: he is writing for the whole Greek-speaking world, to tell them about Jewish origins and the "constitution" given by Moses (1.5). Notice his language here: Moses was a "law-giver," who trained the Jews "in piety and the exercise of the other virtues." These are just the points that he needs to make for Greek readers. Jews are not the bizarre and anti-social people that some claim them to be; they espouse the highest values of all civilized people. Josephus drives the matter home with a thesis statement (1.14):

> But, speaking generally, the main lesson to be learnt from this history by any who care to peruse it is that men who conform to the will of God, and do not venture to transgress laws that have been excellently laid down, prosper in all things beyond belief, and for their reward are offered by God felicity (*eudaimonia*); whereas, in proportion as they depart from the strict observance of these laws, things (else) practicable become impracticable, and whatever imaginary good thing they try to do ends in irretrievable disasters (LCL).

In other words, Jews are exemplary citizens of the empire. They are committed to the bedrock values of Greco-Roman civilization: piety toward God, justice toward humanity, and a firm belief in divine retribution. They have ancient traditions of the noblest character.

In his defense of Judaism here, Josephus repeatedly uses the language of ancient philosophy. The Greek word *eudaimonia* (yoo-die-mo-NEE-uh) in the above quotation, translated "felicity," more literally means "good spirits" (compare "demon" from *daimōn*). It had the sense of happiness or well-being, not unlike our popular term "wellness." Ancient philosophy was not confined to the professor's study and classroom but incorporated much of what we would consider psychology, religion, and the sciences. It embraced the whole quest for knowledge and wisdom. According to Aristotle, the main goal of philosophy was *eudaimonia* (*Nicomachean Ethics* 10.6.1), and by Josephus' time there were various schools that offered recipes for happiness—the Stoics, Epicureans, Cynics, Platonists, Aristotelians, and Skeptics, among others. All of these schools shared a commitment to simplicity of life and "virtue," though they might have defined these terms differently.

Josephus, it seems, is trying to enter Judaism into the marketplace of philosophical positions in the Greco-Roman world. He presents Moses as the Jews' founding philosopher, who first studied the works of God in nature and then drafted a constitution that would match national law with natural law (*Ant.* 1.19–20). By beginning his account with creation (in Genesis 1–11), Moses drew attention to the principles of natural law in order to provide a basis for the civil laws that followed (in Exodus 20). Understanding God as the perfection of virtue, Moses set down laws that would enable humans to imitate that virtue (*Ant.* 1.23). So Josephus claims that the laws of Moses are entirely in keeping with the "nature of the universe" (*Ant.* 1.25). In Josephus' day, the most popular form of philosophy was Stoicism, which held that there was a single unifying principle in all of life, called Nature or Reason, and that happiness could be found in living in accord with that life force. Josephus interprets Moses' laws within this framework. He concludes his preface: "Should any further desire to consider the reasons for every article in our creed, he would find the inquiry profound and highly philosophical" (*Ant.* 1.25).

Philosophical schools in the Hellenistic world tended to place great emphasis on their founders. Even though in fact later members of the schools had unavoidably modified the original teachings, it was customary to portray each school as having a "succession" of great teachers who passed on the original teaching of the founder intact. Manuals that spelled out the succession of teachers for each school circulated widely. This is significant because Josephus too places great emphasis on the *succession* from Moses. He claims that Moses delivered his teaching to the priests and that the high priests, ever since, have been charged with preserving it accurately (*Ant.* 4.209–210, 304; *Ag. Ap.* 2.185). Throughout *Antiquities*, he is careful to enumerate the high priests, and he takes the trouble to note in his conclusion that he has laid out the succession of kings and high priests (*Ant.* 20.224–251, 261). Whereas some Greco-Roman authors had suggested that the Jews' original good ideas about God had been corrupted by later superstition,[7] Josephus insists that not only was Moses' original teaching supremely virtuous, but it was handed down intact to Jews of his own day.

Moses is not the only philosopher in Josephus' presentation of Jewish history. Moses was anticipated by Abraham, who had carefully studied heavenly bodies and was the first to conclude that the ultimate power, God, was one (*Ant.* 1.154–157). While in Egypt, Abraham even taught astronomy and arithmetic to the Egyptians (*Ant.* 1.166–167). After Moses came Solomon, who was thoroughly acquainted with all forms of nature; he surpassed all ancient philosophers in wisdom (*Ant.* 8.42–44). Indeed, Josephus' whole narrative of Jewish history is aimed at demonstrating its preoccupation with the philosophical questions of virtue and well-being. In retelling the biblical stories for Greek readers, he uses the word *eudaimonia* forty-seven times, though it does not appear in the Greek Old Testament. And he regularly pauses, while narrating some biblical scene, to point out who was acting with virtue and who was displaying vice. All of this supports his thesis that those who live virtuously, in accord with Moses' laws, prosper; those who ignore the laws suffer.

Josephus' most striking effort to portray Judaism as a philosophy is his presentation of the Pharisees, Sadducees, and Essenes. As in *War,* he portrays them here as the major sub-philosophies or "schools" within the national philosophy shared by all Jews. He even compares the Essenes to Pythagoreans (*Ant.* 15.371) and the Pharisees to Stoics (*Life* 12). The former share all of their goods and live simple, celibate lives (*Ant.* 18.20); the latter avoid all luxury (*Ant.* 18.15). He says repeatedly that the main issues dividing these schools are the kind that divided the Greek schools—differences over their understanding of human nature, fate, free will, and the soul (*Ant.* 13.171–173). He uses the common technical term for philosophical schools (sg., *hairesis*) to describe the Jewish groups, and even elaborates a little on the "succession of fathers" recognized by the Pharisees (*Ant.* 13.298). We see, then, a sustained effort on Josephus' part to present Judaism as a national philosophy.

At first this tactic seems strange within the context of the ancient world. National religions were usually distinguished sharply from philosophical schools. Most other known religions had an ethnic and geographical base. The worship of Isis, for example, was simply an Egyptian national religion; Cybele was the Phrygian goddess; Mithra was the chief Persian god. As these traditions became known throughout the empire they attracted members from other nations, but they were still largely identified with their ethnic base. Each had its own temples and sacrificial rituals, which could be traced back to time immemorial. The philosophical schools, by contrast, originated with historical founders of the relatively recent past. Without temples or ethnic bases, they did not usually engage in sacrifice and worship but rather devoted themselves to study, teaching, and moral exhortation.[8]

Within this context, on the one hand, Judaism satisfied the normal criteria for a national religion: it had an ethnic and geographical center, with temple, priesthood, and sacrificial system. On the other hand, the earliest Greek observers of Judaism had noted its "philosophical" quality. When Jews were still mainly concentrated in Palestine, some writers described them as "a nation of philosophers."[9] The reasons for this impression seem to lie in those features of Judaism that distinguished it from other national religions, for example: (a) its exclusive belief in one God; (b) its prohibition of images, which betrayed a "philosophical" notion of God; (c) its limitation of sacrifice to one temple, in Jerusalem, so that Jews outside of Jerusalem could only study and teach about God (as did the philosophers) but not perform the rituals; and (d) its preoccupation with study of texts and moral teaching. All of these features made Judaism appear more of a philosophy than a national cult. Several Jewish authors before Josephus had exploited this image,[10] but his extended narrative allowed him to work the theme out in considerable detail.

In addition to presenting Judaism positively as a national tradition of the greatest antiquity (from creation) and highest ethical standards, Josephus wants to confront head on the current slanders about Jewish history. We see this clearly in his presentation of Moses. Against the allegation that Moses was a leper, Josephus emphasizes his remarkable beauty from birth (*Ant.* 2.230–231). He omits the biblical story that had Moses' hand turn leprous as a sign of God's power, for this would have provided more fuel for the slanders. For the same reason, he passes over the Bible's detailed laws about the treatment of leprosy and emphasizes rather that Moses banished all lepers from community life (*Ant.* 3.265–268). He also drops the story of Moses' killing the Egyptian, which might have seemed to confirm the Jews' antisocial behavior, and substitutes a non-biblical account of Moses' military heroism in Ethiopia (*Ant.* 2.238–253). Against the charge that Moses had erected a golden ass's head in the temple, Josephus omits the golden calf episode and the story of Moses' putting his wife and sons on a donkey's back; he carefully describes the interior of the temple to emphasize that no image was permitted there. These changes indicate Josephus' keen sensitivity to the charges that we find in Greek and Roman authors of the period. He wants to show that "our lawgiver was a man of God and that these blasphemous charges brought against us by the rest of men are idle" (*Ant.* 3.180).[11]

One of his most striking alterations to the biblical narrative is his diminution of the idea of "covenant." In the Bible, God establishes a series of special agreements with Abraham, Isaac, Jacob, and Moses. Unlike the earliest covenant, with all humanity through Noah (Gen 9:8–17), these contracts designate Abraham's physical descendants as God's special possession, his "chosen people" who are granted the entire land of Canaan (Gen 15:17–20; 17:1–27; Exod 19:4–6). With the covenant comes the requirement to serve the God of Israel alone and to oppose all other gods in the land. But this exclusivism was seen by Greco-Roman observers as extremely old-fashioned and narrow-minded. Moreover, God's promise of land to Israel was inconsistent with the fact that Rome now ruled the world! To avoid giving his opponents any more ammunition, Josephus systematically removes the stronger covenantal statements from his paraphrase of the Bible (*Ant.* 1.183–185, 191–193). He promises to explain, in a future work, the Jewish practice of circumcision and the dietary laws—covenantal obligations that struck outsiders as antisocial behavior (*Ant.* 1.192; 3.259). And he even declares, against the charge of "atheism," that Moses' law demands respect for the gods and temples of all other nations (*Ant.* 4.207).[12]

Finally, Josephus tries hard to make his narrative resonate with the instincts of his readers. Some leaders, like Moses, Solomon, and the Hasmonean John Hyrcanus, he presents as embodying Plato's ideal of the philosopher-king. Abraham and David, for their part, are heroes like Odysseus—men of great wealth, valor, and prestige. Throughout, he conforms his narrative to the standards of Hellenistic novel writing, which emphasized the characters' thoughts, motives, and emotions. A good example of Josephus' adaptation of the Bible to these ends is his story of Joseph and Potiphar's wife. Whereas the biblical version recounted the episode in a few spare sentences (Gen 39:7–18), Josephus expands it to several pages (2.41–59). The extra space is given over to lengthy reflections and speeches by the characters on virtue, chastity, the sanctity of marriage, and the snare of lust. Josephus manages to sharpen both the erotic tone and the moralizing lesson of the story. He has transformed the brief episode into a miniature novel.

In short, Josephus' *Antiquities* is an all-out campaign to dispel the ridicule and misinformation that characterized literate Roman portrayals of the Jews. It is a massive effort at legitimation, seeking to demonstrate the great antiquity and nobility of Jewish traditions. From the beginning he challenges the reader "to test whether our lawgiver has had a worthy conception of [God's] nature" (1.15). In books 14 and 16, he cites dozens of decrees issued by emperors and lesser governments in recognition of Jewish rights. He includes these, he says, to show "that in former times we were treated with all respect and were not prevented by our rulers from practising any of our ancestral customs," and also "to reconcile the other nations to us and to remove the causes of hatred which have taken root in thoughtless persons among us as well as among them" (16.174, LCL). If Jews in the Greco-Roman world had always been subject to some disdain because of their distinctive customs, the revolt against Rome brought them universal opprobrium. Josephus wrote both *War* and *Antiquities* to try to maintain a secure place for his people in the political-religious scene.

In scope, *Antiquities* is much more extensive than the preface indicates. Josephus claims that he is following the precedent provided by the Greek (Septuagint) translation of the Torah. He says that this translation (made in the third century BC) proves both Jewish willingness to publicize their laws and Greek readiness to hear. But a new translation is necessary because the older one was limited to the laws of Moses (1.5, 9–13). So he will render the whole of the scriptures into Greek without adding or omitting anything (1.17).

This proposal is misleading because: (a) he has used existing Greek translations as the basis for much of his paraphrase; (b) as we have seen, he significantly embellishes, indeed rewrites, the biblical story; and (c) his paraphrase of the Bible covers only *Antiquities* 1–11. The remainder, in books 12–20, mainly repeats and expands the earlier material of *War*—events under the Hasmoneans, the Herods, and the Roman governors before the revolt. Some commentators have noted that Josephus seems to stretch the latter half of *Antiquities* to reach twenty books; for example, book 19 is mainly devoted to a detailed account of the emperor Caligula's death, which seems ill-suited to a work on Jewish history. It may be that he wanted his work to match the twenty books of the *Roman Antiquities,* written a century earlier by Dionysius of Halicarnassus.

The significant overlap between *War* 1–2 and *Antiquities* 12–20 has engendered much scholarly discussion because it turns out that Josephus regularly revises his opinions in *Antiquities* over against *War.* Although earlier scholarship had put this down to his discovery of new sources, that explanation now seems insufficient. Rather, Josephus appears to have changed his mind about some major figures in the interval between *War* and *Antiquities.* He is especially critical now of Herod the Great and his family for their disregard of Jewish law, and he modifies his portrayal of some Hasmonean rulers.

These alterations seem best explained on the following grounds. (a) *Antiquities'* thesis of inevitable divine retribution for good and evil conduct invites some changes in the presentation. For example, Herod, who obviously suffered a tormented end, is now shown to have brought this on himself, whereas in *War* the purpose was to present the Judean king as a Roman ally. The same motive may explain the detailed account of Gaius' death (*Ant.* 19.1–166), since that emperor was the embodiment of wickedness: he had opposed God by demanding that his own statue be erected and worshiped in the Jewish temple. (b) The urgency of the post-war situation has subsided enough with the death of Vespasian and Titus that Josephus need not flatter some of the major players so extensively. Although he maintains his thesis about the Roman right to rule and the Jewish rebels' impudence, he relaxes his effort to isolate the rebels so completely. He concedes that the whole nation felt pressed by the Romans, and that many sympathized with the rebel position; nevertheless, most people still realized the wisdom of cooperation (*Ant.* 18.3). So the rebels were, after all, an aberration. And (c) the vast increase in space that he allots to the post-biblical period requires a great deal of new material. It is that new material in the latter part of *Antiquities* that contains Josephus' only references to figures connected with early Christianity, which will concern us in chapter 5.

THE *LIFE*

Josephus' other two surviving works, the *Life* and *Against Apion*, may be discussed briefly because they are sequels to *War* and *Antiquities*, respectively.

Though a sequel to *War* in content, the *Life* was published as an appendix to *Antiquities*, within two or three years of the larger work's appearance (93/94).[13] It has no preface of its own, but is introduced at the end of *Antiquities* (20.266). It appears with *Antiquities* in all known manuscripts of that work and is cited by Eusebius as part of *Antiquities* (*Eccl hist* 3.10.8). Finally, Josephus closes the *Life* with the claim that he has now completed his account of "our antiquities" (*Life* 430). Why did he append this brief life story to the end of *Antiquities*?

As we saw in discussing Josephus' career, the tract is not really a "life" in the sense of a complete autobiography. It does include some highly stylized references to Josephus' ancestry, birth, and education (*Life* 1–12), and to his post-war activities (*Life* 414–430). But the core of the work (*Life* 28–406) deals in considerable detail with only a five-month period in his life, namely, his tenure as Galilean commander in the revolt.[14] This period became controversial with the appearance of a book by Justus of Tiberias that challenged Josephus' account of his activities in *War*.

That Josephus was deeply provoked by Justus is clear from his remarks about the Tiberian author. He introduces him early in the piece. Upon his arrival in the Galilee, the region he was sent to pacify, he found Tiberias already in revolt (*Life* 32). Over against the peace-loving, "respectable citizens" was a faction that was bent on war with Rome (*Life* 34). This group was led by Justus' father Pistus, who "had a strain of madness in his nature" (recall the importance of a man's pedigree).

A third faction was led by Justus himself, to whom Josephus here devotes considerable space. This man, we are told,
pretended to be hesitant about hostilities with Rome but actually encouraged them. His sole motive was personal power,
which he thought would result from a change of government
(*Life* 36). He tried to stir the Tiberians to revolt by appealing to
their pride: whereas their city had once been the capital of
Galilee, that honor now went to Sepphoris. Nero had trifled
with their city by giving it as a gift to King Agrippa II. They
should avenge their honor by joining the Galileans in fighting
the Romans (*Life* 37–39). In case the reader is in doubt about
Justus' motives, Josephus continues: "he was a clever dema-
gogue and by a charlatan's tricks of oratory more than a match
for opponents with saner counsels" (*Life* 40). Here Josephus
notes that Justus has written a history of "these events"—presumably, of affairs in Tiberias. But Justus has used his considerable training in Greek culture to "disguise the truth."
Indeed, it was to him and his brother that "our ruin was almost
entirely due." Josephus promises to prove this claim as his
narrative unfolds (*Life* 40). So Josephus' own account plays
itself out as a response to Justus.

Plainly, Josephus has been stung. His physical opponent
during the revolt has since become his literary adversary, and
a formidable one—formidable enough for Josephus to write
the *Life* in response. We pause to note that the portrayal of
Justus here does not make complete sense. If he had preached
rebellion as openly as Josephus claims, then he can hardly
have been trying to "feign hesitancy," as Josephus also claims.
We become immediately suspicious when we see that Justus'
motives are alleged to be power-lust and "general depravity"
(*Life* 40), for these are weapons drawn from the arsenal of
polemic, not real psychological motives.

Our suspicion intensifies when we next meet Justus and
find that he is supporting John of Gischala, another of Josephus' adversaries whom we have met before (*Life* 87). So he is
not after personal power. Justus also supports a high-ranking
delegation sent from Jerusalem to remove Josephus. These
four men, with a bodyguard nearly one thousand strong, had
been sent under the authority of the high priest and the respected leaders of the country to arrest our author (*Life* 196–
203). Both John of Gischala and Justus endorsed them (*Life*

192, 279). This means that Justus was not the isolated crank that Josephus wants to portray. Rather, he represented a widespread and credible opposition. Josephus, of course, must now dismiss all of his adversaries—high priest, leading Pharisees, Justus, and the official embassy—as either innately evil or open to bribery (*Life* 195–196).

After describing at length the machinations of the delegation (*Life* 199–335), Josephus turns to address Justus, who has "taken upon himself to write an account of this war" (*Life* 336–338). This second-person confrontation constitutes the heart of the *Life* (336–367). Again accusing Justus of fabrication, he says: "Being, therefore, now compelled to defend myself against these false allegations, I shall allude to matters about which I have hitherto kept silence" (*Life* 338). Indeed, he was silent (in *War*) about the points made by Justus, and we might wonder why. He tries to head off this question by claiming that he was only trying to spare his opponents from undue scorn (*Life* 339). But Josephus was never reluctant to disparage his enemies. Obviously, he had formerly omitted the issues raised by Justus because they were incompatible with his intended self-portrait.

What exactly did Justus say? Since *Life* seems to be a rebuttal of Justus' account, we would not go far wrong if we listed Josephus' positive claims about himself and assumed that Justus had asserted the opposite. In addition, the less flattering admissions that Josephus now makes were doubtless required by incontrovertible evidence presented by Justus. Finally, in his confrontation of Justus, Josephus directly quotes some of his claims. Putting all of this evidence together, we end up with the following general outline:

A. Josephus wrote the *War* to present himself as a wily and resourceful general (though a reluctant participant in the war) enjoying the full support of the central authorities most of the time. His only opponents were a handful of jealous and evil thugs.

B. After the *War* appeared, Justus wrote an impressive history of the whole conflict, including events at Tiberias, Jotapata, and Jerusalem (*Life* 357–358), which presented a very different view. Given Josephus' attack on his rhetorical prowess, we may suppose that the book was widely read and that it caused Josephus significant embarrassment. Its survival into the ninth century indicates that someone found it interesting enough to copy. In general, Justus claimed that:

1. *His* narrative is the truthful one, intended to expose the lies of others like Josephus (*Life* 357).

2. Josephus behaved as a tyrant (*Life* 302), intimidating the city-folk, especially the peace-loving populace of Tiberias, into joining the revolt (*Life* 340, 350).

3. Josephus was not initially commissioned as a general in the Galilee. Rather, he was an independent tyrant and his despotic actions aroused the indignation of the most eminent and fair-minded citizens, not only John of Gischala and Justus' family but also the high priest Ananus, the respected Pharisee Simon ben Gamaliel, and the whole Jerusalem council (*Life* 188–198).

More specifically, Justus may have charged that:

4. Because Justus and his family favored cooperation with Rome, Josephus abused them. His partisans had cut off the hands of Justus' brother, then killed him, and Josephus threatened Justus with the same treatment (*Life* 174–188).

5. Josephus lived in luxury, practiced extortion, and maintained a mercenary army for protection (*Life* 77–78, 284).

6. Josephus authorized the confiscation of imperial corn stores from the villages of Galilee to use the proceeds for fortifications (*Life* 71–73).

7. Josephus supported John of Gischala's profiteering racket in olive oil, needed by Jews of Caesarea Philippi (*Life* 74–76).

8. Josephus' behavior at Jotapata was cowardly (*Life* 357).

C. Josephus wrote the *Life* because his reputation as a captured enemy general was being seriously tarnished by Justus' claims. Those assertions that he could dispute, he did; those that seemed undeniable, he granted but reinterpreted. For example, he allows that he was not initially sent as a general (*Life* 28) but insists that he was *ultimately* confirmed as sole commander (*Life* 310). He also concedes the stature of Simon ben Gamaliel but suggests that the Pharisee's friendship with John of Gischala corrupted him (*Life* 191–192). And he alleges that the high priest had originally supported him entirely (*Life* 194), but changed his mind only when bribed by Simon. (Conveniently, he notes that "everyone in the city remained ignorant of the plot" [*Life* 196].)

We can no longer tell what really happened in the Galilee, though it seems certain that Josephus has some fairly large skeletons in his closet. On the other hand, we cannot check Justus' account for its accuracy, and we should assume (other things being equal) that it was no less deceptive than Josephus'.

AGAINST APION

Josephus' last surviving work was written as a sequel to *Antiquities*. In his view, that long account of Jewish history had failed to accomplish its objective:

> Since . . . a considerable number of persons, influenced by the malicious calumnies of certain individuals, discredit the statements in my history concerning our antiquity, and adduce as proof of the comparative modernity of our race the fact that it has not been thought worthy of mention by the best known Greek historians, I consider it my duty to devote a brief treatise to all these points (*Ag. Ap.* 1.2, LCL).

When Josephus' opponents spoke of the "comparative modernity" of Judaism, they were demeaning it. As we have seen, Greeks and Romans tended to revere what was old and established beyond memory. But Jews did not become well known throughout the Mediterranean until the second century BC. The claim that they were merely a degenerate offshoot of the Egyptians was a serious challenge to their social legitimacy. Rather than rehashing the story told in *Antiquities*, Josephus decides to tackle the issue of Jewish antiquity in a systematic, essay-type format. In so doing, he creates a model of religious apologetics that has seldom been matched.

Josephus did not supply the title "Against Apion"; that originated with those who transmitted his writings. It is not particularly apt, since only the first half of the second volume has to do with Apion. The two volumes have a much broader scope: they are Josephus' most impassioned defense and advocacy of his nation's traditions.

We have no clear idea of the book's date, except that we must allow time beforehand for the dissemination of *Antiquities*, for a largely negative (literary?) response to it, and for the composition of the new work in two volumes. Presumably, those factors would date it in the vicinity of AD 97–100 or later.

Josephus begins the first book with a "digression" (*Ag. Ap.* 1.57) on the general untrustworthiness of Greek authors (*Ag. Ap.* 1.6–56). It is not really a digression, of course, for it immediately removes the assumption that everything worth saying was said by the Greeks. He points out the relative lateness of Greek historians (5th. cent. BC), provides examples of discrepancies among them, and explains these as the result of carelessness and a concern for style over substance. To these practices he contrasts the extreme care of the orientals—Egyptians, Babylonians, and Persians—with their ancient records, and he cleverly includes the Jews among the Easterners. Like the others', the Jews' history has been vouchsafed to the priests (such as Josephus), who have maintained it with scrupulous accuracy (*Ag. Ap.* 1.29).

This attack on the Greeks, already begun in *War* (1.16), is not as daring as we might think at first. Although we as outsiders look on the Romans as having swallowed Greek culture bodily, the Romans themselves did not always see it that way. They took over only what was self-evidently true and right. Many of them resisted "hellenization." In Josephus' day there was already a literary history of criticizing the Greeks, and there were also grand debates between those who preferred "Asian" style to the classical Greek. Most would have granted his point (already made by Herodotus) that the Egyptians and Mesopotamians had more ancient cultures. In challenging the Greeks, therefore, he was on safe ground.[15]

This accomplished, in *Against Apion* 1.58 he sets out a prospectus for the rest of the book. He will: (a) explain why the Greeks were mainly silent about the Jews; (b) prove that they did nevertheless mention the Jews in places; and (c) "show the utter absurdity" of the charges made about Jewish origins. The Greeks knew little about the Jews, he maintains, because the latter had no outlet to the sea but were a quiet, inland, agricultural nation (*Ag. Ap.* 1.60–68). In a brilliant move, he notes that the Romans are also not mentioned by the earliest Greek writers, for the same reasons! But then he shows that the Jews were mentioned in various Egyptian, Phoenician, Babylonian/Persian, and Greek histories (*Ag. Ap.* 1.69–226). The upshot is that the Jews left Egypt nearly a thousand years before the famous Trojan war of remote Greek history (*Ag. Ap.* 1.104—a mistake on Josephus' part). Since most of the documents quoted by Josephus have long since perished, this section of his account is extremely valuable to historians. Finally, having culled from these Gentile historians the points he wanted to make about Jewish antiquity, Josephus takes up their anti-Jewish assertions one by one. His method is first to cite or summarize the author at some length, then to point out the logical contradictions in his account. His tone is extremely sarcastic, which makes it humorous and effective. Josephus shows himself here to possess a wide background in Greek literature and a keenly critical eye.

Josephus ends the first volume rather suddenly, with the note that he has run out of space (*Ag. Ap.* 1.320). Evidently, he became carried away and only now realized that he was at the end of his scroll. So the attack on Apion, which takes up the first half of the second volume (*Ag. Ap.* 2.2–144), and from which the whole book derives its name, simply continues the author-by-author analysis of volume 1. Apion was a famous Egyptian scholar who had moved to Rome to teach rhetoric in the thirties of the first century. Known by several emperors, he wrote books of literary criticism (on Homer) and a comprehensive history of Egypt. He was also an outspoken adversary of the Jewish community in Alexandria. He opposed their bid for Alexandrian citizenship before the emperor Gaius, and his Egyptian history was the source of much misinformation about Jewish origins. Josephus first claims that Apion's assertions hardly require serious refutation, but then he devotes half the volume to that purpose. Obviously, the claims of such an influential scholar, which included the accusation that Jews annually sacrificed and ate a Greek male while swearing hatred of all Greeks (*Ag. Ap.* 2.95), demanded a refutation.

Josephus takes particular delight in the appropriate means by which Apion met his end. This propagandist, who had mercilessly derided circumcision and the Jewish dietary laws, got an ulcer on his genitals that rendered circumcision necessary. But gangrene set in and took his life (*Ag. Ap.* 2.144).

On the theory that the best defense is a good offense, Josephus devotes the rest of this book to a summary description of Moses' laws. Having responded to the false claims about them, he will now present them in their own right, to show that they "promote piety, friendly relations with each other, and humanity towards the world at large" (*Ag. Ap.* 2.146). He begins with a discussion of Moses himself, which praises him as the most ancient of legislators, an outstanding general and leader, and one who devised laws to cover the whole of life. His brilliance lay in his establishing a "theocracy" (Josephus seems to have coined this term), which brought the whole of life under the reign of God, thus creating a blissful

harmony (*Ag. Ap.* 2.179–181). Whereas the elite Greek philosophers had achieved a noble view of God, but kept it to
themselves, Moses had long since made such conceptions the
common property of all Jews (*Ag. Ap.* 2.168–171, 224). Whereas
Plato had posited an ideal republic in which all citizens
knew the laws, Moses made the dream a reality among the
Jews: even the women and children knew the laws (*Ag. Ap.*
2.175, 257).

This panegyric on Moses is followed by a summary of the
laws themselves (*Ag. Ap.* 2.190–219). Josephus begins with the
prohibition of images (always admired by outside observers)
and its philosophical implications. He then describes the restraint of Jewish sacrifice—in one temple only and not as an
occasion for wild partying. He follows with laws relating to the
family and social relationships, including a notice that the
woman "is in all things inferior to [or controlled by] the man"
because authority has been given to the man (*Ag. Ap.* 2.201).
We should take this statement with a grain of salt, since Josephus is selectively choosing items that will appeal to his readers. He continues with an emphasis on the gentleness and
humanity of the laws, then concludes with a promise of "living
again" for those who observe them. Plainly, this is not a pro-
portional summary of the actual laws in the Bible; indeed,
much of what Josephus says (such as concerning the afterlife)
is not in the books of Moses at all. He has chosen a few central
items in order to impress his readers with the humaneness of
Jewish traditions.

The remainder of *Ag. Ap.* (2.220–296) is a fitting conclusion to Josephus' literary career, for it reaches truly sublime
heights. He compares the Jewish laws favorably to the highest
aspirations of Greek philosophers. He elaborates on Jewish
willingness to die rather than transgress the revealed constitution. He even claims that Greek philosophers imitated Jewish laws. Moreover, Jewish customs such as observance of the
sabbath and dietary restrictions have now spread to every
single nation of the earth:

> The greatest miracle of all is that our Law holds out no seduc-
> tive bait of sensual pleasure, but has exercised this influence
> through its own inherent merits; and, as God permeates the
> universe, so the Law has found its way among all mankind (*Ag.
> Ap.* 2.284, LCL).

Though it might seem exaggerated, this assertion of Judaism's appeal is matched by the complaints of Roman literati about the rapid spread of Jewish observance in the world.[16] Josephus uses this appeal to answer his critics: "It follows, then, that our accusers must either condemn the whole world for deliberate malice in being so eager to adopt the bad laws of a foreign country, . . . or else give up their grudge against us" (*Ag. Ap.* 2.285). We are faced with the paradox that, although Roman writers consistently disparaged Judaism, many ordinary folk were attracted by it and even converted.

Josephus closes the book with a stirring encomium on the laws, which should be allowed to speak for itself:

> What greater beauty than inviolable piety? What higher justice than obedience to the laws? What more beneficial than to be in harmony with one another, to be a prey neither to disunion in adversity, nor to arrogance and faction in prosperity; in war to despise death, in peace to devote oneself to crafts or agriculture; and to be convinced that everything in the whole universe is under the eye and direction of God (*Ag. Ap.* 2.294, LCL)?

So much for the old Christian assumptions about Judaism as dull and dry works-righteousness. And so much for the church fathers' belief that the destruction of Jerusalem virtually wiped out the Jews, leaving only an anemic remnant to wander the earth. Jewish sources from the period simply do not support such claims. Christians do well to repudiate them.

CONCLUSION: JOSEPHUS, THE MAN AND THE WRITER

Josephus has usually been either loved or hated. The hatred has stemmed from his personal biography, which, even on the most charitable reading, smacks of opportunism and routine deception. Nevertheless, Christians have tended to value him for what they thought he said about the destruction of the temple and about Jesus as Messiah. This traditional bifurcation of opinion lives on among scholars in a milder form. Those who are concerned with his biography usually regard him with deep skepticism; those who focus on his writings as literary productions tend to admire his dedication to a theme.

It is natural that we should want to choose between these options. We want to know whether Josephus was one of the "good guys" in history or one of the bad guys. Our assessment depends on our starting point. On the one hand, if he could behave like that, then his writings must be dismissed as self-serving rhetoric. On the other hand, if he could write so passionately in defense of his faith, in a time of crisis, then we should give his behavior the benefit of the doubt.

I would propose, however, that we resist our natural inclination to make such neat assessments. Our own experience of the world teaches us that people who are capable of inspiring speech or writing (the two were closely linked in antiquity) often lead less than exemplary lives. This does not mean that their speech is deliberately deceitful; it may reflect their deepest yearnings. People are more complex than the labels "good" and "bad" suggest. We could all be accused of hypocrisy by someone or other, if we were in positions that attracted such attention.

In Josephus' case, we ought to bear in mind three further considerations: (a) his biography is not something that we know, but it must be hypothetically reconstructed from highly stylized accounts; (b) his writings, which are immediately accessible, show him to have labored extensively and persuasively in defense of his people; and (c) in many cases, his duplicity is quite deliberately recounted by *him*, in an effort to demonstrate his resourcefulness. A striking example is *Life* 126–144, in which Josephus not only admits but relishes at length a barefaced lie that saved his life. We can hardly use these rhetorical ploys as evidence against him. I, for one, take his real personality to be unknown. At the same time, I have deep respect and gratitude for the writings that he has left us.

FOR FURTHER READING

On the place of Jews in the Greco-Roman world, see:

- Molly Whittaker, *Jews and Christians: Graeco-Roman Views* (Cambridge: Cambridge University Press, 1984), 1–130 [containing the most important texts in translation, with notes and introductions].

- Menahem Stern, *Greek and Latin Authors on Jews and Judaism*, 3 vols. (Jerusalem: Israel Academy of Sciences, 1976) [which provides the complete texts of relevant passages, in the original language and in translation, with commentary].

- Jerry L. Daniel, "Anti-Semitism in the Hellenistic-Roman Period," *JBL* 98 (1979), 45–65.

Balanced and readable introductions to each of Josephus' writings are offered by:

- Harold W. Attridge, "Josephus and his Works," in *Jewish Writings of the Second-Temple Period* (Compendia Rerum Iudaicarum ad Novum Testamentum 2.2; ed. Michael Stone; Assen: Van Gorcum; Philadelphia: Fortress, 1984), 185–232.

- Per Bilde, *Flavius Josephus between Jerusalem and Rome* (Sheffield: Sheffield Academic Press, 1988), 61–122.

Of the older general introductions, the following article, by a great Josephus scholar, stands out:

- Benedictus Niese, "Josephus," *ERE* vol. 7, 569–79.

A fine introduction to the major themes of *Antiquities*, although it only deals specifically with the first eleven volumes, is:

- Harold W. Attridge, *The Interpretation of Biblical History in the* Antiquitates Judaicae *of Flavius Josephus* (Missoula: Scholars, 1976).

Introductions to *War* and *Life*, from quite different perspectives, are to be found in:

- Shaye J. D. Cohen, *Josephus in Galilee and Rome. His Vita and His Development as a Historian* (Leiden: E. J. Brill, 1979).

- Steve Mason, *Flavius Josephus on the Pharisees: A Composition-Critical Study* (Leiden: E. J. Brill, 1991).

Although it does not deal systematically with the literary features of *War* or *Life*, this book sheds much light on both works:

- Tessa Rajak, *Josephus: The Historian and his Society* (London: Duckworth, 1983).

NOTES

1. Cicero, *For Flaccus* 28.69; in Whittaker, *Jews and Christians*, 118.

2. So H. St. John Thackeray, *Josephus: the Man and the Historian* (New York: Jewish Institute of Religion, 1929), 27.

3. See Menachem Stern, "Josephus and the Roman Empire as Reflected in *The Jewish War*," *JJC*, 71–80.

4. So Hecataeus of Abdera, cited in Whittaker, *Jews and Christians*, 37.

5. For numerous examples of these claims, see Whittaker, *Jews and Christians*, 16–62.

6. Tacitus, *Histories* 5.4, cited by Whittaker, *Jews and Christians*, 20.

7. Cf. Strabo, *Geog.* 16.2.34–7, 49.

8. See Nock, *Conversion.*

9. So Clearchus of Soli and Hecataeus of Abdera, ca. 300 BC; cited in Josephus *Ag. Ap.* 1.179, and Diodorus Siculus 40.3.1–5.

10. Cf. the Alexandrian Jewish writings of Aristobulus, "Aristeas," and Philo.

11. Cf. Gohei Hata, "The Story of Moses Interpreted within the Context of Anti-Semitism," *JJC*, 180–97.

12. Josephus is able to build here on the the Septuagint at Exod 22:28. Whereas the original Hebrew text (Exod 22:27) had said only that "You shall not curse your God," the third-century BC Greek translators rendered it "You shall not blaspheme gods" without qualification.

13. *Life* 359 assumes the recent death of King Agrippa II. His death has recently been dated to ca. 95 by Seth Schwartz, *Josephus and Judean Politics* (Leiden: E. J. Brill, 1990).

14. The detailed account begins after the defeat of Cestius Gallus (late November, 66) and concludes with Vespasian's arrival in Galilee (May, 67).

15. See, for example, the work on rhetoric entitled *To Herrenius* 4.1–4.

16. See Whittaker, *Jews and Christians*, 85–91. Seneca, for example, is said to have lamented that "the practices of this villainous race have become so influential that they are now accepted throughout every land. The vanquished have given laws to their victors!" (*On Superstition,* cited by Augustine, *City of God* 6.11, trans. Whittaker, *Jews and Christians*, 88).

4 Who's Who in the New Testament World?

The three preceding chapters dealt with Josephus on his own terms; the next three will deal with New Testament questions. That is, we shall now take issues that arise for us as readers of the NT and present them to Josephus for clarification. Because we now have some familiarity with his world of thought, we should be well positioned to understand his replies. The illumination to be gained from Josephus is potentially infinite, however, so we shall need to restrict our enquiries in some way. I propose in this chapter to consider selected groups of people in the NT world who are discussed by Josephus. Chapter 5 will narrow the focus to figures from the early Christian tradition who are mentioned by Josephus. Then, in chapter 6, we shall look at parallels between Josephus and Luke–Acts. A concluding chapter will both summarize the results of our study and suggest some wider aspects of Josephus' significance.

If we want to study the background of the NT—historical, political, social, geographical—everything that Josephus wrote is relevant to some degree. All we can do in this chapter is ask him about some obvious, representative features of the NT world. I have selected the following groups of people: Herod the Great and his family; the Roman governors of Judea; the Jewish high priesthood; and the Jewish religious parties (especially Pharisees and Sadducees). My goal in discussing these groups is to provide examples of how one can read Josephus' "evidence" about any given topic within the context of his own thought. The point is not, in the first instance, to discover the *truth* about these people, which would require the massive

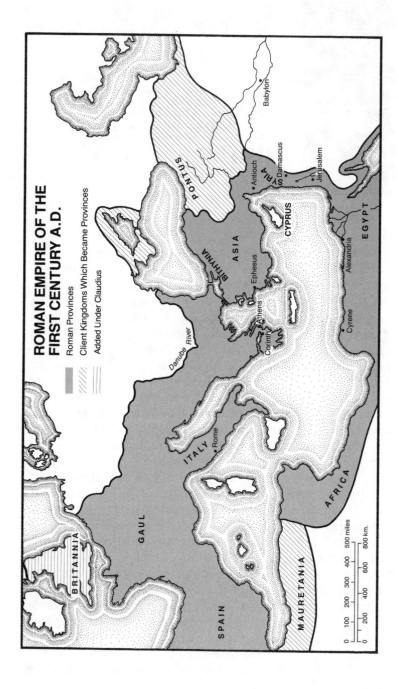

ROMAN EMPIRE OF THE
FIRST CENTURY A.D.

Roman Provinces

Client Kingdoms Which Became Provinces

Added Under Claudius

investigation of all relevant sources that typifies the large manuals of Jewish history. Our purpose is rather to understand how these groups function in Josephus' narratives, and what *he* wants to say about them. With such experience, I hope, the reader will then be able to consult the text of Josephus itself on any number of other questions that might be of further interest. So this is not a comprehensive treatment of the NT background; it is rather a primer for further study.

HEROD THE GREAT AND FAMILY

Of the various political figures who provide the setting for the Gospels and Acts, Herod the Great and his descendants are the most prominent. Four generations of the Herodian family are mentioned in the NT.

(a) The infamous King Herod himself (reigned 37–4 BC) ruled all of Palestine[1] at the time of Jesus' birth (Matt 2:1–19; Luke 1:5).

(b) At Herod's death, his kingdom was partitioned by the Roman emperor Augustus and given to three of Herod's sons; but none of them was granted the title of king, which Herod had enjoyed.[2] Archelaus became ethnarch or "national ruler" and was given the heartland of Judea, Samaria, and the coastal plain. He was hated by his subjects and, proving hopelessly incompetent, was removed by the Romans in AD 6. Herod's son Antipas, by contrast, governed Jesus' home region of Galilee for more than forty years, throughout Jesus' entire life (4 BC–AD 39), along with the region of Perea across the Jordan River. It was this tetrarch, or "ruler of a quarter," who executed John the Baptist (Matt 14:1; Luke 3:19), and he also played a role in Jesus' death (Luke 13:31; 23:6–12). Still a third son, Philip, was made tetrarch of the more remote northern and eastern parts of Herod's kingdom (AD 4–34). His only claim to fame in the NT is the notice that his wife Herodias had been taken by his brother Herod Antipas (Matt 14:3–4; Mark 6:17–18; cf. Luke 3:1).

(c) Herod Agrippa I, a grandson of Herod the Great, was king over his grandfather's entire territory for a critical four-year period in the young church's history (AD 41–44).[3] He executed the apostle James, brother of John, and imprisoned Peter, who then miraculously escaped (Acts 12:2–19).

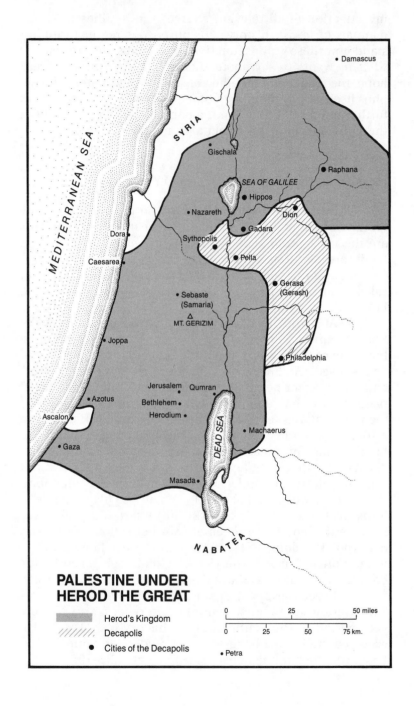

PALESTINE UNDER HEROD THE GREAT

	Herod's Kingdom
///////.	Decapolis
●	Cities of the Decapolis

Major Figures in the Herodian Family

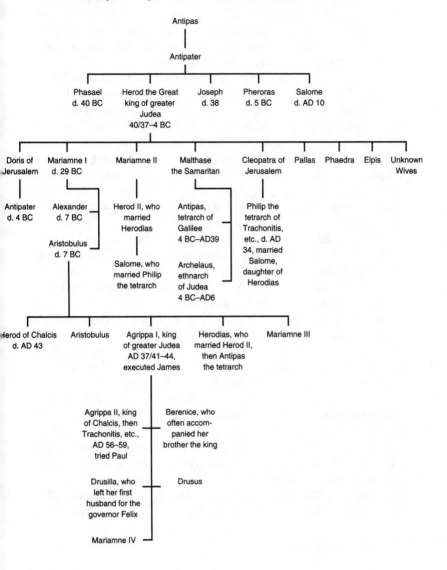

(d) Finally, Agrippa II, son of Agrippa I and great-grandson of Herod the Great, served as king, first of Chalcis in Lebanon (AD 48–52) and then of the former territories of Philip in the northeastern region of Palestine (AD 53–93).[4] This is the King Agrippa who, while visiting the new Roman governor in Caesarea (about AD 59), interviewed Paul and found him innocent of any serious charge (Acts 25:13—26:32).

It is a compelling example of Josephus' importance for NT studies that the above sketch, basic though it seems, could not have been written without his help. Obviously, the family of Herod played a major role in the lives of Jesus and the first Christians. But remarkably, the Gospel writers refer to this dynasty in the vaguest of terms. Only the author of Luke–Acts displays any interest in clarifying the relations among various rulers, and even he is often unclear. Mark, for his part, says that it was a "King Herod" who executed John the Baptist, after offering his step-daughter as much as half of his "kingdom" (Mark 6:14–29). But the Baptist's ministry was under Herod's son Antipas. And Josephus insists, at some length, that none of Herod's sons was permitted to be a king or to have a kingdom (*War* 2.20–38, 93–100). Significantly, Matthew and Luke both call this Herod (Antipas) the *tetrarch* (Matt 14:1; Luke 3:19), in agreement with Josephus. But then Acts refers to Agrippa I as simply "Herod the king" (12:1) and to his son (Agrippa II) as "Agrippa the king" (25:13) without any further explanation. We should be in a sorry state indeed if we did not have the accounts of Josephus for clarification.

I have argued, however, that it is insufficient for us merely to rip out from Josephus' accounts those bits of information that help us, while discarding the rest like old rags. Josephus has both a sustained interest in and outstanding sources for his accounts of the Herodian dynasty. He uses these rulers to illustrate major themes of his various works. If we are to understand his "evidence" about the family of Herod, we must first examine the roles that these figures play in his stories.

In the *Jewish War*

In general, as we saw in the last chapter, the entire family of Herod appears rather differently in *War* and *Antiquities*. In *War*, we first meet Herod's father Antipater, the clever governor of Idumea. Through courage and shrewd diplomacy, Antipater manages to win successive favors from various Roman leaders, culminating in the governorship of Judea, which Julius Caesar grants him in about 47 BC. He appears as a staunch ally of the Romans and a vigorous opponent of all rebellion (1.201–203). His son Herod is first appointed by his father as governor of Galilee, where he too rids the country of rebels and is thus deeply admired by the people. Some people oppose Herod, to be sure, but these are "malicious" advisors of the high priest and "knaves" (*War* 1.208, 212). Herod appears throughout as brave (1.369–385, 429–430), virtuous, compassionate (1.295), pious (1.354–357), aided by providence (1.331, 341), and especially devoted to his family (1.263–267). This might seem difficult to maintain in view of the fact that he would ultimately murder his own wife and several sons, but Josephus explains these acts as the result of vicious intrigues against the king: he was the innocent victim of his own devotion to his wife Mariamne, who was his undoing (1.431–440).

The *War* says little about the tenure of Herod's sons in their respective jurisdictions but focuses rather on the turbulence that arose in Judea while they were away in Rome bidding for the right to succeed Herod. In describing the rebellion at home, Josephus takes the opportunity to illustrate his major themes: that only a few of the Jews had rebellious instincts, even though the masses had real grievances (2.73, 84–89); that the rebel leaders were really tyrants, out for personal power, who squabbled among themselves and terrorized other Jews (2.56–65); and that the Roman authorities, by contrast, were mild and supportive of the innocent population (2.75–78). Significantly, right where we might expect Josephus' account of the Herodian princes' governments, he inserts his lengthy account of the Essenes' politically docile mode of life, in contrast to that of the rebel faction (2.118–166). This interlude is intended to divert the reader's attention from the messy affairs of Judean politics, toward the philosophical heart and soul of Judaism.

Herod's grandson, King Agrippa I, appears in *War* mainly as a central figure in Roman political circles, for he served as intermediary between the new emperor Claudius and the Roman senate, which initially opposed Claudius (2.204–213). And Herod's great-grandson, Agrippa II, makes a long speech to those rebelling against Rome in AD 66, in which he argues that God is now with the Romans; he castigates the rebels for their belligerent, non-Jewish behavior (2.345–404).

Obviously, Josephus' description of the Herodian dynasty in *War* has been tailored to fit that work's broad apologetic agenda. These important figures illustrate his claims that the majority of Jews have always been well disposed to the Romans, who now rule by God's permission, and that rebellion is alien to Jewish ancestral custom. He even offers the Romans an implicit paradigm for their treatment of the Jews after the recent rebellion of AD 66–74: just as the Romans had not allowed earlier rebellions in Judea to weaken their support for the Herodian family and its supporters, so also now they should not harass all Jews for the troubles caused by a few renegades.

In the *Jewish Antiquities*

Because the purpose of *Antiquities* is somewhat different from that of *War,* Josephus uses the family of Herod to different effect in this narrative. To begin with, the larger scope of *Antiquities* allows him to devote much more space to the Herodian dynasty; King Herod alone receives three entire books (books 15 to 17). Much of the new coverage serves to point out the moral and religious shortcomings of Herod's family. This new theme is plainly geared to illustrate one of *Antiquities'* theses—that, according to the ancient and noble traditions of the Jews, those who stray from the laws come to a disastrous end. Since Herod and many of his successors came to disastrous ends, and since Josephus has available excellent accounts of Herod's reign (see below), he elects to use this first-rate material to develop his argument.

The new angle is already apparent in Josephus' discussion of Herod's father Antipater, who is now introduced to the reader as a "rabble-rouser" or troublemaker: he gains influence in Judea as a result of his scheming, lies, and secret intrigues (14.8–18). Likewise, Herod himself appears as a violator of the nation's laws. Whereas *War* had attributed such charges to some "malicious" members of the high priest's entourage (1.208), *Antiquities* makes it clear that Herod really was a violator who literally got away with murder. He is opposed in court by one Samaias, "an upright [or righteous] man and for that reason superior to fear" (14.172). When Herod is appointed king by the Romans, the legitimacy of his rule is now questioned (14.403). Indeed, the Jewish nation as a whole seems to oppose his rule (15.8–10). Josephus elaborates considerably on Herod's execution of the high priest Hyrcanus: in *War*, this had been merely an unfortunate incident that was part of Herod's domestic trouble (1.433–434); now Josephus concludes firmly against Herod, that it was an act contrary to both justice and piety (15.182). Josephus goes on to assert that Herod's introduction of Greek-style games and institutions into Jerusalem was a perversion of Jewish ancestral custom and a cause of the city's later destruction (15.267; cf. 328). And the king's impious act of opening David's tomb brought God's wrath on his family (16.179–188).

In several revealing passages, Josephus reflects on Herod's character. In one, he takes issue with those who find him paradoxical because of his combination of generosity and cruelty. Josephus himself believes that these apparently conflicting tendencies arise from a single motive, namely: unbridled greed and ambition. Herod was generous only when it served his ends; otherwise he was harsh, immoderate, bestial, and evil. Josephus hastens to add that Herod's character stood in opposition to the values of Jewish law and tradition (16.150–159). In another place, Josephus recognizes the role of "fate" in Herod's career and also assigns some blame to his sons. But he is strongest in his denunciation of the king himself, who had an "irreligious spirit" and a mind that could not be turned from evil (16.395–404). While narrating Herod's death, Josephus describes him as "cruel to all alike and one who easily gave in to anger and was contemptuous of justice" (17.191). *Antiquities* dwells at length on the horror of Herod's worsening illness and declares that his unparalleled suffering was the result of his sacrilege (17.150–152). This new moralizing in *Antiquities* is calculated to demonstrate the work's thesis that the wicked suffer divine retribution.

The same thesis explains the significant new information about Herod's son Antipas, who governed Galilee from 4 BC to AD 39. The tetrarch, we are now told, built the city of Tiberias over a former graveyard, in violation of Jewish law (Num 19:11–16). He had to bribe and force the poor into living there, for he knew that he had built it in contravention of religious law (18:36–38). Most noteworthy for us is the complex of events associated with Antipas' marital affairs. Married for some time to the daughter of a neighboring Arab king, the tetrarch fell in love with his step-brother's wife Herodias while on a trip to Rome. (This brother was a son of Herod the Great by his wife Mariamne II, daughter of the high priest Simon.) These two conspired to elope, but Herodias would marry him only if he dismissed his Arab wife; and thus they plotted. Their proposed marriage, of course, flatly violated Jewish law, which prohibited a man from marrying the wife of a brother who was still alive.

But Antipas' first wife got wind of the plot and escaped to her father, the Arabian king, who took the opportunity to settle by war an old boundary dispute with Antipas. In the ensuing conflict, Antipas was soundly thrashed and his army would have been destroyed, says Josephus, had the Romans not intervened (18.109–124). It is within this story of Antipas' affairs that Josephus includes an account of John the Baptist (18.116–119). The tetrarch's execution of this good and righteous man, says Josephus, was held by many Jews to be the cause of his military defeat (18.116).[9] Josephus pointedly concludes that his whole narrative of Herod's family is germane to his account because it demonstrates that no degree of worldly power will succeed if it is not matched by piety toward God. This lesson contributes to the "moral instruction of mankind" (18.128).

The brief career of King Agrippa I is described in much greater detail in *Antiquities* than in *War*. It is shaped to illustrate both sides of Josephus' thesis: the righteous prosper and the wicked suffer. On the one hand, the king successfully intercedes with the emperor Gaius Caligula, who temporarily stays the order that would have put his statue in the Jewish temple (18.297–301). Later, Agrippa persuades the emperor Claudius to speak in favor of Jewish rights in Alexandria and around the empire (19.279, 288). Thus Agrippa is a key figure in Josephus' larger claim that Roman emperors have consistently recognized the legitimacy of Jewish traditions. Further, Agrippa champions the "laws of his fathers" by demanding the punishment of some men who had erected a statue of the emperor in a Jewish synagogue (19.299–311). Indeed, Josephus claims that he "scrupulously observed the traditions of his people" and neglected nothing in the way of proper observance and sacrifice (19.331).

On the other hand, Josephus relates that the young Agrippa had been a hopeless profligate who had recklessly depleted his funds and managed to offend many Roman aristocrats who had initially befriended him (18.143–204). He was at one point imprisoned by the emperor Tiberius for his impudent hope that this emperor would soon die and be replaced by Agrippa's friend Gaius. It seems to have been Agrippa's early exercise of improper ambition that came back to haunt him at the end. Josephus relates that when Agrippa attended games in Caesarea, the sun reflected off his clothing in such a way that he appeared superhuman. Some of the nobility hailed him as divine, and, since he did not correct them, he was immediately felled with a heart attack, which five days later proved fatal (19.343–352). Once again, Josephus' thesis is illustrated: those who violate the laws are punished.

Agrippa II is not a major figure in *Antiquities,* though he does play an important role in the appended *Life.* Significantly, Josephus mentions widespread rumors of an incestuous relationship between Agrippa II and his widowed sister Berenice (Be-re-NI-kay; 20.145) and also Agrippa's unprecedented violation of Jewish custom by building an addition to his palace that enabled him to watch sacrifices in the temple (20.191). Josephus does not draw out the consequences of these actions, perhaps because Agrippa II was still alive in 93/94 when Josephus completed *Antiquities.* But Josephus repeatedly appeals to Agrippa in support of his own trustworthiness, and even cites two of the king's sixty-two letters in this regard (*Life* 364). So it would not have been in Josephus' interest to dwell on Agrippa's shortcomings!

The differences between *War* and *Antiquities* in their portrayals of the Herodian dynasty have usually been explained on the bases of: (a) Josephus' new sources in *Antiquities*; and (b) some shift in his own thinking and/or circumstances that made him either less charitable or more honest concerning this powerful family. Both of these factors seem beyond dispute. His generally positive portrayal of Herod in *War* accords with what he later dismisses, in *Antiquities,* as the flattering whitewash written by Herod's aide Nicolaus of Damascus, who "wrote to please him and be of service to him, dwelling only on those things that redounded to his glory" (*Ant.* 16.184). Nicolaus had written a universal history in 144 books, perhaps the largest of its kind, and had included several books on Herod's reign. It seems that Josephus relied heavily on this work when writing *War*, for which it served his purposes adequately: it showed the Judean king's great favor and prestige in Roman circles. By the time he writes the latter part of *Antiquities*, having lived and studied in Rome another twenty years, he is aware of several other sources on Herod and uses them to expand and qualify the earlier account (*Ant.* 15.174).

While speculating on the reasons for those changes, however, we must not forget that the literary aims of *War* and *Antiquities* are different. Even in *War* Josephus lets slip some indirect religious criticisms of Herod (*War* 1.649–650; 2.84–86), but to dwell on them there would not have helped his argument. In *Antiquities*, by contrast, his purpose is to show that divine judgment inexorably follows departure from the laws of Moses; so his treatment of Herod's career is replete with illustrations of this point. It is this change of purpose in *Antiquities* that explains his willingness to employ the new sources and the critical language.

In the New Testament

We may now ask how the NT references to the Herodian family might be better understood against the background of Josephus' portrayals. The only actions of Herod the Great described by a NT writer come in Matthew's infancy narrative (Matt 1–2). This is the story of the Persian astrologers, the magi, who follow a star to Jerusalem in search of the newborn "king of the Jews." When Herod hears of this birth, he orders that all male children in the vicinity of Bethlehem two years of age or younger (in accordance with the time of Jesus' birth) be killed (Matt 2:16). Joseph and Mary flee to Egypt, however, and while they are there Herod dies. Joseph intends to return home to Judea but, finding that Herod's son Archelaus has come to power, settles instead in Nazareth of Galilee (2:19–23).

The atmosphere of this story fits well with Josephus' descriptions of Judean life under Herod and Archelaus: many Jews at the time lived in great fear, and any rival claimant to the title "King of the Jews" would have been ruthlessly exterminated. Such a story would have resonated with people living in the region who knew the Herodian legacy. It is strange, though, that Josephus does not mention any slaughter of male children near Bethlehem, right at the end of Herod's reign where his account is most detailed. Such a monstrous action could hardly have escaped public notice. Josephus would arguably not have mentioned it in *War* even if he had known about it because that work holds Herod up as a fine example of good Jewish-Roman relations. But in *Antiquities,* as we have seen, the gloves come off and Josephus goes into all sorts of grisly details about the king's rule, in order to explain the unparalleled suffering that eventually killed him. In this context, in which he dwells on much less dramatic infractions of the law, it would plainly have served his purpose to mention a massacre of infants; that would have been Herod's basest action. The probability, therefore, is that Josephus did not know the story of the massacre, although he had not only Nicolaus' history but also several other accounts of Herod's reign at his disposal. Further, it seems clear that Luke did not know the story, for in his account Joseph and Mary come from Nazareth to Bethlehem for a census and then return home after Jesus' birth (Luke 2:1–39); there is no room here for Matthew's two years in Bethlehem followed by a sojourn in Egypt.

In the case of Herod Antipas too, much of the Gospel material is well complemented by Josephus' account. In particular, the Gospels' notice that the Baptist was imprisoned for criticizing the tetrarch's marriage to his sister-in-law Herodias makes abundant sense. Josephus says only that John was imprisoned because he had a large following and therefore was suspected of revolutionary motives; but in view of what was going on at the time of John's arrest, it would not contradict Josephus' point if the preacher had also said of Herodias "It is not lawful for you to have her" (Matt 14:4). Also compatible with Josephus' portrayal is Luke's account of Antipas as "that fox" who was seeking to kill Jesus (Luke 13:31) and participated in his trial (23:6–12).

Significant problems arise, however, when we compare Mark's and Josephus' accounts of John the Baptist's death. Chief among these are Mark's claims: (a) that the tetrarch Antipas was "King Herod" (6:14); (b) that Herodias had been Philip's wife (6:17), whereas Josephus claims that she had been the wife of Herod the Great's son by Mariamne II; (c) that Antipas was involuntarily trapped by his own oath into executing John, for he knew him to be righteous, heard him gladly, and wanted to keep him safe (6:20), whereas Josephus had Antipas arrest and execute John out of sheer self-interest (agreeing with Matt 14:5; Luke 3:19); and (d) that Herodias' daughter, a noblewoman who *was* married to the tetrarch Philip, according to Josephus, was brought in to dance for the viewing pleasure of Herod and his friends (Mark 6:21–29).

In making historical determinations about this episode, one ought to note: (i) that Matthew, by radically abbreviating the story, removes or mitigates many of these problems; (ii) that Luke, who also used Mark as a source and seems to have known a good deal about Herod Antipas, omits the story of the party altogether; (iii) that later manuscripts of both Matthew and Luke omit the name "Philip" from the designation of Herodias' former husband (presumably since Josephus' writings were becoming known when the texts were copied); and (iv) that one cannot easily challenge Josephus' account of the Herodian family tree because it is a tightly woven and intricate whole, based on excellent sources; the Gospel of Mark, for its part, has no sustained interest in Antipas but mentions only this single episode. Like Matthew and Luke, the Gospel that we call "Mark" is really an anonymous document; we do not know who wrote it or where his information came from.

Within the NT corpus, King Agrippa I and his son Agrippa II appear only in Acts. The story of Agrippa I, in Acts 12, corresponds well to the general tone of Josephus' account in *Antiquities*. The comment that because Agrippa's execution of James "pleased the Jews" he also arrested Peter (Acts 12:3) fits with Josephus' observation that the king, unlike his grandfather, devoted himself to Jewish life and causes. Since Josephus presents this as something of a shift from Agrippa's earlier prodigality, we should probably understand it as a strategy for ruling, a means of maintaining popular support, more than a heartfelt commitment to Jewish tradition. The claim in Acts that Agrippa was trying to maintain the favor of the Jewish people presupposes the kind of political motivation that Josephus asserts. Moreover, Josephus and Acts (12:22) agree that the king died because he accepted praise as a god.

As we have come to expect, however, the details in Acts do not correspond exactly to those offered by Josephus. Whereas Josephus had claimed that Agrippa I was stricken with a heart attack in the theatre at Caesarea, after failing to correct those who hailed him as a god, and died five days later, Acts has him seated on his throne in the palace at Caesarea. A delegation from Tyre and Sidon had come to appease the king's anger, and when he had finished a speech to them, these Gentiles hailed him as a god. Then "immediately an angel of the Lord struck him, because he did not give the glory to God; he was eaten up with worms and expired" (Acts 12:23). Interestingly, Acts mentions that Agrippa had first put on his royal robes (12:21), but it does not say with Josephus that the glimmer of the robes inspired the worship. Why, then, are the robes mentioned? It almost seems as if the author (we do not know who wrote Luke and Acts) has Josephus' story in mind—that he has adapted Josephus' story for his own narrative purposes (see chapter 6). Once again, Josephus' evidence cannot be easily dismissed, since he was in close contact with the king's son (Agrippa II), from whom he even cites personal letters (*Life* 363–366); he had detailed information about both father and son.

As for Agrippa II, the account in Acts of his interview with Paul (25:13—26:32) dovetails nicely with Josephus' portrayal. Josephus nowhere mentions Paul, and that is probably evidence of the limited impact that Christianity had on the turbulent life of first-century Judea. Josephus does mention several other persecuted leaders of small groups, and Paul is mistaken for one of these, according to Acts 21:38. (More about that in chapter 6.)

But the story of Paul's hearing before Agrippa II matches Josephus' account in its repeated reference to his companion Berenice (Acts 25:13, 23; 26:30). Acts does not explain that she is Agrippa's sister, nor does it divulge why she is there, since she does not figure into the exchanges with Paul. But once we know Josephus' account, the episode takes on a poignantly sarcastic tone. Here is the great king in all his pomp (25:23), brought in by the Roman governor Festus because of his purported expertise in things Jewish (25:26), which the governor lacked. Indeed, Paul repeatedly appeals to the king's familiarity with Jewish teaching: "With all that I am being accused of by the Jews, King Agrippa, I consider myself fortunate that I am to defend myself before you today, above all because you are expert in Jewish customs and issues" (26:2–3, 26–27). But if the reader is supposed to realize that this august Jewish leader, who presumes to try Paul, is all the while sitting next to the sister with whom he is having an incestuous affair, in violation of the most basic Jewish laws, then the whole trial becomes a comedy. Paul's appeals to Agrippa's Jewish knowledge are really devastating barbs.

None of this requires that either the author of Acts or his first readers knew Josephus' writings, since the rumors about Agrippa II and Berenice circulated widely. But the fact that, in its stories of both Agrippa I and Agrippa II, Acts seems almost to ride "piggy-back" on Josephus' accounts, forces us to examine more closely the relationship between these two works. We shall do so in chapter 6. For now, we simply note that while the NT accounts of the Herodian family fit with the general portrayal of their character and motives drawn in Josephus' *Antiquities*, the details sometimes differ.

THE ROMAN GOVERNORS OF JUDEA

Closely related to the family of Herod were the Roman governors of Judea. The whole of Palestine had fallen under Roman control in 63 BC, with the arrival of the general Pompey. But the Romans were disinclined to invest their own administrative and military resources into the rule of a faraway territory unless it were absolutely necessary. So for a couple of decades (63–40 BC), they were content to let the native Jewish dynasty, the Hasmoneans (who had been ruling for about seventy-five years before the Romans arrived), continue to serve as high priests with some political control over internal Jewish affairs. But the last representatives of the Hasmonean dynasty proved politically weak, and that is why Herod's father, an Idumean, could insinuate himself into Judean affairs. Ultimately, Herod himself achieved the remarkable privilege of ruling as "king" under Roman patronage (appointed in 40, ruled 37–4 BC). But when Herod's son Archelaus was banished for incompetence (AD 6), the Romans finally decided that it was time to make Judea an imperial province, bringing it under the direct control of Roman governors and armies.

The Political World of Josephus and the New Testament

High Priests	Governors in Judea/Samaria	Emperors	Rulers in Galilee/Perea
Simon son of Boethus (5 BC) Mattaiah / Joseph / Joezer / Eleazar / Jesus son of See (5 BC–AD 6)	Herod the Great (40/37–4 BC) Archelaus (4 BC–AD 6) Coponius (6–9)	AUGUSTUS (27 BC–AD 14)	Herod the Great (40/37–4 BC) Herod Antipas (4 BC–AD 39)
Ananus (6–15)	Ambivulus (9–12) Rufus (12–15) Valerius (15–26)	TIBERIUS (14–37)	
Ishmael b. Phabi / Eleazar / Simon (15–18)			
Joseph Caiaphas (18–37)	Pontius Pilate (26–36)		
Jonathan and Theophilus b. Ananus (37–41)	Marcellus (37) Marullus (37–41)	GAIUS CALIGULA (37–41)	
Simon Cantheras / Matthias / Elionaeus / and Joseph b. Camei (41–47)	King Agrippa I (41–44) Fadus (44–46)	CLAUDIUS (41–54)	King Agrippa I (41–44) Fadus (44–46)
Ananias b. Nebedaeus (47–59)	T.J. Alexander (46–48) Cumanas (48–52) Felix (52–59/60) Festus (59/60–62)	NERO (54–68)	T.J. Alexander (46–48) Cumanas (48–52) Felix (52–56) King Agrippa II (56–95)
Ishmael b. Phabi II (59–61) Joseph and Ananus II (62) Jesus b. Damnaeus (62-64?)	Albinus (62–64)		
Jesus b. Gamaliel (64-65?) Matthias b. Theophilus (65–67)		GALBA / OTHO / VITELLIUS (68/69)	
Phanni b. Samuel (67–70)	Florus (66–70)	VESPASIAN (69–79)	
	Bassus (70–72) Silva (72–75) Commodus (75–80)	TITUS (79–81)	
	Salvidenus (80–86) Longinus (86–95) Campanua (95–?)	DOMITIAN (81–96) NERVA (96–98)	Campanua (95–?)
		TRAJAN (98–117)	

Of the fourteen governors who served between AD 6 and the outbreak of the Jewish revolt in AD 66, only three are mentioned in the NT. Most famous is Pontius Pilate, who executed Jesus. Antoninus Felix and Porcius Festus appear in Acts' account of Paul's arrest and imprisonment. We shall examine Josephus' accounts of these men in the context of his larger portrayals of the Roman governors.

In the *Jewish War*

In *War,* Josephus uses the Roman governors to introduce at least two nuances into his general thesis about the Jewish revolt. First, he wants to show that, although the vast majority of Jews were peace-loving and did not desire rebellion, they had to contend with numerous provocations from the later governors. The rebels were grossly misguided, to be sure, but one can see the reasons for their hostility. Those who opposed rebellion were not themselves enamored of the Romans but rather exercised the Jewish virtues of patience and self-control. So Agrippa II is made to say: "Granted that the Roman ministers are intolerably harsh, it does not follow that all the Romans are unjust to you" (*War* 2.352, LCL). The rebels, by contrast, displayed an un-Jewish zeal for confrontation from the beginning.

Second, Josephus has to explain the conspicuous fact that, in spite of his own peace-loving inclinations, he himself ended up as a "general" in the rebel cause. Today, we can understand such a paradox in view of the many current examples of Middle-Eastern leaders who are thoroughly "Westernized" but find themselves fighting against "the West" under social-political constraint. But Josephus does not explore this paradox. Describing his appointment as general, he simply remarks that the Jewish rebels in AD 66 "won over those who still favoured Rome—both by force and by persuasion" (2.562), leaving open the possibility that he was coerced into fighting. Thus he was appointed a general, and so was John the Essene (2.567), even though the Essenes have already been portrayed as peaceful and politically docile (2.140–142). His point seems to be that by the end of 66, with the initial success of the rebels and the atrocities of the last Roman governors, even the most moderate aristocrats, including himself and the high priestly family, were caught up in the swirl of events. But to make this case plausible, he must recount the misdeeds of the last governors.

The first governor, Coponius (AD 6–9), is mentioned only in passing (2.117–118). With his arrival in AD 6, Judea fell under direct Roman administration and so was subject to direct "tribute" payments. Josephus takes this opportunity to introduce Judas the Galilean, the archetypal rebel, who immediately called for revolt on the ground that Jews should have no lord but God (2.118). This notice permits him, in turn, to discuss at length the three legitimate "schools of Jewish philosophy," which hold no such views (2.119–166). Of Coponius himself, Josephus remarks only that he held the "equestrian" rank (of the Roman lower nobility) and that he came with full powers, including that of capital punishment (2.117). This last point has stimulated much scholarly discussion because of its possible bearing on the thorny question whether the *Jewish* court was also permitted to execute criminals (e.g., in the case of Jesus). We cannot discuss that question here because Josephus does not pose it. We may note, however, that Josephus seems to mention Coponius' power here in order to set the stage for the subsequent actions of the governors, who will indeed execute Judean provincials at their discretion. So the notice helps to build a sense of tension that steadily increases throughout the remainder of the book. His point is not that the Jewish court or anyone else was deprived of the power to execute, only that Coponius *had* it.

Interestingly enough, for the NT reader, in *War* Josephus omits any mention of the next three governors but chooses to discuss Pontius Pilate's career (AD 26–36) at some length (2.169–177). He relates two episodes that illustrate this man's insensitivity and cruel capriciousness. First, upon his arrival in Judea, Pilate arranged to have standards of the emperor Tiberius, with sculpted images attached, brought into Jerusalem during the night. The Jews saw this as a violation of the second commandment (Exod 20:4), which prohibited the making of images.[6] Jewish refusal to tolerate images of God was well known throughout the Roman world, and Josephus portrays Pilate's action, "by night, under cover," as a deliberate offense. But the Jews responded with overwhelming zeal. Masses of them visited Pilate's residence in coastal Caesarea (where governors preferred to stay) and lay motionless on his lawns for five days. Finally, he summoned them to a hearing in the outdoor theatre, surrounded them with troops, and threatened to kill them if they remained obstinate. But they offered their necks to his soldiers' swords, preferring to die than to violate their laws. Impressed by their "superstition" (from his perspective), Pilate ordered the standards removed from Jerusalem (2.174).

In the second episode, Pilate was not so pliable. He had appropriated funds from the temple treasury to pay for the construction of an aqueduct, to carry water to Jerusalem. Josephus does not say that this action violated Jewish law, but he does say that the indignant Jerusalemites surrounded Pilate as he heard cases, and protested angrily. Pilate, however, had taken the precaution of planting "plain-clothes" soldiers among the crowd. At the appropriate moment he signalled for them to draw their clubs and beat the protesters. Josephus says that many Jews perished, either from the blows or from being trampled in the escape. Thus, under Pilate, the Jews were reduced to fearful silence (2.177).

Inscription bearing the name of the Roman governor Pilate.
Photo courtesy of Southwest Missouri State University.

It is noteworthy that Josephus begins his account of the governors' escalating offenses with the tenure of Pilate. This man was removed from office in the year before Josephus' birth, and Josephus doubtless grew up hearing tales of Pilate's behavior. A Jewish contemporary of Pilate, Philo of Alexandria, heard a good deal about Pilate and listed his crimes: "the briberies, the insults, the robberies, the outrages and wanton injuries, the executions without trial constantly repeated, the ceaseless and supremely grievous cruelty" (*On the Embassy to Gaius* 302). Philo may be exaggerating here for his own literary purposes: he wants to use the wicked Pilate as a foil for the virtuous Emperor Tiberius, who opposed Pilate's misdeeds. Nevertheless, where there is smoke there is fire. Philo's depiction explains why Josephus chose to begin his account of governors' offenses with Pilate. Also noteworthy is Josephus' admission that "the Jews," without distinction, were upset by these provocations. It was not the rebels alone who opposed such insensitive acts.

In *War* Josephus does not mention Pilate's replacement, for the period after Pilate (AD 37–40) was overshadowed by one of the greatest provocations in Jewish history to that point. The emperor Gaius Caligula, motivated by a desire to be worshiped, ordered that a statue of himself be installed in the Jewish temple. He sent the general Petronius with three legions to execute the order (2.184–187). The Jewish populace was so horrified that its leaders met the general in the coastal city of Ptolemais and followed him to Galilean Tiberias for an audience. The general spoke about his duty to enforce the order, the Jews about their duty toward their laws. Once again, they declared themselves ready to die rather than violate the law. Petronius, amazed at their persistence, ultimately decided that it would be better for him to risk death in failing to implement the order than to drive the nation to rebellion (2.201–202). In the end, Gaius was assassinated in Rome and Petronius was relieved of the order. But once again, Josephus makes it clear that this provocation, following soon after Pilate's odious tenure, was indeed an affront to Jewish laws and was thus opposed by all Jews alike.

Significantly, Josephus passes over the next two governors (Cuspius Fadus, 44–46, and Tiberius Julius Alexander, 46–48), after the reign of King Agrippa I (AD 41–44), with the simple notice that they, "by not violating the local customs, preserved the nation in peace" (2.220). Once again, whereas the rebels were consistently and philosophically opposed to Roman rule, most Jews were quite willing to cooperate as long as they were not asked to disregard their laws.

With the arrival of Cumanus (AD 48–52), relations between Jews and Romans deteriorated quickly. Josephus narrates three episodes representative of his misconduct, which was so egregious that the emperor Claudius finally tried and banished him. First, at a Passover feast early in his tenure, a Roman soldier standing on the roof of the temple portico turned his back to the crowd, raised his robe, and "mooned" the pilgrims in the temple courtyard, while making noises to match the gesture. Some of the outraged worshipers, the "hot-headed youths and those rebellious by nature," began to pelt the soldiers with stones. A riot ensued, and Josephus claims that more than 30,000 Jews were killed in the conflict (2.224–227). The number seems high, but Josephus later claims that at least 2.5 million persons normally gathered in Jerusalem for Passover (*War* 6.423–425), several times the normal population of the city.

In the second episode under Cumanus, some Jewish terrorists attacked and robbed one of the emperor's slaves. In the aftermath, a Roman soldier who was searching for the culprits found a Torah scroll and threw it into a fire (2.228–231). Once again the local Jews protested en masse to the governor. In this case, Cumanus thought the wiser course was to execute the guilty soldier. But tensions had been raised.

The events that brought Cumanus' governorship to a close began when a Galilean Jew was murdered by some Samaritans while traveling to Jerusalem for Passover (2.232). Some Galileans immediately set out for Samaria to retaliate, and the Jewish authorities implored Cumanus to intervene and punish the guilty Samaritans before the Galileans did. But Cumanus, occupied with other matters, brushed them aside. At that point many Jerusalemites, especially the terrorists and rebels, hurried off to Samaria for revenge; they massacred the villagers of one region. Now Cumanus was forced to act, and his troops killed many of the Jews who had attacked the Samaritans (2.236). Some of the Jews escaped, however, and continued to foment strife all around the country (2.238).

Finally, the governor of Syria, a superior to the governor of Judea, intervened. He crucified the Jewish prisoners taken by Cumanus, but also sent the Jewish and Samaritan leaders as well as Cumanus himself to Rome to explain their actions. With King Agrippa II's support in Rome, the Jewish case persuaded the emperor Claudius, and he banished Cumanus (2.245–246).

These stories provide clear examples of Josephus' thesis: the Jews were pressed beyond all reason by several of the Roman governors, but most of them, and certainly their leaders, had the wisdom to refrain from confronting the Romans. They had no intention of bringing Roman wrath on Jerusalem and the temple (2.237). What distinguished the rebels from the Jewish mainstream was their obstinate and reckless commitment to the path of war, which ultimately brought destruction on the city.

Josephus' accounts of Antonius Felix (AD 52–59?) and Porcius Festus (59–62?) are ambivalent. On the one hand, they dealt severely with both terrorists and the many religious impostors ("pseudo-prophets") who appeared at the time (2.253–265, 271). Since Josephus detests both groups, he seems to be grateful for the governors' efforts. As an example, he describes the "Egyptian pseudo-prophet" as a "charlatan" who had attracted some 30,000 "dupes" as followers; this deceiver intended to take Jerusalem from the Romans and install himself as tyrant (2.262). Josephus claims that when Felix sent the infantry against him, "the whole [Jewish] population" joined the soldiers, for they too were scandalized by such behavior. (According to Acts 21:38, right about this time Paul was mistaken for the Egyptian. See chapter 6.) On the other hand, Josephus points out the partiality of the governor and his troops toward the Greek-speaking citizens of Caesarea in their disputes with the Jewish residents; on one occasion Felix confronted the Jews and killed many of them (2.270). Josephus says nothing about Paul's appearances before Felix or Festus.

With Albinus (AD 62–64), who succeeded Festus, Josephus says that provincial affairs reached a new low. This governor, he claims, used his authority to steal private property and to exact extraordinary taxes. Moreover, he encouraged bribery from all sides, and emptied the prisons of all the terrorists who had formerly been put away: only those who were unable to bribe the governor remained in confinement. So the country exploded in factional strife, with numerous rebel groups intimidating the peaceful folk into submission, plundering at will, and killing those who demurred (2.275). Josephus flatly states that Albinus acquiesced in all of this, abetting the rebel cause, because his cooperation had been bought (2.274).

Finally, *War* asserts that Albinus' successor, Gessius Florus (AD 64–66), made his predecessor look like the "best of men" (2.277). The detailed account of Florus' government (2.277–343) inevitably draws the reader into sympathy with the rebel cause, in spite of Josephus' denunciation of the rebels. This is part of his literary art. While evoking understanding for the plight of the Jews, he simultaneously castigates the rebels for not displaying the (heroic) endurance that Jewish tradition taught (cf. 2.343–357, 393, 410, 412–414). As for Florus, he was violent, shameless, cruel, and crafty (2.278). He not only sided with the Greeks against the Jews and accepted bribes, but also pilfered funds from the temple in Jerusalem (2.293). When some young Jews made fun of this by passing around a basket for the needy governor, he became enraged and turned his soldiers loose in the market square, to kill and plunder at will (2.293–306). He even crucified upper-class Jews who held Roman citizenship and noble status—an unprecedented travesty (2.308). Josephus claims that Florus actually plotted to stir up rebellion: he told his soldiers not to return a greeting from the people, so that, when the people complained, the soldiers would have reason to cut them down (2.318–329).

War's portrayal of Florus' term effectively climaxes its general point about the Roman governors' administration. In effect, Josephus concludes: If anyone had reason for rebellion, we did, but the rebels were *still* wrong. Although we did suffer under incompetent and cruel governors in Judea, the Roman empire as a whole was obviously established by God's will; otherwise it could not have succeeded. So rebellion against it was wrong.

In the *Jewish Antiquities*

In its treatment of the Roman governors, *Antiquities* does not differ substantially from *War*. It agrees that they oppressed the Jews beyond reason, and that they reached their nadir in Gessius Florus (64–66). This governor "constrained us to take up war with the Romans, for we preferred to perish together rather than by degrees" (*Ant.* 20.257). As in *War*, Josephus allows that the whole nation, himself included, was by necessity caught up in the final catastrophic war. Only now he hints that for a short time he actually supported the war. But *Antiquities* also sustains, and even intensifies, *War*'s disparagement of those who were rebellious by disposition. In keeping with its thesis, it devotes more space to the theme of the Jews' collective sins as the cause of their catastrophe. In addition to these emphases, the longer account in *Antiquities* adds a significant amount of detail and makes a few minor changes.

Although *Antiquities* mentions the names of the governors between Coponius and Pontius Pilate, this is mainly to provide a framework for Josephus' chronicle of the high priests, in whom he has a great interest (18.30–35). The early governors themselves are dispensed with quickly. A significant addition is his notice that the occasion of Judas' rebellion in AD 6 was not merely the incorporation of Judea as a Roman province but the attendant census of property for taxation purposes, administered by Quirinius the governor of Syria (18.2). This census is mentioned in Luke 2:2 as the occasion for Jesus' birth; it will be discussed in chapter 6.

Like *War*, *Antiquities* presents Pontius Pilate (AD 26–36) as the first example of the governors' abusive behavior toward the Jews. Josephus now stresses Pilate's guilt in the episode of the military standards by noting that previous governors had taken care to remove the standards when entering Jerusalem (18.56). He also adds the story of how Pilate dealt with a Samaritan messianic figure who led his followers to Mt. Gerizim in Samaria; Pilate killed many of them (18.85–87). Most significant for us, Josephus introduces into this account of Pilate's tenure his trial and execution of Jesus (18.63–64). This passage has almost certainly been retouched by Christian copyists of Josephus' text. We shall consider it in chapter 5.

Concerning Cuspius Fadus (AD 44–46), who followed King Agrippa I, Josephus adds significant details to the brief mention in *War*. First, he notes that Fadus permitted the auxiliary troops made up of locals (Gentiles) from Caesarea and

Sebaste to stay in Judea, contrary to the emperor Claudius' orders, and that these men contributed to the final revolt by their aggravation of the Jews (19.366). Second, however, Josephus credits Fadus with prudence in his dealings with the Jewish terrorists who were removed from Judea (20.5). Likewise, Fadus is praised for his handling of "a certain impostor" named Theudas. This man, who is also mentioned in Acts 5:36 (see chapter 6), rallied a huge popular following. Claiming to be a prophet, he promised to part the Jordan river. But Fadus' men fell upon the crowd, killed many, and cut off Theudas' head (20.99). Here is another example of Josephus' supporting what he considered to be the legitimate role of the governors—to maintain order and to prosecute troublemakers.

Tiberius Julius Alexander (AD 46–48) is an interesting case. In *War* he appeared as a strong supporter of Vespasian during the revolt, and little is said about his governorship. *Antiquities* continues this restraint. It adds that Alexander crucified the rebel sons of the arch-rebel Judas the Galilean, which seems to be meant as a compliment (20.102). But Josephus also blurts out the quick notice that "this man did not remain within the traditional customs" (20.100)—apparently, that he was a Jew who had given up the distinctive practices of Judaism. This tentative assertion reflects the tendency of *Antiquities* to point out who was or was not faithful to the Jewish laws, though it would have been more compelling if Josephus had related some awful consequence of Alexander's non-observance!

In general, *Antiquities* is milder on Cumanus (AD 48–52) than *War* had been. Josephus now says that the Roman soldier at Passover exhibited his "genitals," not his backside, to pilgrims in the temple courtyard (20.108). Perhaps this act intended ridicule of Jewish circumcision. In any case, we are now told that Cumanus first pleaded with the offended Jews not to riot, but to set aside their "lust for revolution" (20.110). Only when this failed did he send troops to confront the Jews; even then, most of the casualties died while trying to flee the soldiers. Remarkably, *Antiquities* devotes less space than *War* to the Jews' outrage at the soldier who destroyed a copy of the Torah (20.116); Cumanus handles the affair prudently. Yet *Antiquities* gives much more attention than *War* to the conflict between the Galileans and Samaritans (20.118–136). It now claims: (a) that many Galileans were murdered (not just one);

(b) that Cumanus was bribed by the Samaritans not to punish the offenders; and (c) that Quadratus, governor of Syria, quickly determined that "the Samaritans had been responsible for the disorder" (20.129). This elaboration seems intended to support Josephus' general position, common to *War* and *Antiquities*, that the Jews were not troublemakers by nature.

New material about Felix (52–59?) in *Antiquities* includes the information that he contracted an unlawful marriage with Drusilla, sister of King Agrippa II, who was already married to the king of Emesa; that king had converted to Judaism and undergone circumcision in order to be her husband (20.143). It is probably no coincidence that Josephus immediately reports the tragic death of the son who was born of this illicit relationship (20.144). He goes on to say that the death of the high priest Jonathan, incidentally mentioned in *War*, was actually plotted by Felix: the governor was fed up with the high priest's constant admonitions to improve the government (20.162). In *Life*, Josephus will later claim that Felix sent some priests, "excellent men" and friends of Josephus, to face trial in Rome on a "minor and insignificant charge" (13).

Josephus is clear about the misdeeds of Felix, and claims that the governor would have been punished by the emperor had not Felix's brother Pallas been influential with Nero (20.182). Indeed, it seems that Felix's misconduct was notorious. The Roman historian Tacitus, who had no interest in siding with the Jews, singles out Felix among the Judean governors as one who "practised every kind of cruelty and lust, wielding the power of a king with all the instincts of a slave" (*Histories* 5.9).

Whereas *War* had said that Porcius Festus captured and killed large numbers of terrorists (2.271), *Antiquities* says only that there were large numbers of *sicarii* (see chapter 6) in Judea during his governorship, not that Festus did anything about them (20.185–187). Yet Josephus goes on to say that Festus "also" sent troops against "a certain impostor," who promised salvation and respite to those who would follow him into the wilderness (20.188). It is noteworthy: (a) that Josephus seems to have had the *War* passage in his mind while writing this part of *Antiquities*, and so understood (but forgot to say) that Festus put down the rebels; (b) that the unnamed deceiver sounds very much like Theudas, under Fadus' tenure, who was also called "a certain impostor"; and (c) that *War* had spoken of several such deceivers, who wanted to lead people out into the wilderness, under Felix's government (2.259). Josephus may have transferred this problem to help fill out his account of Festus' tenure.

New to *Antiquities* is the notice that Festus died in office (20.197). This sets the stage for Josephus' account of the death of James, Jesus' brother, who is stoned along with other Christians while there is no governor in Judea. Josephus castigates the high priest who was responsible for this action (20.200–201). We shall discuss the episode in chapter 5.

Antiquities is milder than *War* toward Albinus (AD 62–64). It says only that he began his government by taking every possible precaution to ensure peace in Judea; to that end, he "exterminated most" of the *sicarii* (20.204). Those prisoners who were obviously guilty of serious crimes he executed; those who were guilty of minor infractions he released. Josephus presents this as a fair policy, even though it had the unwanted effect of filling the country with terrorists (20.215)—quite a different emphasis from *War*.

With his account of the evil Gessius Florus (AD 64–66), Josephus brings to a close the narrative of *Antiquities*. As in *War*, this governor marks the ultimate deterioration of Roman government in Judea. Strangely, Josephus compares him to Albinus (20.253) as he had done in *War*, but this makes little sense in *Antiquities* because this work has not treated Albinus harshly. Once again, it seems that Josephus has *War* in mind as he writes *Antiquities*; he even takes over the exact language of the earlier work (*War* 2.277 // *Ant.* 20.254). And, having stated that Gessius' actions compelled the Jews to revolt, he refers the reader back to his precise account in *War*. This reference indicates that Josephus does not see himself as presenting a radically new version in *Antiquities*.

Indeed, there is no simple way to categorize *Antiquities'* changes to *War's* portrayal of the Roman governors. In general, Josephus maintains his position that (a) the governors from Pilate onward behaved intolerably, yet (b) the Jewish rebel-terrorists had the wrong attitude and were even more to blame for the catastrophe that befell the city (cf. 20.166, 180–181). The larger scope of *Antiquities* allows for the introduction of significant new material on the governors. Some of this has the effect of moderating their atrocities or emphasizing the misdeeds of some Jews at the time; this tendency supports *Antiquities'* thesis that departure from the traditional Jewish laws brings catastrophe. Occasionally, as with Felix and Pilate, the new material heightens the governors' misconduct. At bottom, Josephus and his readers simply assumed that Roman provincial governors were all going to behave in a greedy and violent manner, that they accepted these posts in order to enrich themselves. Josephus even claims that the emperor Tiberius knew this, and so allowed governors like Pilate to remain for long periods. Better to let them remain and govern moderately, after satisfying their greed, than to replace them quickly with others who would bleed the country, for "It is in the nature of all government to practice extortion" (20.172).

In the New Testament

How does Josephus' portrayal of the Roman governors shed light on the various NT presentations? If we read Acts with Josephus' accounts in mind, we find a piquant irony, as we did in Acts' portrait of King Agrippa II. On the surface, these governors are praised for their great beneficence toward the Jews. The Jewish spokesman who accuses Paul before Felix declares: "Being favored with abundant peace through you, and in view of the reforms that have come to this nation through your concern, most excellent Felix, in every way and everywhere we receive [this] with all gratitude" (Acts 24:2–3). Paul sustains the congeniality: "Since you have been a judge to this people for many years, I readily speak in defense of my case" (24:10). Acts presents the governors as defenders of Roman justice: they agree with Paul that they cannot condemn a man unless his accusers are present to make a cogent case (24:19; 25:16). As in the case of Jesus, these model magistrates find in Paul "nothing deserving of death" (25:25; cf. Luke 23:15, 22). It is a consistent theme of Luke–Acts that, whereas the Jews relentlessly persecuted Jesus and his followers, the Roman officials in Judea consistently found the Christians innocent. This theme arises from obvious social constraints on Christians at the time of Acts, which we shall discuss in chapter 6.

But knowing Josephus' account allows us to penetrate beneath the surface. Thus when we read that Felix came with his wife Drusilla to visit Paul while the latter was in chains (24:24), we recall that Drusilla, the object of Felix's overwhelming passion (according to Josephus) had abandoned both her lawful husband and Jewish custom when she succumbed to Felix's enticement. And Felix was notorious for his cruelty toward the Jews. Now, when this couple came to visit Paul, according to Acts, the preacher discussed with them "justice, self-control, and coming judgment" (24:25). Why these themes in particular, and not the resurrection of Jesus or faith in Christ, which dominate the book elsewhere? Their significance would not be lost on the reader who knew Josephus' accounts. Whether the reader was expected to know this background or not, the author of Acts plainly has some such information in mind, for he describes Felix's reaction to this exhortation as follows: "Felix became afraid and answered, 'Go away for now; when I have opportunity I shall send for you'" (24:25). Paul's discussion of justice, self-control, and coming judgment seems to have been carefully tailored to the governor's situation. The writer even notes that Felix expected to receive a bribe from Paul (24:26).

What is peculiar here is that the narrative of Acts almost *assumes* knowledge of an account such as Josephus'. That is, Acts itself only praises the conduct of the governors; it is not clear on internal grounds why Felix (with Drusilla present) should have been upset by a discourse on self-control and coming judgment, or why this great "reformer" should have expected a bribe. These details make sense only if we have another perspective, like that offered by Josephus. An intriguing question, then, is: What did the author of Acts expect his readers to know in advance? This question, in turn, depends on the identification of his readers (Jews? Gentiles? Roman elites? urban provincials? of which province[s]?). Without resolving that thorny issue here, we may at least conclude that the author of Acts has "encoded" his story with irony. If some of his readers knew other perspectives, as the author did, then they would have been party to the irony. Otherwise, the book's regular appeal to Roman decency over against Jewish malice would provide the key motif.

Much more difficult to understand in the light of Josephus are the Gospels' presentations of Pontius Pilate. Whereas Josephus (like Philo) treats him as the prototype of the cruel,

capricious, and insensitive Roman governor, slaughtering
Jewish provincials on a whim, the Gospels all show him insisting on Jesus' innocence, and deeply concerned that he receive
a fair trial. Even here, Luke–Acts is the most intelligible of the
Gospels against Josephus' background. When Jesus first plans
to come to Jerusalem, he sends some people ahead to make
sure that he can pass through Samaria, which lay between
Galilee and Judea (Luke 9:51–56). But his delegation is rebuffed, for the Samaritans will not let him pass if he is headed
for the Passover in Jerusalem. This episode accords perfectly
with Josephus' story about the Galileans who were killed en
route to a Passover feast in Jerusalem—twenty years later,
under Cumanus. The author seems to know a lot about the
tensions that Josephus reports. Even the disciples' hostile response to this rejection (9:54) is typical of the Galilean response described by Josephus.

As for Pilate, some of Luke's characters allude to certain
Galileans "whose blood Pilate mingled with their sacrifices"
(13:1). Josephus does not mention Pilate's attack on any Galileans, though he does describe: (a) Cumanus' later confrontation of Galileans and Judeans who took vengeance on the
Samaritans for the murder(s) mentioned above and (b) Pilate's
attack on a Samaritan leader and his followers. At least we can
say that this notice in Luke matches the atmosphere of Pilate's
tenure evoked by Josephus; it may even be that Luke has imperfectly remembered some specific story in Josephus. Also
matching Josephus' portrait is Luke's claim that Herod Antipas
of Galilee and Pilate "became friends" on the day of Jesus'
trial (23:5). We have seen that Luke does not like Antipas; the
connection with Pilate implies that the two were partners in
mischief.

The most serious difficulties come with the other Gospels. In Mark, the Jewish plot against Jesus that was hatched
early in the Gospel (3:6) comes to a climax with his arrest by a
delegation from the "chief priests and scribes" (14:43). Bent
on killing him (14:1), the Jewish leaders have no qualms about
sentencing him to death on trumped-up charges (14:59–65).
They have no concern for justice or due process; the distinguished judges even beat him and spit on him (14:65). But
then Jesus appears before Pilate, who marvels at Jesus (15:5).
This judge of character knows that the Jews oppose Jesus out

of envy (15:10) and tries to release him by the clever ploy of offering them either Jesus or the convicted murderer Barabbas (15:9). But these Jews are so opposed to Jesus, the story says, that they prefer the murderer and thus foil Pilate's plan. Even so, he pleads with them: "Why, what did he do wrong?" (15:14). But in the end, in spite of his own feelings, Pilate feels compelled by the Jewish crowd to condemn Jesus to death (15:15).

This unusual presentation of Pilate as a sensitive and just man, as a pawn in the hands of the Jewish leaders, is intensified in Matthew. This Gospel says that Pilate's wife, having suffered in a dream because of this "righteous man," told her husband not to harm Jesus (27:19). The dutiful and conscientious governor even declares his innocence in Jesus' death with the *Jewish* symbol of washing his hands (27:24; cf. Deut 21:6–9). Who then is responsible? The author leaves no doubt that it is "all the Jewish people" and their descendants (27:25), who deliberately assume the blame. Once again, Pilate appears here as the instrument of the Jewish leaders who had long since plotted against Jesus. Though committed to justice, he was compelled to carry out the people's wishes.

The author of John seems to be aware of the problem of reconciling Pilate's reputation with the claim that he was innocent in Jesus' death. So he begins his relatively lengthy exchange between Jesus and Pilate by having the governor act in a suitably cavalier and distracted manner. He says to the Jewish leaders, "You take him and judge him by your own law" (18:31). In response to Jesus, he scoffs "Am I a Jew?" (18:35). And this jaded bureaucrat poses to Jesus the famous rhetorical question, "What is truth?" (18:38). His soldiers, in character with Josephus' portrayal, beat and mock Jesus even before the trial (18:2–3). Still, Pilate quickly becomes afraid when he hears that Jesus calls himself the son of God (19:8—not mentioned in the other accounts) and wants to release him in response to Jesus' wise answers (19:12). He protests on behalf of Jesus' innocence, and John seems to say that he even handed Jesus over to the Jewish leaders so that they would conduct the execution (19:16). Only John answers the question why, if Pilate was innocent in Jesus' death, he was involved at all. John has the Jewish leaders remind the Roman governor that only he has the power of capital punishment (18:31).

A particular problem in the Gospel accounts is their claim that Pilate used to release a criminal chosen by the Jews every year at Passover (Mark 15:6; Matt 27:15; John 18:39). The story is difficult for several reasons: (a) it violates both Jewish and Roman law, according to which the guilty, especially murderers, must be punished; they cannot simply be freed by public vote; (b) it is not attested anywhere else in Jewish or Roman history and literature; (c) according to Josephus, feasts such as Passover were precisely the occasions when the Romans were most concerned about maintaining order, and so were most severe in their punishments (*War* 2.10–11, 42, 224, 232–234); (d) if Pilate could release one man to the crowds, he could presumably also have released Jesus; (e) Luke, who seems most familiar with Roman law, transforms the story so that Pilate simply yields to popular demand for Barabbas as a one-time concession, not as an annual custom (23:18); and (f) Barabbas is a peculiar name because it means "son of a father," which is hardly a distinction. None of this means that the episode is impossible, only that it is difficult to understand. On the other hand, the story does fit well with the Gospels' attempts to demonstrate the depth of Jewish opposition to Jesus: given the opportunity to choose him over a convicted terrorist, they chose the terrorist.

The Gospels' attempts to relieve Pilate of any guilt and to place it squarely on Jewish heads are understandable in light of the Christians' social-political situation after AD 70: the Jews were already considered troublemakers as a result of their failed revolt, and the Christians were in desperate need of a claim to legitimacy. Christians had to explain to the Roman world (and to themselves) how it happened that their Lord had been crucified by a Roman governor. It was natural that in such circumstances, the Jewish role in Jesus' death would be exaggerated and the Roman role minimized. And it was inevitable that Christian portrayals written in these circumstances would conflict with the writings of the Jewish author Josephus, who had no need to whitewash the governors' activities. Those activities were so notorious that Josephus could cite them as causes of the revolt while still maintaining that Jews were on the whole committed to peace with the central, divinely supported Roman government.

THE JEWISH HIGH PRIESTS

A third important group in the background of the NT that also looms large in Josephus' writing is the Jewish priesthood. In the Gospels' accounts of Jesus' death, the "chief priests" appear regularly as his opponents (Matt 16:21; 20:18; Mark 8:31; Luke 9:22; 19:47; John 7:32; 11:47–53; 12:10). The high priest hosts Jesus' trial and passes judgment on him (e.g., Mark 14:53–64). And the book of Hebrews presents the risen Jesus as the heavenly high priest (Heb 5:10; 7:26). Josephus, for his part, is proud of his priestly heritage. We have already seen that he presents the high priests as the "successors" of Moses, the guardians of the teaching that was given to Israel. Under the direction of the high priest, the priests serve as teachers and administrators of the divinely revealed laws.

But Josephus cannot simply praise the high priesthood as the authorized vehicle for transmitting Moses' teaching, for recent Jewish history, up to the revolt against Rome, involved individual high priests in various ways. Especially in *Antiquities,* therefore, where Josephus wants to expose Jewish sins as a cause of the calamity, he must also recount in detail the lawless actions of priests and high priests. In other words, he must at the same time maintain his ideal portrait of Judaism as an ancient and established tradition and explain how it was that such a noble tradition recently fell to such ignominious depths. The high priests figure on both sides of the ledger.

To understand Josephus' remarks, it is helpful to have some background knowledge of the high priesthood. In the biblical story, God designates Moses' brother Aaron as the first high priest. Once the sacred tent (or "tabernacle") is in place, God takes up residence above the box called the ark of the covenant in the "most holy place"—the innermost cube-shaped room (Exod 25:22). The high priest performs the critical role of mediator between God and the people, for he is the only one who may enter the holiest place, and that but once a year (Exod 29:44; Lev 16:2–5). This chief of all the priests is charged with representing the people to God, by supervising the whole sacrificial system and representing God to the people by ensuring that the divine teachings are propagated and observed (Lev 10:8–11). Under King Solomon (tenth century BC), the temple of Jerusalem was built as a permanent replacement for the tent, where God met Israel. All descendants of Aaron were priests by birth, though only those without physical defects could serve in the temple. The high priesthood, however, became customarily associated with a small group of priestly families—first, the sons of Zadok (tsa-DOKE), who was high priest under David and Solomon, then a progressively restricted group of clans.

The book of Deuteronomy reflects what we might call a separation of powers among the priesthood, the Israelite king, and authorized prophets: the man with executive political power must still learn and observe the laws taught by the priests (Deut 17:14–20). And everyone must listen to the prophet who declares God's will (18:15–22). But after the Babylonian exile (586–538 BC), there were no longer kings or regular prophets in Israel, so the high priest inevitably assumed such political functions as the Jews retained under foreign domination. By about 300 BC, perhaps much earlier, he had become head of a senate or "council of elders" (*gerousia*), the precursor of the Sanhedrin mentioned in the Gospels. After the exile, the high priest's power was determined by the degree to which the foreign master (Persian, Macedonian, Egyptian, Syrian, Roman) wished to interfere directly. At two points in particular, we see the foreign political rulers breaking with Jewish tradition by deposing legitimate high priests early in their tenure (they normally served for life) and replacing them with others who would serve the king's interests better. Such aggressive rulers were the Seleucid King Antiochus IV (175–164 BC) and Herod the Great (37–4 BC).

In the *Jewish War*

In *War*, Josephus effectively uses the case of the high priesthood to isolate the rebels as untypical of mainstream Jews, in keeping with his literary aims: the priesthood in general represents traditional, established Judaism, opposed to the "innovations" of the terrorists. In the very first paragraph, therefore, he introduces himself as a priest from Jerusalem (1.3). There were priests and high priests throughout the Greco-Roman world, in every significant town, for they ran the temples of the various regional gods. In those other religions, priestly families often handed down the sacred craft from one generation to another. But at the same time, the role of chief officiator or "high priest" was usually a civic honor, to which noted citizens were elected on an annual basis. The Jews, however, had a rigidly maintained caste system in which priesthood was determined by lineage. As in some other oriental countries, one could not choose either priesthood or high priesthood as a vocation. Greco-Roman readers were fascinated by the exotic ways of the East, with their mysterious and powerful priests, and Josephus plays to this audience by identifying himself as a priest.

In describing his surrender to Vespasian, which we have discussed in another context, Josephus exploits his priesthood at a key moment—to explain how it was that he came to know of Vespasian's future. Having appealed to some "nightly dreams" in which God revealed the future to him, he continues: "He [Josephus] was not unfamiliar with the prophecies of the sacred books, being himself a priest and a descendant of priests" (3.352). This association of the Jewish priesthood with both traditional wisdom and mysterious power is a consistent theme in Josephus' writings. He goes on to claim that he had regularly predicted the future (3.406). Moreover, he has already said that his favorite Hasmonean ruler, John Hyrcanus, uniquely combined the rule of the people with high priesthood and a prophetic gift: "For so closely was he in touch with the Deity that he was never ignorant of the future" (1.69, LCL). Josephus' Hasmonean ancestry and priestly descent are prominent features of his self-understanding.

In accord with its priestly bias, Josephus' *War* presents the rebels as violators of both the sacred temple precincts and the priestly traditions. When the governor Gessius Florus pillages the temple and is mocked by some young upstarts, it is the chief priests and eminent citizens who appeal to him (in vain) for clemency, wishing to maintain peace (2.301). While the governor plots to further aggravate the populace, the chief priests earnestly assemble the people and plead with them, against the rebels' policies, to show courtesy to the Roman soldiers, so as to avoid irreversible damage to the holy place (2.318–324). Even when Florus ridicules this policy by attacking the Jews, and though a rash young priest persuades other priests to stop offering sacrifices on behalf of the Romans, Josephus claims that "the chief priests and the notables stren-

uously admonished them not to give up the traditional offering for the rulers" (2.410). The chief priests and other leaders
accuse the rebels of "introducing a strange kind of worship"
that did not admit sacrifices for rulers (2.414). They then produce "priestly experts in the traditions, who reported that all
of their forebears had welcomed the sacrifices of foreigners"
(2.417). Finally, when Jerusalem is under siege, it is the chief
priests who take up the Romans' offer of surrender and quit
the city (6.114). In spite of the actions of some younger priests
who were deceived by the rebels, therefore, Josephus aligns
himself with the priestly establishment in solid opposition to
the revolt.

Most revealing of *War*'s perspective is a lengthy passage
in which Josephus fumes against the rebels for their unprecedented violation of priestly tradition (4.147–325). He has already told us that, once they had gained control of Jerusalem,
the rebels first burned down the house of the former high
priest Ananias, then murdered him along with his brother
(2.426, 441). But now, most outrageous of all, they dare to elect
their own high priest: "Abrogating the claims of those families
from which in turn the high priests had always been drawn,
they appointed to that office ignoble and low born individuals,
in order to gain accomplices in their impious crimes" (4.148,
LCL). Josephus says that they convened one of the twenty-four
priestly clans and cast lots for a high priest. As it happened,
the lot fell to a simpleton who lived in the countryside and did
not even understand what the high priesthood was. But the
rebels used this turn of events to their advantage, dragged the
reluctant man out of his home, and dressed him up as high
priest. They made their new "high priest" the object of much
sport and laughter (4.155–157).

We must remember that this is entirely Josephus' perspective. Historically speaking, the legitimacy of the high
priesthood had often been ignored: the Seleucid kings and
later Herod the Great appointed whomever they wished to the
office. And an insistence on choice by lot probably reflected
the rebels' protest against the corruption of the office under
the wealthy, traditional high priestly families. But this historical perspective only serves to highlight Josephus' literary aim,
which is to remove the rebels completely beyond the pale of
normal Judaism.

In response to the rebels' actions, Josephus continues, the eminent former high priests Ananus and Jesus met with the people and severely chastised them for not preventing this outrage against the sacred office (4.160). *War* devotes a good deal of space to the speeches of these two leaders, in which they complain that murderers have now polluted God's sanctuary (4.163, 242). Ananus even leads the people against the rebels, but the zealots receive support from Idumeans, who come up from the south. Together, the Jewish rebels and Idumeans defeat the chief priests. Finally, the Idumeans murder Ananus and Jesus; they again flagrantly violate Jewish custom by casting the corpses out of the city without burial (4.316–317).

The aristocratic priest Josephus claims that these outrages against temple and priestly tradition were the causes of God's punishment: "the capture of the city began with the death of Ananus; the collapse of the walls and the destruction of things Judean began from that day, in which they saw the high priest, the governor of their own salvation, slaughtered in the heart of the city" (4.318). Josephus proceeds to give a eulogy of Ananus as a man of noble birth, the highest honor, and the greatest integrity, a man committed to peace or, if war was necessary, to fighting only in a disciplined and careful manner (4.320). In other words, Ananus functions as a mouthpiece for Josephus' own views on the revolt. In this way, the high priests serve to establish *War*'s thesis concerning the non-traditional, un-Jewish character of the rebels.

In the *Jewish Antiquities*

In *Antiquities, Life*, and its sequel, *Against Apion*, the high priests are even more prominent than in *War*. On the one hand, the high priesthood is the cornerstone of Josephus' argument that Jewish traditions have been handed down intact from the time of Moses. On the other hand, and in some tension with this theme, individual high priests are exposed as sinners whose transgressions brought God's punishment on Jerusalem.

We have seen that one of Josephus' techniques in *Antiquities* is to present Judaism as an ancient *philosophy*—a school of virtue, founded by Moses, which offers *eudaimonia*, or happiness, to those who follow its precepts. Within this scheme, the high priests have a critical function as Moses' "successors," who transmit the founder's teachings unchanged from generation to generation. So Aaron, the first high priest, is introduced with considerable fanfare. Josephus describes his special clothing in detail and then attributes to Moses a speech in praise of Aaron that has no parallel in the Bible (3.151–192). Among Aaron's virtues, significantly, is the gift of prophecy (3.192). In his subsequent narrative of Israel's history, Josephus regularly introduces the high priest where he is not mentioned at all in the Bible: a striking example is Josephus' paraphrase of Joshua, which has the great commander routinely turning to the high priest and his "council of elders" for advice (*Ant.* 5.15, 43, 55–57). These embellishments offer a fascinating insight into how Josephus assumed that things should work, based on conditions of his own day, even though the Bible said nothing about them. For him, the high priest is the authorized head of Jewish public life. In accordance with this view, Josephus spells out the identity of the current high priest as his narrative progresses. Most significantly, in his conclusion to the lengthy *Antiquities*, he thinks it important to recap the whole "succession" of high priests from Aaron to the end of the recent war (20.224–251, 261)—a span of two thousand years.

The centrality of the high priesthood to Josephus' understanding of Judaism is spelled out in his apologetic work *Against Apion*. Contrasting the Jewish historical records with the untrustworthy Greek accounts, he argues that the Jews entrusted their writings to "chief priests and prophets" who preserved them through the ages with scrupulous accuracy (*Ag. Ap.* 1.29). Notice again his connection of the priesthood with prophecy. And the high priests have been the guarantors of this tradition (1.36). Josephus wants to present Judaism as a beautiful and harmonious system, working in accord with the laws of nature:

> Could there be a [constitution] more splendid and just than that which makes God the master of everything, assigns the greatest matters to the administration of the priests as a unit, and then entrusts to the supreme high priest the direction of the other priests? . . . . This [responsibility] included scrupulous care for the law and for the various pursuits of life (*Ag. Ap.* 2.184–187, author's translation).

Picking up on the biblical notice that Moses entrusted the laws to the priests (Deut 31:9, 25; cf. *Ant.* 4.304), Josephus presents the high priest as conductor of an orchestrated effort to preserve and disseminate the divine teachings.

But *Antiquities* must also demonstrate its thesis that violation of the Jewish laws leads to disaster. Within this scheme, Josephus does not hesitate to point out the shortcomings of individual high priests who departed from the traditions and consequently suffered for it. These included the greedy and mean-spirited Onias, who brought the Jews to the brink of disaster (12.158), and the later Hasmonean high priests, who brought about the end of Jewish independence through their internecine strife and murder (cf. 13.300–319, 431–432).

Most revealing are *Antiquities'* revisions of *War's* portraits of the high priests in the years before the revolt. Ananus, whom *War* had praised as a moderate and virtuous man, over against the violent rebels, is introduced in *Antiquities* 20.199 as "rash and conspicuously bold in manner." This Sadducean high priest took advantage of the governor's absence in Judea after the death of Festus by convening the Sanhedrin and passing a death sentence on James, the brother of Jesus, and some others. Evidently, the high priest could convene the Sanhedrin only with the permission of the Roman governor. Ananus' mischievous behavior earned him the opposition of the law-abiding Jews, the new Roman governor, and King Agrippa II, who removed him from the high priesthood (20.200–203). This is the same high priest who later, along with a chief priest named Jesus, accepted bribes in order to oust Josephus from his command in Galilee (*Life* 193, 196). Then the distinguished former high priest Ananias is described as one who freely engaged in bribery; his servants were "utter rascals," who would rob the tithes from the poorer priests, leaving them to starve to death (20.206–207, 213). It was this sort of lawlessness among the aristocracy that brought destruction on Jerusalem (20.214, 218).

What are we to make of these changes between *War* and *Antiquities* concerning the pre-war high priests? No one can deny that Josephus frequently contradicts himself in small matters, even within his own chronicles of the high priests. But the obvious shifts here are not mistakes. They are better explained as resulting from a change of literary aim. We have seen that

Josephus takes his theses very seriously, and so spells them out in elaborate prefaces. Since *War* is a tightly written attempt to isolate the rebels from the Jewish mainstream, it is not the place for him to expatiate on the high priests' shortcomings; he wants rather to make the sole point that the high priests represented the normal establishment over against the rebels. *Antiquities* assumes the same general thesis but also intends to demonstrate the efficacy of Jewish laws by proving that transgressors are invariably punished. In this context it is important to point out Jewish sins, even those of the high priests, that contributed to the recent divine punishment. Josephus' careful selection of "what to include" is not much different from what most of us do when we make different kinds of arguments from a single body of evidence.

In the New Testament

Josephus' portrayals of the high priests shed considerable light on the NT. First, they explain how it is that the high priest appears in the NT as the head of a council, the Sanhedrin, composed of the eminent citizens, leading Pharisees, and Sadducees (Mark 11:27; 14:1, 53; Acts 5:21–39; 22:30—23:10). This constellation is apt to seem strange, both because the OT does not put the high priest at the head of a council and also because Pharisees and Sadducees are not supposed to get along (see below). Even a modern scholar expresses his bafflement at the NT accounts:

> Anyone with knowledge of the religious and political scene at this time in Judaea feels the presence of an important problem here: the High Priest was not a Pharisee, but a Sadducee, and the Sadducees were bitterly opposed to the Pharisees.[7]

But Josephus everywhere assumes that the high priest is the head of the Jewish council, and that this council comprises eminent citizens of all parties (e.g., *War* 2.411; *Life* 21); indeed, it is the chief priests who send a delegation composed mainly of Pharisees to replace him as Galilean commander (*Life* 193–197). In Josephus' mind at least, the various parties could work together in government, in spite of their real and deep differences.

Second, Josephus describes a coincidence of interest between Jewish chief-priestly circles and the Roman government. He presents the chief priests by and large as favoring cooperation with Rome, even in the face of severe provocation. Not only do these eminent citizens support the governors' harsh treatment of political terrorists and religious fanatics, they also cooperate in removing such troublesome individuals. A particularly interesting case concerns one Jesus son of Ananias, a common peasant who predicted the fall of the temple four years before the outbreak of the revolt. For more than seven years, especially at festivals, he would cry, "Woe to Jerusalem!" and "A voice against Jerusalem and the sanctuary, a voice against the bridegroom and the bride, a voice against all the people." The exasperated temple leaders punished him without success, and eventually passed him over to the Roman governor. As he would not answer any questions, he was flayed to the bone and released on grounds of insanity (*War* 6.300–309). This cooperation of the leading citizens with the Romans, when it came to a person who had disrupted the already tense festival periods in Jerusalem, fits with the general picture of political relations painted by Josephus. This picture in turn helps one to imagine some cooperation between the Jewish leadership and the Roman governor in the trial of Jesus.

Third, Josephus often confuses the reader by speaking of various individuals as "high priest" at the same time, or by calling someone high priest when he was no longer in office (e.g., *War* 2.441; *Ant.* 20.205; *Life* 193). Yet the Bible and Josephus both insist that only one person can serve as high priest at one time. On closer examination, we realize that Josephus allows former high priests to retain the title and prestige of the office as long as they live. Perhaps this usage reflects his assumption that high priests *ought* to serve for life. In any case, we have a similar confusion in the Gospels and Acts. Luke 3:2 and Acts 4:6 mention several high priests (especially Annas and Caiaphas) as though they were current. More baffling yet, John 18:12–28 has Jesus interrogated by Annas (=Ananus I), who is first called "the father-in-law of the high priest" (18:13) but is then addressed as "high priest" (18:15, 19, 22). And when Jesus' interview with the high priest is finished, he is sent in chains to "Caiaphas the high priest" (18:24). If the authors of Luke and John made the same assumptions as Josephus, and expected their readers to do so, then their accounts become somewhat less puzzling. Ananus I was an extremely distinguished high priest in Josephus' view, for five of his sons followed him in office (*Ant.* 20.197–198). So it makes sense that the Gospel authors would remember his name in conjunction with Caiaphas, the serving high priest at the time of Jesus' trial.

Fourth, on a more theological level, Josephus plainly regards the high priesthood and the temple service as the heart and soul of Judaism. This is important because several modern scholars have argued that the whole priesthood was reduced to the status of mere "functionaries" by the rise of the Pharisees and/or scribes in the two centuries before Jesus.[8] Although some Pharisees may have had such a perspective, however, Josephus the priest enthuses about the vitality of the priesthood. Josephus' perspective helps to make sense of an essay like Hebrews, which presents Jesus as a new and ideal high priest. If the priesthood were no longer a vital force, this author would merely be dredging up old images.

JEWISH HIGH PRIESTS AD 6 TO 70

Jesus son of See (to AD 6)	*Ant.* 17.341
*Ananus (=Annas) I (AD 6–15)	*War* 2.240; *Ant.* 18.26, 34
Ishmael son of Phabi I (AD 15–16)	*Ant.* 18.34
Eleazar son of Ananus (AD 16–17)	*Ant.* 18.34
Simon son of Camith (AD 17–18)	*Ant.* 18.34
*Joseph Caiaphas (AD 18–37)	*Ant.* 18.35, 95
Jonathan son of Ananus (AD 37)	*Ant.* 18.95, 123
Theophilus son of Ananus (AD 37–41)	*Ant.* 18.123; 19.297
Simon Cantheras son of Boethus (from AD 41)	*Ant.* 19.297, 313
Matthias son of Ananus	*Ant.* 19.316, 342
Elionaeus son of Cantheras (AD 44)	*Ant.* 19.342; 20.16
Joseph son of Camei	*Ant.* 20.16, 103
*Ananias son of Nebedaeus (AD 47–59)	*War* 2.243, 409–442; *Ant.* 20.103, 131
Ishmael son of Phabi II (AD 59–61)	*Ant.* 20.179, 194
Joseph Kabi son of Simon (to AD 62)	*Ant.* 20.196
Ananus (=Annas) II son of Ananus (AD 62)	*War* 2.563, 648–653; *Ant.* 20.197, 203
Jesus son of Damnaeus (AD 62–64)	*Ant.* 20.203, 213
Jesus son of Gamaliel (AD 64–65?)	*Ant.* 20.213, 223
Matthias son of Theophilus (AD 65–67)	*Ant.* 20.223
Phanasus (=Phanni) son of Samuel (AD 67–70)	*War* 4.155; *Ant.* 20.227

* Appears in NT

Yet Josephus presents the NT reader, once again, with difficulties as well as assistance. A notable difficulty is the question of who was the serving high priest at the time of Jesus' trial. This problem is only partly solved by the custom of allowing former high priests to retain the title. For Josephus presents a fairly clear chronicle of the first-century high priests, and even where his dates are not precise, we can usually figure them out within a year or two on the basis of current events mentioned in the surrounding narrative.

As the table above indicates, Caiaphas was high priest throughout Jesus' adult life, and throughout the governorship of Pilate (26–36), who ordered that Jesus be executed.

But the Gospel writers, as a group, do not seem to have a clear idea of who the high priest was at Jesus' trial. The earliest of them, Mark, simply says that Jesus was interrogated and sentenced to death by "the high priest" and council (14:53—15:1). It is peculiar that Mark, like all of the Gospel writers, knows the name of Pilate (15:1), whom he presents as innocent in Jesus' death, but that he does not disclose the name of the one truly responsible, the high priest. Matthew makes up for this deficiency. Following Mark's narrative closely, when he comes to the mention of the high priest he identifies this villain as Caiaphas.

Mark 14:48–54

48 "*Have you come out to arrest me with swords and clubs, as if against a robber?* 49 *Day after day* I was with you *in the temple teaching, and you did not arrest me!* But *in order that the scriptures might be fulfilled.*" 50 *And leaving him,* they *all fled.* 51 And a certain young man was following him, wearing only a linen cloth over his naked body. And they seize him, 52 but, abandoning the linen cloth, he fled naked.

53 And they *led Jesus off to the high priest,* and all the chief priests, and *the elders,* and *the scribes* assembled. 54 And *Peter, from a distance,* followed *him.*

Matthew 26:55–58

55 "*Have you come out to arrest me with swords and clubs, as if against a robber? Day after day I* sat *in the temple teaching, and you did not arrest me!* 56 Now this all happened *in* order that *the scriptures* of the prophets *might be fulfilled.*" Then *all* the disciples, *leaving him, fled.*

57 Now those who had seized him *led Jesus off to* Caiaphas *the high priest, where the scribes* and *the elders* had gathered. 58 But *Peter* was following *him from a distance.*

This passage illustrates the standard view that the author of Matthew used Mark as a source. On the one hand, we see extensive verbal agreements between the two texts, to a degree that one does not find in independent accounts of the same event. Greek (the original language of the Gospels) offers countless possibilities for expressing similar ideas, but these two authors basically agree in their choice of sentence structure, vocabulary ("as if against a robber," "day after day," "led Jesus off"), word order, and in their manner of weaving together different plots (Jesus with the high priest, Peter in the courtyard). Such differences as remain are usually explained as Matthew's attempt to improve the story, thus: (a) he substitutes other conjunctions and sentence structures to replace Marks' monotonous "and"; (b) he completes and clarifies Mark's sentence about the fulfillment of scripture; (c) he omits the story about the naked young man, which might have seemed both irrelevant to the story line (since he does not appear again) and not entirely in good taste. Most important for us: Matthew seems to think it necessary to identify the high priest, since he plays such a crucial role in the story of Jesus' trial. His insertion of the name Caiaphas agrees with Josephus' chronicle.

Luke's Gospel also seems to follow Mark as a source, but like Mark, Luke declines to name the high priest *within the trial narrative itself* (cf. Luke 22:54). Yet the omission is more understandable in Luke's case because he has already identified the various rulers at the beginning of his Gospel. There, he says that John the Baptist began preaching "under the high priest [singular] Annas and Caiaphas" (Luke 3:2). This is a peculiar construction because the singular "high priest" does not match the pair of names that follows. If we suppose that Annas, as a *former* high priest of distinction, offered the serving high priest his ongoing counsel, we are still left with the problem that Caiaphas' name should have appeared first; having been in office for a decade or more, he was no novice. In this awkward construction, however, the name of Caiaphas is left dangling, and it seems that Luke thinks of Annas as the high priest. The problem is compounded by Acts 4:6. Describing the situation shortly after Jesus' death, that passage says that the Jerusalem council met "with Annas the high priest, and Caiaphas, John, and Alexander, and whoever was of the high priestly family." This text plainly sets Caiaphas on a level with several other members of "the family"; the author implies that Annas was the serving high priest.

In other words, if we had only Luke–Acts, we would not have guessed that Caiaphas was high priest during Jesus' trial (according to Josephus and Matthew), for this author implies that Annas held the office. Josephus is also confusing at times in his usage of the title "high priest," but the difference is that he clarifies the situation, if we but read on for a few paragraphs. Luke does not, so it remains a question whether he knew who was high priest at the time of Jesus' death. Nevertheless, Luke's later identification of Ananias as serving high priest at the time of Paul's arrest, under the governorship of Felix (Acts 23:2; 24:1), agrees with Josephus.

We have already noted the problem in John's Gospel, which has Jesus first appear before the "high priest" Annas, father-in-law of the high priest Caiaphas, and then has him sent to the (serving) high priest (John 18:13–24). Much of this apparent confusion, we saw, could be explained by Josephus' use of "high priest" to designate also former high priests. Josephus does not say that Annas was Caiaphas' father-in-law, and the omission seems odd in view of his claim about Annas' great influence through his five sons, but the relationship is nonetheless plausible. Yet two problems remain: (a) John repeatedly identifies Caiaphas as "high priest that year" (11:51; 18:13). A non-Jewish reader would presumably infer that the Jewish high priest, like many others in the Greco-Roman world, was annually elected as a civic official. Even though the high priesthood had lost its life-long tenure by Jesus' time, however, it was by no means an annual position. According to Josephus, Caiaphas held it for about eighteen years. (b) The other problem is that John makes the trial before Annas the main one and omits any mention of what happened before Caiaphas, the serving high priest. Moreover, Peter's denial is set within the framework of the trial before Annas (18:13–24; cf. Mark 14:67 on Peter's warming himself by the fire). So, in spite of the partial help that we get from Josephus' liberal use of the title "high priest," John's narrative remains a problem.

In sum: on the one hand, it is remarkable that the Gospel authors unanimously and without equivocation know that the Roman governor at the time of Jesus' death was Pontius Pilate, and yet he is said by all of them to have been a mere pawn in the hands of the Jewish leaders. On the other hand, Mark does not even name the chief Jewish official; Matthew seems to have researched or recalled that his name was Caiaphas; Luke implies that he was Annas; and John makes Caiaphas an annually appointed high priest but places Jesus' significant trial before Annas.

The most obvious conflict between Josephus and the NT authors concerns the general character of the "chief priests." Josephus regards the high priestly class as the vital center of Judaism and its typical leaders as deeply pious, cultured, moderate men like himself. This broad perspective makes his isolation of unworthy high priests that much more significant. The NT authors usually portray the whole Jewish leadership as ignorant of God's designs and opposed to Jesus' mission. Notice their tendency to implicate "all" or "the whole" of the "chief priests, elders, and scribes." It is a high priest who declares the fateful sentence against Jesus, and a high priest who leads the attack against Paul.

Who is right? Were the chief priests sincerely committed to their faith, or were they self-satisfied enemies of the truth? I would suggest that the question cannot be resolved in such terms. But Josephus' portrayal forces us to realize that the Gospels represent only one perspective on the Jewish leadership. The Gospels' accusations, made in the heat of controversy, should not be taken as objective facts: it is not as if the chief priests arose every morning wondering what kinds of evil they could perpetrate in the world. They were public figures with a high profile. We do not have access to their private thoughts and goals. All we have are images left from one of their followers (Josephus) and several of their opponents (the NT writers). Inevitably, such figures attract admiration and hostility, depending on whom you ask.

PHARISEES AND SADDUCEES

We come finally to the Jewish groups most frequently mentioned in the Gospels and Acts, the Pharisees and Sadducees. Once again, Josephus is our only contemporary source of information about these groups outside the NT. Like the high priests, the Sadducees and Pharisees appear in two quite different contexts in Josephus' writings. On the one hand, he wants to work them into his immense tapestry of idealized Judaism, with which he is trying to impress his readers—an awe-inspiring tradition that deserves respect. On the other hand, he must also relate Jewish history in a plausible way, to explain how the Jews have fallen on such dreadful times. Within this story, some Sadducees, but especially the Pharisees, play a critical, destructive role.

Unlike the family of Herod and the high priests, the Pharisees and Sadducees do not perform significantly different functions in *War* and *Antiquities*. Indeed, they are not major figures in *War*; and the two sides of the portrayal appear throughout Josephus' works. Instead of examining *War* and *Antiquities* in isolation, therefore, we shall first consider how the Pharisees and Sadducees support Josephus' idealizing presentation of Judaism, and then we shall examine how these groups functioned in his account of Jewish history.

In Josephus' Ideal Portrait of Judaism

It is intriguing that no NT author mentions the Essenes, for Josephus always includes them with the Pharisees and Sadducees in his idealizing portraits of Judaism. Of the three groups, in fact, it is the Essenes who elicit his highest praise. Characteristic of these idealizing portrayals is Josephus' claim that the three groups represent "philosophical schools" within the larger national philosophy of Judaism (see chapter 3). Judaism represents a high philosophical culture, comparable to that of the Greeks, with its own spectrum of philosophical opinion.

In *War* 2.162–166, having lavishly praised the Essenes as a class by themselves, he simply places the Pharisees and Sadducees on opposite ends of the philosophical spectrum: the Pharisees affirm the activity of fate and the immortality of the soul (2.163); the Sadducees deny both positions, insisting on absolute freedom of will and rejecting afterlife with its rewards and punishments (2.164–165). It was customary for those who wrote summaries of Greco-Roman philosophy to align the various schools on two poles, according to their affirmation or denial of such principles (cf. Diogenes Laertius,

Lives of Eminent Philosophers): Josephus does the same for the Pharisees and Sadducees, after distinguishing the Essenes as a unique group.

Josephus compares the three schools again in *Antiquities* 13.171–173. Here, he adjusts the spectrum to include all three schools, so that the Essenes take up the fatalist wing, the Sadducees take their place on the opposite end, but now the Pharisees assume the middle ground, for they assign some matters to fate and others to free will.

In his third passage on the Jewish philosophical schools (*Ant.* 18.11–23), Josephus again uses them to represent normal Judaism, over against the rebels, who introduced a bizarre "fourth philosophy" (*Ant.* 18.9, 24). Once again he mainly sketches different views of fate and immortality among the three "ancient" schools. But he also mentions a dispute between Pharisees and Sadducees over authority: the Pharisees have their own special tradition in addition to the scriptures, whereas the Sadducees accept only the biblical laws (18.12, 16). Josephus had not originally mentioned this issue, probably because it would detract from his depiction of a cosmopolitan Judaism engaged with the issues common to all humanity. Nevertheless, this dispute over authority came up unavoidably in one of his stories (*Ant.* 13.288–298); now that he has explained the point anyway, he is willing to restate it in this summary.

A final passage in *Life* (10–12) merely recalls that the Jews have three "philosophical schools" so as to explain Josephus' training in each.

It should be noted that Josephus' idealizing portrayal of the three traditional schools does not by itself imply that he is personally committed to any of them. On the contrary, his autobiography claims that he did not find any of them personally satisfying, so he became a student of the desert monk Bannus (*Life* 10–11; see above, chapter 2). He groups the schools together because: (a) he wants to impress his readers with the depth and variety of Judaism and (b) he wants to expose the rebels as anti-social renegades from the traditions. Whereas the other three schools deal with common human issues, only the rebels separate themselves and therefore deserve the charge (often leveled against all Jews) of misanthropy. In his narrative Josephus occasionally mentions, incidentally, that some noted Pharisees were among the moderate leaders who opposed the revolt (*War* 2.411; *Life* 21); like the school passages, these notices serve to isolate the rebels from the mainstream population.

Within this ideal presentation, however, one can easily detect that Josephus is less than enthusiastic about the Sadducees and Pharisees. Only the Essenes receive unqualified praise. Josephus consistently offers them to the reader as exemplary Jews. They lead an admirably simple, philosophical life, according to a strict regimen. Holding all their possessions in common, they renounce both marriage[9] and slave ownership. They are masters of their emotions and impervious to pain. They possess secret knowledge, by which they can perform cures and predict the future. Their virtue is unmatched, whether by Greeks or barbarians (*Ant.* 18.20). Josephus even declares that those who once sample their doctrines are irresistibly attracted (*War* 2.158), which has led more than one scholar to suggest that Josephus wanted to pass himself off as one of them. Indeed, he describes Bannus, the only one who could satisfy his philosophical quest, in language that recalls the Essene lifestyle (*Life* 11).

Although Josephus concedes that the Sadducees count some of the worthiest citizens among their members, their denial of fate and the afterlife seem to him irreligious. His attack on Epicurean philosophy for its rejection of divine providence (*Ant.* 10.277–281) applies equally well to the Sadducean position (*War* 2.164). And his firm belief that Moses promised a blissful future existence to those who obey the laws (*Ag. Ap.* 2.218; cf. *War* 2.157) flatly contradicts the Sadducean view (*War* 2.165; *Ant.* 18.16). Of course, it would hurt his case to denounce the Sadducees when he is appealing to their legitimate status, over against the rebels' innovations. So the school passages omit any forthright attack on the group. Nevertheless, the attentive reader knows that Josephus' recognition of the Sadducees' historic legitimacy does not entail his own allegiance. Even within the school passages, he cannot resist noting that the Sadducees, perhaps like the Cynics in this regard, behave in a rude and disputatious manner (*War* 2.166; *Ant.* 18.16).

Josephus has no quarrel with the philosophical views of the Pharisees: he agrees with their belief in an afterlife, rewards and punishments, and also with their acceptance of both providence and free will. He thinks that these principles are taught in the Jewish laws (cf. *Ant.* 16.396–399). Indeed, most people hold such views, Josephus says, and that is why the Pharisees are the most influential school: their beliefs resonate with the mainstream of the populace (*Ant.* 18.15). But notice how he phrases this point. His Greek says that the Pharisees "as chance would have it" (*tynchanousin*) are the most persuasive of the schools (*Ant.* 18.15). This phrase (which he repeats in the same sentence) is clarified by his subsequent remark that even the most eminent Sadducees must defer to "what the Pharisee says" (18.17) and by his further claim that the Essenes excel all others in virtue (18.20). That the Pharisees enjoy the greatest popular support is not something over which Josephus exults. Similarly in *War* he presents the Pharisees as "the foremost" of the schools in popular influence (*War* 2.162; cf. 2.411), but his summary presentation of them, after his lengthy disquisition on the Essenes, is hardly to be taken as flattery.

Still another subtle jibe is his notice that the hated rebel faction, which "sowed the seeds of every kind of misery" with its murderous behavior (*Ant.* 18.6–8), was co-founded by Judas *and* Saddok, a Pharisee (18.4). To be sure, he explains that the Pharisees were not as a group inclined to revolt (18.23); otherwise his attempt to isolate the rebels would be ineffective. But then, why raise the Pharisaic connection at all? This note does not flatter the Pharisees. Like the Sadducees, they are coopted to show that the Jews have old and established philosophical schools. But even in this context Josephus is less than enthusiastic about either party.

In Josephus' Historical Narrative

Outside of these idealizing passages, Josephus' narrative of Jewish history consistently sets the Essenes in a radiant light, but deprecates both Sadducees and Pharisees. He speaks glowingly of Judas the Essene, who never once erred in his predictions (*War* 1.78–80); he praises John the Essene, who was appointed like him as a commander in the revolt, as a man of "first-rate prowess and ability" (*War* 3.11); and he asserts that many Essenes had been granted a knowledge of the future because of their virtue (*Ant.* 15.371–379). Essenes reliably predicted the rise and fall of both Herod the Great and his son Archelaus (*Ant.* 15.371–379; 17.346). These narrative accounts support the prominence given to the Essenes in the school passages: they appear as the spiritual heroes of the Jewish world.

The Sadducees per se do not play a regular part in Josephus' narratives. This is noteworthy because he claims that Sadducees are "men of the highest standing" (*Ant.* 18.17), a wealthy elite with no following among the masses (13.298). It seems probable, therefore, that many of the "eminent citizens" who shared Josephus' moderate outlook on the revolt and whom he praises for their wisdom, were in fact Sadducees. But then it is striking that he never mentions their Sadducean links in any positive context. The only time he raises the issue is when he criticizes the high priest Ananus for unlawfully convening the Sanhedrin in order to try James. He explains there that Ananus "followed the school of the Sadducees, who are, when it comes to judgments, savage beyond all other Jews" (*Ant.* 20.199, author's translation). Interestingly, Ananus' Sadducean affiliation had not come up in *War*, where Josephus had praised his *virtues*.

That this group has negative associations in Josephus' mind is confirmed by the only other story he tells about them. When his favorite ancestor, the Hasmonean ruler John Hyrcanus, was accused of holding the high priesthood unlawfully, a Sadducean at court persuaded Hyrcanus that the Pharisees were responsible for this insult. The Sadducee inflamed his anger and "worked on him" until he abandoned the Pharisees in favor of the Sadducees (*Ant.* 13.293, 296). These unflattering references to the Sadducees complement Josephus' distaste for their philosophical teachings. They may also explain why he does not usually disclose the party affiliation of the leading Jewish moderates: he likes their politics in spite of their religious-philosophical views.

Of the three recognized schools, only the Pharisees play an ongoing role in Josephus' narratives. He presents them throughout as the dominant party in Jewish society, but also as troublemakers for those in power—from Josephus' beloved Hasmonean ancestors to Herod the Great to Josephus himself.

In *War* 1.110–114, he describes the actions of the Pharisees under the Hasmonean Queen Alexandra Salome. He has already said that the Hasmonean dynasty reached its greatest moment under John Hyrcanus and steadily declined thereafter (1.69). The downward spiral began with a disastrous one-year reign of Hyrcanus' son Aristobulus, who imprisoned his entire family out of suspicion and ultimately killed his most loved brother (*War* 1.77, 81). It continued with Alexander Janneus, who at first seemed to be a moderate ruler (1.85) but ended up in a brutal civil war with his unhappy subjects (1.91, 97). Queen Alexandra, Janneus' widow, is introduced as a ray of promise: a frail, pious woman, who was indeed gentle and scrupulous in observing the sacred laws (1.108). She wisely gave the high priesthood to her elder, docile son, and confined her younger son, a "hot-head," to private life (1.109). But her downfall, and so the continuing decline of the Hasmonean dynasty, was the result of the Pharisees' activity: this powerful group took advantage of her religiosity to insinuate themselves into power (1.110–111). They quickly took de facto control of domestic affairs and launched a reign of terror (1.113–114), which left the country in disarray (1.117).

Significantly, Josephus retells the story in *Antiquities* in a way that changes the roles of several key characters. He now claims that the queen actually contrived with her dying husband to grant the Pharisees full domestic power as a way of conciliating the masses (*Ant.* 13.399–400). This is not the frail old woman of *War,* but a strident and determined ruler who "showed none of the weakness of her sex" (*Ant.* 13.430). She was not duped by the Pharisees, but deliberately gave them their desired power as part of a strategic alliance. Josephus also changes his view of her sons, for he now thinks that the younger Aristobulus, a man of action and character, should have been given the high priesthood (13.407, 417, 423). But in the midst of this revision, the Pharisees maintain their consistent role as villains: Josephus presents them as troublemakers who disrupted the peace that would otherwise have prevailed under Alexandra (13.410); he expands greatly on their victims' plight (13.411–417); he claims that they "played drunken games" with the Hasmonean house (13.426). He concludes at length that Alexandra's experimental alliance with them was an unqualified disaster, which sealed the dynasty's fate (13.430–432). Since he is himself a proud descendant of the Hasmoneans, his bitterness is palpable.

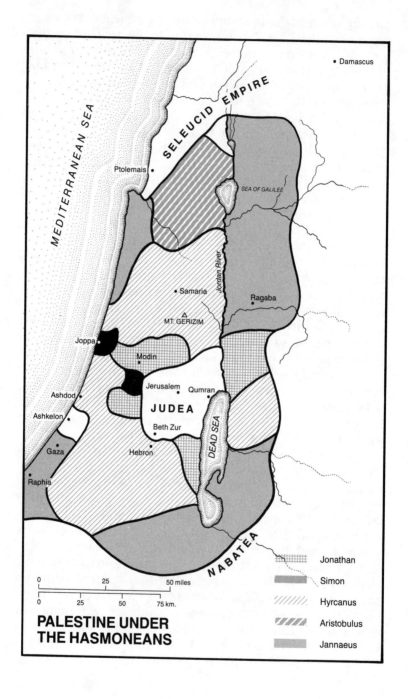

PALESTINE UNDER
THE HASMONEANS

The Hasmonean Dynasty

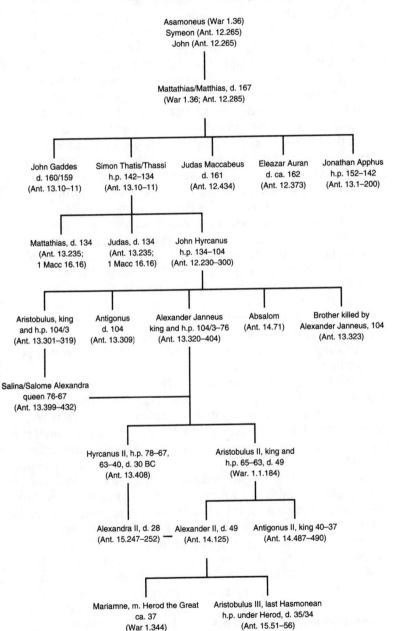

Asamoneus (War 1.36)
Symeon (Ant. 12.265)
John (Ant. 12.265)

Mattathias/Matthias, d. 167
(War 1.36; Ant. 12.285)

John Gaddes
d. 160/159
(Ant. 13.10–11)

Simon Thatis/Thassi
h.p. 142–134
(Ant. 13.10–11)

Judas Maccabeus
d. 161
(Ant. 12.434)

Eleazar Auran
d. ca. 162
(Ant. 12.373)

Jonathan Apphus
h.p. 152–142
(Ant. 13.1–200)

Mattathias, d. 134
(Ant. 13.235;
1 Macc 16.16)

Judas, d. 134
(Ant. 13.235;
1 Macc 16.16)

John Hyrcanus
h.p. 134–104
(Ant. 12.230–300)

Aristobulus, king
and h.p. 104/3
(Ant. 13.301–319)

Antigonus
d. 104
(Ant. 13.309)

Alexander Janneus
king and h.p. 104/3–76
(Ant. 13.320–404)

Absalom
(Ant. 14.71)

Brother killed by
Alexander Janneus, 104
(Ant. 13.323)

Salina/Salome Alexandra
queen 76-67
(Ant. 13.399–432)

Hyrcanus II, h.p. 78–67,
63–40, d. 30 BC
(Ant. 13.408)

Aristobulus II, king and
h.p. 65–63, d. 49
(War. 1.1.184)

Alexandra II, d. 28
(Ant. 15.247–252)

Alexander II, d. 49
(Ant. 14.125)

Antigonus II, king 40–37
(Ant. 14.487–490)

Mariamne, m. Herod the Great
ca. 37
(War 1.344)

Aristobulus III, last Hasmonean
h.p. under Herod, d. 35/34
(Ant. 15.51–56)

In *Antiquities,* Josephus includes a story about the Pharisees in his account of John Hyrcanus' peerless government (13.288–298). Whereas *War* had simply noted that Hyrcanus faced opposition from some of his "envious countrymen," whose rebellion was quashed (1.67), *Antiquities* clearly identifies the leaders of this agitation as Pharisees. This school has such great influence with the masses that they are easily able to stir up trouble even for a king and a high priest (13.288). Given Josephus' attitude toward all forms of rebellion and his fondness for John Hyrcanus, we cannot interpret this description of the Pharisees as anything but hostile. To document his charge, Josephus recounts a traditional story about a dispute between Hyrcanus and the Pharisees (13.289–296). It occurred at a banquet, at which a guest named Eleazar boldly demanded that Hyrcanus give up the high priesthood because the circumstances of his birth disqualified him for that office. Notice: the traditional story itself is not anti-Pharisaic. It does not clearly identify Eleazar as a Pharisee, and it insists that "all the Pharisees" were indignant over the charge (13.292). The story seems to come from circles in which both the Pharisees and the Hasmoneans were well thought of. It was the Sadducee Jonathan, as we saw before, who used the issue to create a rift between Hyrcanus and the Pharisees. But Josephus takes over this legend and furnishes it with an introduction that is plainly hostile to the Pharisees.[10]

At the end of the story of John Hyrcanus' break with the Pharisees, Josephus appends an important footnote (ancient writing offered no comparable technique) on the differences between Pharisees and Sadducees, in order to explain what it was that Hyrcanus abrogated when he annulled Pharisaic law (13.297–298). The essential point is that the Pharisees accept certain ordinances that are not among the laws of Moses but issue from a "tradition of fathers"—the Pharisees' name for their living tradition. But the Sadducees claim to accept only what is written in Moses' laws. This difference represents a major source of controversy, though the conflict is alleviated by the fact that the Pharisees have massive popular support whereas the Sadducees persuade only a wealthy few. We may note here that although Josephus is plainly not a Sadducee, his own view of Moses' constitution, as a comprehensive written code not to be tampered with, seems to correspond to that of the

Sadducees. At least, he nowhere else mentions such an extra-biblical tradition that he accepts. And he speaks of the laws as revealed entirely to Moses, in writing, and inviolable for all time.

During the reign of Herod the Great, the Pharisees appear in a similar light, as powerful yet baneful influences. As with Queen Alexandra, this is all the more noteworthy because Josephus' portrait of Herod changes significantly between *War* and *Antiquities*. In *War*, where Herod appears as a victim of domestic plots, the Pharisees are simply part of the intrigue, bribed for their services by Herod's scheming sister-in-law (*War* 1.571). Although Josephus is eager in *Antiquities* to illustrate Herod's lawlessness, it does not follow that Herod's opponents automatically become virtuous. On the contrary, he maintains his stern portrayal of the "female clique" that plotted the king's demise (*Ant.* 17.32–40). He now elaborates on the involvement of the Pharisees, whom he numbers at more than 6000: this was a group that "thought very highly of its precision with respect to ancestral custom, and pretended [to observance] of such laws as the Deity approves" (17.41, author's translation). These men, who dominated the female clique, used their religious authority to "combat and injure" the king (17.42). They did this by manufacturing false predictions, in which they promised Herod's brother and sister-in-law (who had paid their fine for not swearing an oath of allegiance) that they would become rulers after Herod's removal (17.43). The Pharisees also secured the support of a eunuch named Bagoas by promising the poor fellow that he would sire a future (messianic?) king of Israel (17.45). Josephus leaves no doubt, in spite of his animosity toward Herod, that this sort of behavior was scandalous.

The only Pharisee who receives unqualified praise from Josephus is one Samaias, "an upright man and for that reason superior to fear" (*Ant.* 14.176). He was the only member of the Jewish court who was willing to stand up and confront the young Herod when the latter was charged with executing bandits in the Galilee without due process. But significantly, Josephus neglects to mention, while praising the man's virtues, that he was a Pharisee. This piece of information turns up only incidentally in the following volume (15.3). As with the Sadducean high priest Ananus, Josephus does not connect Samaias' admirable qualities with his party allegiance.

Finally, Josephus' account of his "command" of Galilee during the revolt includes considerable attention to the actions of some high-ranking Pharisees. They become involved in the story, he says, because of his opponent John of Gischala, who competed with him for influence in the region. John was able to win the support of his friend Simon, son of Gamaliel, a very prominent Pharisee (*Life* 190). Josephus has no choice but to concede Simon's credentials (191), but he immediately goes on to say that Simon tried to persuade the Jerusalem authorities to remove him from his position (193). When Simon's first bid was unsuccessful, this reputed Pharisee resorted to underhanded bribery (195)—a tactic that was successful (196). Moreover, once the council had decided to remove Josephus, moreover, they sent a delegation of four dignitaries, accompanied by sufficient troops, to do the job. Three of the four delegates were also Pharisees. Predictably, Josephus accuses his adversaries of all sorts of crimes: they were deceitful, slanderous, and violent (*Life* 216, 233, 237, 245, 261, 274, 281, 301–303); one of the Pharisees was "a wicked man and an evildoer" (290).

All of this vitriol is to be expected where Josephus is defending himself. In this case, it happens to be Pharisees who run afoul of his self-vindication. But this episode in his own career makes his overall portrayal of the Pharisees' activities in Jewish history consistent: they use their great reputation for religious scrupulosity, and consequent influence with the masses, to effect their own political goals. They typically resort to bribery, intrigue, and even violence to accomplish their ends. So their actions belie their popular reputation for piety. It is not one of Josephus' major literary goals to denigrate the Pharisees. But if *we* ask what he says about the group, it is that they have exercised a detrimental influence on Jewish history, from their destructive actions under the independent Hasmonean state to their plots against Josephus.

In spite of this consistent presentation, it has usually been thought that Josephus either was a devoted Pharisee or wanted to present himself as one. How could such a view have arisen? In describing his adolescent philosophical quest (considered in chapter 3), Josephus claims that, having studied with the Pharisees, Sadducees, and Essenes and found them unsatisfying, and having then studied with Bannus for three years, he returned to the city (Greek *polis; Life* 10–12a). The following line has usually been translated: "and began to conduct myself according to the rules of the sect of the Pharisees" (Whiston, 1737) or "I began to govern my life by the rules of the Pharisees" (Thackeray, 1926). Thus, virtually every commentator has taken the statement to be Josephus' claim that he became a Pharisee or joined the Pharisaic school. In a recent book, however, I have argued that such a translation overlooks the context: Josephus has already said that he studied with the Pharisees, but he dismisses that conventional experience as unsatisfactory.[11] So it makes no sense for him to say, without explanation, "Then I became a Pharisee." That statement would be especially puzzling in view of his descriptions of the Pharisees, which do not endear them to the reader.

Further, the Greek sentence actually has two parts. The main verb (*politeuesthai*), which has usually been taken to mean "behave" or "conduct my life" is better translated as "take part in public affairs." That is how Josephus normally uses the word elsewhere. Furthermore, that fits the context, in which he is about to describe his public career (*Life* 13ff.). So: he returned from the desert to the city (*polis*) and began to engage in public affairs (*poli-teuesthai*). The second part of the sentence is a dependent clause, "following the school of the Pharisees." Thus, Josephus' public career entailed following the Pharisees. What does this mean? As we have seen, he consistently presents the Pharisees as the dominant school in Jewish political life: all the "religious" aspects of life follow their plan (*Ant.* 18.15), and even the most eminent Sadducees must defer to the Pharisees when they assume public office (*Ant.* 18.17). Whether any of this is historically true[12] is not germane to understanding Josephus' point. He *claims* that the Pharisees controlled public life, so it makes sense within his presentation that his own beginning in civic affairs would entail deference to the Pharisees. This does not mean that he became a Pharisee, just as it does not mean that office-holding Sadducees had to become Pharisees.

In the New Testament

How do Josephus' portrayals of the three main Jewish schools assist the reader of the NT? As we have come to expect, they are both supportive and problematic.

On the supportive side, Josephus agrees with the Gospels' general assumption that the Pharisees were the most prominent group in Palestinian Jewish life. They seem to represent the recognized religious authority. Moreover, they appear in the Gospels as scrupulous in their observance of the Jewish law, especially concerning sabbath observance, tithing, and religious purity laws. Thus Matthew's Jesus uses them as illustrations of scrupulosity: when laying down an extreme standard for his own followers, he can do no better than admonish them to be even more righteous than the scribes and Pharisees (5:20); that is understood to be a tall order. Josephus does not mention tithing and purity, perhaps because they would not be easily understood by his readers, but he does often say that the Pharisees are reputed to be the most precise interpreters of the laws.

Paul's claim that he had been a Pharisee or held to a Pharisaic view of the law before his conversion to Christianity (Phil 3:5) also illustrates that the Pharisees were a prominent, well-known school in the first century. Interestingly, Paul elsewhere says that he had been zealous, while still in Judaism, for the "traditions of my fathers" (Gal 1:14). This phrase is very close to the one that Josephus uses for the Pharisees' special tradition in *Antiquities* 13.297. It is also paralleled by Mark, who explains that the Pharisees wash their hands before eating, "observing the tradition of the elders" (Mark 7:3).

Some scholars have labeled both Jesus and Josephus as Pharisees because they agree in various ways with Pharisaic positions. We have seen that there is no good reason to think that Josephus was or wanted to be seen as a Pharisee, for he was highly critical of the group. There is a superficial similarity here with Jesus, who charges the Pharisees with hypocrisy. But there is an important difference. Josephus writes as a member of the aristocratic elite: he looks down his nose at the Pharisees for being mere pretenders. He is convinced that priests like him are the real adepts in the law, and even trustworthy prophets; they are the traditional heart and soul of Judaism. So he feels qualified to dismiss the Pharisees' reputation among the naive masses as unfounded. And his criticisms of the Pharisees are at the highly political level, which would interest only a politico like himself. He is convinced that they contributed to the downfall of his Hasmonean ancestors, and he accuses some of them of trying to subvert his own career. Josephus' critique of the Pharisees shows that, although he portrays them as the dominant party, they did have literate opponents, and not exclusively among the Sadducees. It was quite possible to dislike the Pharisees and still stand wholly within Judaism.

Jesus, for his part, is portrayed as moving about the peasant population of Galilee and criticizing the Pharisees mainly for their hypocrisy. Hypocrisy is the characteristic charge of the disaffected and the injured, those who are hurt by the failure of those in power to live up to their stated principles. (It is still probably the most common charge leveled against Western governments.) Jesus' classic statement is given in Matthew 23:2–3:

> The scribes and the Pharisees sit upon the seat of Moses. Whatever they might say, therefore, do and observe; but do not act according to their behavior, for they say and do not perform!

We see here what is plainly an in-house criticism. The Pharisees' legitimacy as scriptural interpreters is assumed and is not an issue. The only issue is their behavior: like all preachers and politicians, they inevitably draw the charge of "Hypocrite!" from some of their compatriots. So Josephus and Jesus both castigate the Pharisees, but from quite different perspectives and for different reasons.

In confining the Sadducees' appearance to Jesus' last days in Jerusalem (Mark 12:18–27), the Gospels agree with Josephus' limitation of their influence. Like Josephus, the Gospel authors also know that this group denies resurrection and afterlife (Mark 12:18; Acts 23:8). According to Acts 23:8, the Sadducees deny the existence of angels and spirits. Although Josephus does not mention this point, it fits well with his claim that the Sadducees accept only what is written in the law. The Torah (Gen—Deut) assumes that death is the end of life, and it has no explicit view of angels and demons. Developed belief in such powers, with named archangels and demons, begins to appear in Jewish writings only with the very latest biblical books, from about 200 BC. So the Sadducees' rejection of heavenly beings would fit with their dismissal of afterlife, since neither is clearly developed in the laws of Moses. Josephus' notice that the disagreement between Pharisees and Sadducees led to serious conflicts also fits well with the presentation of Paul's trial before the Sanhedrin in Acts 23. All he had to do was mention resurrection and "a great clamor arose" between the Sadducees and Pharisees (23:9).

Conspicuously absent from the NT are the Essenes, of whom Josephus speaks most fondly. There seems to be a good reason for this absence: since Josephus claims that the Essenes lead quiet lives, removed from public affairs, they would have little occasion to run into conflict with Jesus and his followers. If the Essenes were to be found in "each town" of Palestine (*War* 2.124), they must have been known to Jesus. Given their simple and virtuous lifestyle, however, it may well be that Jesus' followers too admired them. Indeed, in the book of Acts, as we shall see, the role that should belong to the Essenes (according to Josephus' presentation) is taken by the early Christian movement. We must reserve that discussion for chapter 6.

Some of the apparent problems created by Josephus' accounts of the schools may be solved with relative ease. For example, his focus on the issue of fate and free will as the central issue distinguishing the schools does not appear at all in the NT. Nevertheless, from his own writings we can tell that he dwells on that issue mainly in order to dignify the Jewish schools by making their subjects of discourse sound like those of the Greco-Roman schools. That he deliberately refrains from mentioning more "Jewish" themes, which might have reinforced his readers' prejudices about the backwardness of Jewish culture, is clear from his later admission that the main controversy between Pharisees and Sadducees was over the question of authoritative traditions. Once this issue is on the table, he leaves it there, for it is in fact the central issue from which the others flow (cf. *Ant.* 18.12). But his attempt to conceal this question suggests that he consciously omitted other matters as well, perhaps matters relating to ritual purity, tithing, and the like, that appear in the NT but would be of no interest to his readers.

Still, some tensions remain. For example, Matthew tends to group the "Pharisees and Sadducees" together as Jesus' opponents; the Pharisees and Sadducees who come to John for baptism are rebuffed (Matt 3:7). This tandem also tests Jesus by requesting a sign from heaven (Matt 16:1). Jesus, in

turn, tells his disciples to beware of the "leaven" of the Pharisees and Sadducees, by which he means their teaching (Matt
16:12). This pairing is strange in view of Josephus' account,
because recognizing their quite different social constituencies
and outlooks on religion, one would not expect the Pharisees
and Sadducees to spend a lot of time together, outside of the
governing council where their cooperation was necessary. Moreover, none of the other Gospels cites the Pharisees and Sadducees working together like that. Luke simply has "the crowds"
coming out for baptism and being rebuffed by John (Luke 3:7).
In Mark 8:11, it is the Pharisees alone who seek a sign from
him. In Mark 8:15, it is the leaven of the Pharisees and of *Herod*
that the disciples are warned against. From all of this it appears that the pairing of "Pharisees and Sadducees" in Matthew is not meant to designate Jesus' actual adversaries but as
an inclusive phrase, probably encapsulating the entire Jewish
leadership.

Again, Luke's claim that "the Pharisees were lovers of
money" (Luke 16:14) is hard to square with Josephus. Although
he dislikes the group, he does concede that they lead a simple
lifestyle, not yielding to luxury (*Ant.* 18.12). To be sure, he does
accuse them of both offering and accepting bribes, but these
are isolated incidents and do not imply a luxurious lifestyle.
The charge of being a lover of money was a standard polemical
tactic in antiquity, and it still shows up today. It gained cur-
rency with Plato's attack on the "sophists"—philosophers who
made a living by traveling around and teaching philosophy to
upper-class youth. It was repeated endlessly by philosophers
who attacked their competition as unworthy practitioners,
and it seems to have been used against Paul as well (1 Thess
2:5, 9). It seems safest to take the charge in Luke as this kind
of stock polemic rather than as a telling statement about the
Pharisees' general behavior.

In examining Josephus' portrayals of the family of Herod,
the Roman governors, the high priests, and the Jewish religious parties, we have learned a lot about the background of
the NT. This does not mean that we have taken Josephus as
some sort of repository of facts. Rather, we have tried to understand his presentations of these groups within the context
of his own literary aims. Only when we have completed that
task have we asked about his significance for NT interpreta-

tion, and it turns out that his significance is multifaceted. In some cases, he confirms points made in the Gospels. In others, his information almost seems necessary to a proper interpretation of the NT, especially of some passages in Acts. In still other cases, such as his portrait of Pontius Pilate or his dating of the high priests, Josephus' perspective helps us to appreciate that the NT documents too are products of a given time and place, and so have their own limited perspectives. His accounts help us to sharpen our awareness of the NT authors' literary aims, and to realize that they too do not represent objective facts but rather interpretations of facts.

FOR FURTHER READING

General treatments in English of Josephus and the NT world have fallen out of fashion in recent decades. As we have noted, however, all handbooks on the historical environment of the NT depend heavily on Josephus. Of these, the most essential are:

- Emil Schürer, *The History of the Jewish People in the Age of Jesus Christ* (3 vols. in 4; rev. and ed. Geza Vermes, Fergus Millar, Martin Goodman, and Matthew Black; Edinburgh: T. & T. Clark, 1986–1987).

- S. Safrai and M. Stern, eds., *The Jewish People in the First Century* (2 vols.; Compendia Rerum Iudaicarum ad Novum Testamentum, Section One; Assen: Van Gorcum; Philadelphia: Fortress, 1987).

These handbooks include some assessment of Josephus' literary aims, whereas most others are concerned with a larger historical construction. Beyond these, one might look at books and essays on Josephus' treatments of the various groups in question, such as:

- Arnold H. M. Jones, *The Herods of Judaea* (Oxford: Clarendon, 1967).

- Stewart Perowne, *The Life and Times of Herod the Great* (London: Hodder and Stoughton, 1956).

- Samuel Sandmel, "Herod (Family)," *IDB*, vol. 2, 584–94.

- Paul Winter, "Pilate in History and in Christian Tradition," in his *On the Trial of Jesus* (rev. and ed. T. A. Burkill and Geza Vermes; Berlin-New York: W. de Gruyter, 1974), 70–89.

- Clemens Thoma, "The High Priesthood in the Judgment of Josephus," *JBH*, 196–215.

- Steve Mason, "Priesthood in Josephus and the 'Pharisaic Revolution,' " *JBL* 107 (1988), 657–61.

- Jacob Neusner, *From Politics to Piety: the Emergence of Pharisaic Judaism* (Englewood Cliffs, N.J.: Prentice-Hall, 1973), 45–66 (for a famous but no longer tenable treatment of Josephus' Pharisees).

- Anthony J. Saldarini, *Pharisees, Scribes and Sadducees in Palestinian Society* (Wilmington: Michael Glazier, 1988), 79–198 (on the Pharisees, Sadducees, and others in Josephus and the NT, with special attention to social history).

- Steve Mason, *Flavius Josephus on the Pharisees* (Leiden: E. J. Brill, 1991).

NOTES

1. That is, Judea, Samaria, Galilee, Trans-Jordan, Idumea, and the coastal plain—what would later be called Palestina by the Romans.
2. For the division of Herod's kingdom, see Josephus, *War* 2.94–98.
3. On Agrippa I, see Josephus, *War* 2.214–222; *Ant.* 19.292–352.
4. On Agrippa II, see Josephus, *War* 2.223–284; 3.56–57; *Ant.* 20.104, 138–140.
5. We shall consider Josephus' discussion of the Baptist more closely in chapter 5.
6. Josephus says that the laws forbade erection of images "in the city," but there is no such specific law.
7. Hyam Maccoby, *The Myth-Maker: Paul and the Invention of Christianity* (San Francisco: Harper, 1986), 8.
8. See S. N. Mason, "Priesthood in Josephus and the Theory of a 'Pharisaic Revolution,' " *JBL* 107/4 (1988), 657–61.
9. It should be noted that Josephus alludes to "another order of Essenes" (LCL) that allows marriage (*War* 2.160). This is an odd exception and stands over against evidence elsewhere in Josephus

and Philo (e.g., *Hypothetica* 11.14–17). It is generally held that the Essenes repudiated marriage.

10. In their belief that Josephus was himself a Pharisee, many scholars have suggested that he did not write the introduction to the story, that it comes from one of his sources and does not reflect his views. This view is untenable, however, since: (a) the author refers to his earlier remarks on the schools (cf. 13.171–173); (b) his language about their influence with the masses establishes a theme that continues throughout *Antiquities* (cf. 13.298; 14.400; 18.15); and (c) the language about success producing envy is quite characteristic of Josephus, even in his autobiography (*Life* 80, 85, 122, 204, 423), where reliance on sources is unlikely. For a full discussion, see Steve Mason, *Flavius Josephus on the Pharisees* (Studia Post-Biblica 39; Leiden: E. J. Brill, 1991), 213–45.

11. See the preceding note.

12. Many scholars in the last few decades have come to doubt the old view, based largely on Josephus, that the Pharisees were the dominant group in Jewish society before the temple fell in AD 70. So Rudolf Meyer and H. F. Weiss, *TDNT*, vol. 9, 31; Morton Smith, "Palestinian Judaism in the First Century," in *Israel: Its Role in Civilization* (ed. Moshe Davis; New York: Harper & Brothers, 1956), 67–81; Jacob Neusner, *From Politics to Piety: The Emergence of Pharisaic Judaism* (Englewood Cliffs, N.J.: Prentice-Hall, 1973); Anthony J. Saldarini, *Pharisees, Scribes and Sadducees* (Wilmington: Michael Glazier, 1988), 157, 211, 214, 229. E. P. Sanders, *Judaism: Practice and Belief, 63 BCE–66 CE* (London: SCM; Philadelphia: TPI, 1992), 380–490, credits the Pharisees with popularity but not social control in pre–70 Judea. This may be a helpful distinction, though it is not made by Josephus.

5 Early Christian Figures Mentioned by Josephus

The most obvious reason for Christian interest in Josephus is that he mentions three prominent NT personalities: John the Baptist, Jesus, and Jesus' brother James. I have delayed considering those figures until now because the passages in which they appear are not central to Josephus' literary aims. All three occur only in the potpourri of material that he includes in *Antiquities* 18–20 to fill out that rambling narrative, but those are not the first places one should look to understand Josephus. In my view, his significance for the NT reader would remain almost as great if he had said nothing about John, Jesus, and James.

Nevertheless, he does mention them, and his unique perspective is helpful for NT interpretation. Of the three passages, the one concerning John the Baptist is the most revealing. Josephus' description of Jesus is full of problems, but most of those seem capable of resolution. His reference to James, though very brief, is also useful. Even as we turn to consider his discussions of these figures, we need to keep in mind everything that we have observed so far about his literary aims.

JOHN THE BAPTIST

It is a mark of Josephus' complete isolation from the early Christian world of thought that he devotes significantly more space to John the Baptist than to Jesus—even if we admit his account of Jesus as it stands (but see below). He mentions the

Baptist while discussing the marital indiscretions of Herod Antipas, which we considered in chapter 4. Recall that the tetrarch's passion for his brother's wife led him to abandon his own, who happened to be the daughter of the neighboring king, Aretas IV. That king was already upset with Antipas over a border dispute. When he heard his daughter's story, he engaged Antipas in battle and routed his army. Josephus comments:

> But to some of the Jews the destruction of Herod's army seemed to be divine vengeance, and certainly a just vengeance, for his treatment of John, surnamed the Baptist. For Herod had put him to death, though he was a good man and had exhorted the Jews to lead righteous lives, to practise justice [*dikaiosynē*] towards their fellows and piety [*eusebeia*] towards God, and so doing to join in baptism. In his view this was a necessary preliminary if baptism was to be acceptable to God. They must not employ it to gain pardon for whatever sins they had committed, but as a consecration of the body implying that the soul was already cleansed by right behaviour. When others too joined the crowds about him, because they were aroused to the highest degree by his sermons, Herod became alarmed. Eloquence that had so great an effect on mankind might lead to some form of sedition, for it looked as if they would be guided by John in everything that they did. Herod decided therefore that it would be much better to strike first and be rid of him before his work led to an uprising, than to wait for an upheaval, get involved in a difficult situation and see his mistake. Though John, because of Herod's suspicions, was brought in chains to Machaerus, the stronghold that we have previously mentioned, and there put to death, yet the verdict of the Jews was that the destruction visited upon Herod's army was a vindication of John, since God saw fit to inflict such a blow on Herod (*Ant.* 18.116–119, LCL)

So in Josephus' view, John was a good and virtuous teacher, well respected among the Jews. His unjust death once again exposed the lawlessness of the Herodian family. In keeping with the thesis of *Antiquities*, Antipas was quickly punished by God for his misdeeds.

Since John died before Josephus' birth, the historian must be recounting a tradition, either oral or written. Perhaps the legend of the Baptist was so famous that Josephus knew it from childhood and simply chose to insert it here in his account of Antipas' rule. Or perhaps his written source for the political history of the period referred to John's death. In any case, Josephus tells the story in his own way, to make his own points. Most obviously, he welds the episode into his ongoing demonstration that violation of the divine laws brings inevitable punishment.

Notice also that Josephus reduces the content of John's preaching to the maxim "piety toward God and justice toward one's fellows." This is Josephus' usual way of describing Jewish ethical responsibility.[1] Against the charges that Jews were atheists and haters of humanity, he says that all Jewish customs (*ethē*) are concerned with "piety [toward God] and justice [toward humanity]" (*Ant.* 16.42). He ascribes this pair of virtues to the great kings of Israel (*Ant.* 7.338, 342, 356, 374; 9.236) and paraphrases David's deathbed speech to Solomon so as to include them (*Ant.* 7.384). He even claims that the first two oaths sworn by Essene novices were "to behave with piety toward God and with justice toward their fellows" (*War* 2.139, author's translation). This terminology, which summarizes the popular morality of the Greco-Roman world, is part of Josephus' apologetic arsenal: he wants to present Judaism as a philosophical tradition that embraces the world's highest values.[2] John the Baptist appears as another Jewish philosopher, a modern heir of Abraham, Moses, and Solomon. But he is a persecuted philosopher of the sort familiar to Josephus' readers, condemned by an unjust ruler for his fearless virtue (see chapter 6).

How does Josephus' account of John relate to the Gospels' portrayals? On the one hand, it offers striking independent confirmation of John's demand that people coming for immersion first repent and resolve to behave righteously. In Josephus' words, "They must not employ it [baptism] to gain pardon for whatever sins they had committed, but as a consecration of the body implying that the soul was *already* cleansed by right behaviour" (*Ant.* 18.117). In the language of the Gospels:

Matt 3:7–10	Luke 3:7–9
But when he saw many of the Pharisees and Sadducees coming for immersion, he said to them:	He used to say to the crowds that came out to be immersed by him:

"Brood of vipers! Who warned you to flee from the coming wrath? Produce, therefore, fruit worthy of repentance, and do not consider saying among yourselves 'We have Abraham for a father.' For I am telling you that God is able to raise up children for Abraham from these stones. But the axe is already being set at the root of the trees; so every tree that does not produce good fruit is being rooted out and thrown into the fire" (author's translation).	"Brood of vipers! Who warned you to flee from the coming wrath? Produce, therefore, fruits worthy of repentance, and do not begin to say among yourselves 'We have Abraham for a father.' For I am telling you that God is able to raise up children for Abraham from these stones. But the axe is already being set at the root of the trees; so every tree that does not produce good fruit is being rooted out and thrown into the fire" (author's translation).

The Gospel of Luke elaborates on the kind of behavior that was required:

> Now the crowds used to ask him, "What, then, should we do?" And he would answer, "A person who has two coats should give to someone who has none, and a person who has food should do the same." Tax collectors would come to be immersed and would say to him, "Teacher, what should we do?" He said to them, "Do not make a surplus, beyond what is scheduled for you." And soldiers would ask him, "What about us? What should we do?" He said to them, "Do not extort or blackmail, but be content with your wages" (Luke 3:10–14, author's translation).

There is, to be sure, a difference of tone between Josephus' and the Gospels' accounts. His discussion of soul and the body and of "right action" is a translation of John's preaching into the philosophical language that he typically uses to describe Judaism. There is also a difference of content, to which we shall return below. Nevertheless, Josephus and the Gospels agree that John typically demanded repentance as a prior condition of immersion.

Some scholars have found a problem in the different reasons given for John's arrest. Josephus says that it was because of the preacher's great eloquence; in a period marked by successive popular movements that made the authorities very nervous, his popularity seemed sure to lead to disturbances. Just as the Roman governors of Judea did not hesitate to destroy such movements in Judea proper, so the tetrarch of Galilee and Perea thought it best to nip this group in the bud by destroying its leader. (Notice, however, that whereas Josephus usually detests such popular leaders, he only speaks well of John.) The Gospels, for their part, claim that Antipas killed

John because the preacher had denounced the tetrarch's un-
lawful marriage to his sister-in-law: "For John was saying to
Herod, 'It is not lawful for you to have your brother's wife' "
(Mark 6:18; Matt 14:4; Luke 3:19).

On examination, the two explanations are not mutually
exclusive, but actually fit together quite well. The Gospels do
not explain any details of the marital affair, and Josephus'
account provides helpful background. Luke, at least, allows
that the Baptist made many other criticisms of the ruler (Luke
3:19). Conversely, although Josephus does not mention John's
criticism of the tetrarch's marriage, we have seen that he
greatly simplifies John's preaching in schematic form. Such
popular movements were inherently anti-establishment, and
it would make sense if John or his followers had spoken
against Antipas' lawlessness. Moreover, if John did chastise
the tetrarch on this score, that would lend a kind of poetic
justice to the story, for he receives his punishment at the hand
of the abandoned wife's father. That connection may even
explain why this particular military defeat was traditionally
seen as punishment for Antipas' treatment of John.

Yet we see an obvious and major difference between Josephus and the Gospels in their respective portraits of the
Baptist. To put it bluntly, Josephus does not see John as a
"figure in the Christian tradition." The Baptist is not connected with early Christianity in any way. On the contrary,
Josephus presents him as a famous Jewish preacher with a
message and a following of his own, neither of which is related
to Jesus. This is a problem for the reader of the NT because the
Gospels unanimously declare him to be essentially the *forerunner* of Jesus the Messiah.

Mark, the earliest Gospel, sets the tone. He opens his narrative with a composite quotation from the prophets that interprets John as one who prepares for the Lord's coming (1:2–3):

> Just as it is written in Isaiah the prophet,
> "Look, I am sending my messenger before your face,
>   who will prepare your way,
> the voice of one who cries in the desert,
> 'Prepare the Lord's way; make his paths straight!' "

Although Mark attributes the quoted words to Isaiah, the first
two lines are a paraphrase of Malachi 3:1; Matthew (3:3) and

Luke (3:4) correct the oversight. For Mark, as for the early Christians generally, the title "Lord" refers to Jesus and not God as in the OT.[3] So John plays a key role in the story of salvation: he comes as a herald to prepare the way for Jesus. Mark's description of his preaching stresses its preparatory role: what he said to the people when he immersed them was that someone mightier was coming, who would immerse them in "holy spirit," and that he was totally unworthy of the coming one's company (1:7–8).

> The more powerful one is coming after me, the thong of whose sandals I am unworthy to stoop down and untie. I immersed you in water, but he will immerse you in holy spirit.

Thus John's preaching is basically forward-looking, pointing ahead to Jesus. He predicts the arrival of the Spirit in the church. Significantly, Jesus' career does not begin (in the synoptic Gospels) until the forerunner is in prison, having completed his role (Mark 1:14).

Matthew and Luke continue and develop this portrayal of John as herald. They agree that he played the role of Elijah, who, according to Malachi 4:5, would come before the "day of the Lord," to reconcile families so that the day of judgment would not be too catastrophic (Matt 11:14; Luke 1:12–17). He is a close ally of Jesus, drawing his power from the same source (Matt 11:16–19; 21:23–27); Luke even says he is a cousin (1:36). Nevertheless, when John is still in the womb he and his mother recognize the priority of Jesus and Mary (Luke 1:41–42). Matthew and Luke strictly relegate John to the old order, before Jesus' coming: "Among those born of women, none greater than John the Baptist has arisen; yet he who is least in the reign of heaven is greater than he" (Matt 11:11; Luke 7:28). He represents the highest point of the "law and prophets," before the coming of the gospel (Matt 11:13; Luke 16:17). Because "Luke" also writes Acts, he has considerable opportunity to emphasize John's preparatory function: he repeatedly notes that John's immersion in water anticipated the outpouring of the Spirit, the characteristic mark of the young church (Acts 1:5; 11:16).

The independence of the Fourth Gospel from the first three is indicated by its claim that Jesus and John worked side by side before John was arrested (John 3:22–23) and by its pointed denial of the Elijah role to the Baptist (1:21). But otherwise it maintains the synoptics' tendency both to claim John as a herald for Jesus and to distinctly subordinate him to Jesus. While introducing Jesus to the reader as the light of the world, the author takes the trouble to note that John was *not* the light of the world, but only bore witness to it (John 1:6–8). The Baptist says that his whole reason for immersing people was that he might reveal Jesus to Israel (1:31). Once he has fulfilled this mission, he releases his own disciples to follow Jesus (1:37). Then he utters the classic statement of Christian self-negation: "He must increase, but I must decrease" (3:30).

From beginning to end, therefore, the Gospels incorporate John wholly into the Christian story of salvation. His basic mission was to prepare the way for Jesus, to identify and "anoint" the Messiah. So too his preaching was entirely contingent on the future: what he preached about was Jesus' coming.

We have seen, however, that Josephus mentions nothing of John's association with Jesus. In Josephus' account, John has a large following and a self-contained message with its own logic. He does not encourage his students to follow Jesus. On the contrary, Antipas can only disperse his followers by getting rid of him. This difference of portrayal forces us to ask whether it is more likely that Josephus has taken a figure who was a herald for Jesus and, erasing his Christian connection, made him into a famous Jewish preacher, or whether the early Christian tradition has coopted a famous Jewish preacher as an ally and subordinate of Jesus.

The answer seems clear. On the one hand, Josephus had no discernible reason to create a famous Jewish preacher out of one of Jesus' associates. He has no sustained interest in John, but mentions him quite incidentally in his description of Antipas' government. He has already mentioned Jesus and will mention James, so he is not dedicated to removing all traces of Christianity from his writings. On the other hand, we can easily see in the Gospels themselves, in spite of their overall tendency to make John into a subordinate herald, traces of another story—one that left the Baptist with his integrity, his own message, and his own following.

John's integrity appears, for example, in the passages cited above, in which he plainly tells his audience what is required of them—not to believe in Jesus, but to behave generously toward one another, especially to the poor. We see it also in passages that reflect differences of practice between John's and Jesus' followers on the matter of fasting and diet (Mark 2:18; Matt 11:18–19). Most impressive, however, is the account in Acts 19:1–5. At Ephesus, some years after the deaths of both Jesus and John, Paul comes upon a group of "students" or disciples:[4]

> Paul passed through the upper district and came to Ephesus. When he found some students there, he said to them, "Did you receive holy spirit with your faith?" They said to him, "But we did not hear that there was a 'holy spirit.' " So he said, "With what, then, were you immersed?" And they said, "With the immersion of John." But Paul said, "John immersed with an immersion of repentance, saying to the people that they should trust in the one coming after him; this one is Jesus." When they heard that, they were immersed in the name of the Lord Jesus.

The students report that they have never heard of "holy spirit," and the author connects this with the fact that they are disciples of the Baptist, having experienced only his immersion. Interestingly enough, Paul also has to explain to them that the coming one announced by John was in fact Jesus. The function of the story in Acts seems clear enough: Luke wants to show that the outpouring of the Spirit is the hallmark of the young church; he takes over this tradition about John's disciples as one example of the many groups, Jewish and Gentile, that joined the church and received the Spirit. But the story seems to be at odds with his earlier presentations of the Baptist (in Luke), according to which John's primary concern, indeed his mission from birth, was precisely to declare the arrival of Jesus and to announce the coming baptism in the Spirit. This unassimilated tradition suggests, therefore: (a) that John's followers survived his death, were still known as an independent group, and had spread to Asia by the middle of the first century, and (b) that John's preaching was not contingent on either the arrival of Jesus or a future Spirit-immersion.

Another passage that points in the same direction tells of an enquiry about Jesus' identity by John. It comes as something of a surprise to the reader of Matthew and Luke that, after John has recognized Jesus while still in the womb (Luke), after he has immersed Jesus, witnessed the descent of the dove, heard the heavenly voice, and knowingly declared his unworthiness to baptize Jesus—all of which are presented as the climax of his career—he should later hear about Jesus' wonderful deeds and innocently send messengers to ask, "Are you the coming one or should we wait for another?" Thus:

Matt 11:2–6	Luke 7:18–23
Now when John, in prison, heard about the accomplishments of the Christ, he sent word via his students and said to him, "Are you the coming one, or should we expect another?"	John's students reported to him concerning all of these things. And John, calling in two of his students, sent them to the Lord saying, "Are you the coming one or should we expect another?" When they had come to him, the men said, "John the Baptist sent us to you saying, 'Are you the coming one, or should we expect another?' " In that hour, he cured many of diseases and torments and evil spirits and he granted sight to many who were blind.
And Jesus answered and said to them, "Go and report to John what you hear and see: the blind see again and the lame walk, lepers are cleansed and the deaf hear, the dead are raised and the poor receive good news. Happy is the one who takes no offense at me."	And he answered and said to them, "Go and report to John what you saw and heard: the blind see again, the lame walk, the lepers are cleansed and the deaf hear, the dead are raised, the poor receive good news. Happy is the one who takes no offense at me.

The standard solution to the problem is to suppose that John was beginning to have some doubt about Jesus' messiahship. Thus the force of his question would be, "I thought that you were the Messiah. If you are, when are you going to do something Messiah-like (take political control, expel the Romans, etc.)?" It has sometimes been thought that Jesus' miracles disturbed John, for he wanted a political leader, not a healer. So the story would present the beginning of John's doubt about Jesus. Indeed, the closing line suggests that this is how Matthew and Luke understood it.

The problem with this interpretation is the internal logic of the story. Read by itself, it clearly implies the beginning of John's *interest* in Jesus as Messiah. He hears about Jesus' wonders and so is encouraged to ask whether Jesus is the coming one. In quiet response, Jesus performs more wonders in the presence of John's messengers, thus evidently confirming that he *is* the coming one. The sense is one of discovery and excitement. John's students return to him and report that what they had heard about Jesus is true! They have seen it with their own eyes. Although it is conceivable that the story has to do with John's doubt, it seems more adequately explained as an incident remembered by Jesus' followers in which the great Jewish preacher expressed an initial interest in Jesus' work. That explanation would fit with both Josephus' presentation of John as an independent figure and the NT passages (above) that assume the ongoing vitality of the "Baptist movement."

In sum, then, Josephus' account of John the Baptist, independent as it is from the tendencies of the Christian tradition, forces us to ask whether the wilderness preacher has not been posthumously adopted by the church in a way that he did not anticipate. It seems clear enough that he did immerse Jesus, among many others, and that this event marked a watershed in Jesus' life. Jesus' immersion by John caused problems for early Christians, for they then had to explain why Jesus was immersed "for the forgiveness of sins."[5] It is unlikely, therefore, that Christians created the story of Jesus' baptism. But since the renowned Jewish preacher had immersed him, the early Christian retelling of the story increasingly coopted John into the Christian story, gradually diminishing his own message and making him a prophet for the church. This kind of process seems inevitable with famous and well-liked people: notice how Jesus himself has been adopted by Marxists and Capitalists, Enlightenment thinkers and fundamentalists, not to mention virtually every world religion. Josephus' account of John helps us to see another side of him, independent of the young church's perspective.

Yet we have seen that Josephus has his own biases. He too has schematized John's preaching to fit his overall story. John is made to speak, in Josephus' language, of "justice toward one's fellows and piety toward God." In this case, the Gospels can help us to interpret Josephus, for they provide more information about the Baptist's language. If we strip away the obvious Christian themes overlaid on John's preaching in the Gospels, we find an underlying core of Jewish "apocalyptic" thought—that is, a declaration that the fiery judgment of God was about to fall on the world, bringing an end to this present evil age. Thus:

Matthew 3:12	Luke 3:17
His winnowing fork is in his hand, and he will clear his threshing floor and gather his wheat into the storehouse, but the chaff he will burn up with inextinguishable fire.	His winnowing fork is in his hand, to clear his threshing floor, and to gather the wheat into his storehouse, but the chaff he will burn up with inextinguishable fire.

Or again:

> But the axe has already been set to the root of the trees; so every tree that does not produce good fruit is being rooted out and thrown into the fire (Matt 3:10//Luke 3:9).

The idea of coming fiery judgment was quite common in ancient Jewish imagination. In that hot and dry region, the image of precious bodies of water (lakes and rivers) turned to *fire* was an especially terrifying symbol of punishment. So we find many references to lakes or rivers of fire in apocalyptic writings from the time. Daniel already envisaged a river of fire streaming from God's throne, into which the evil fourth beast would be thrown (Dan 7:9–11). Another famous apocalyptic text draws this picture of the judgment:

> In the meantime I saw how another abyss like it, full of fire, was opened wide in the middle of the ground; and they brought those blinded sheep, all of which were judged, found guilty, and cast into this fiery abyss and they were burned (1 Enoch 90.26).[6]

The Dead Sea Scrolls (1QH 3.27–32) and the book of Revelation (20:10) use the same imagery. What distinguished John's preaching, and may have suggested his nick-name "the Baptist," was that he offered a symbolic immersion in water *now* instead of the coming immersion in fire, to those who would repent and behave righteously.

If this apocalyptic message was the core of John's preaching, then both Josephus and the NT writers have obscured it to some degree. The NT writers did so, perhaps unconsciously, as they reinterpreted John's role within their view of history. Josephus, for his part, was wary of presenting Judaism in apocalyptic terms because that would not favorably impress the audience he was trying to reach. Upper-class Roman readers could be expected to take a dim view of any apparent disloyalty to Rome's divine mission. The recently failed revolt in Judea, which had brought the Jews such bad press, had been partly fueled by apocalyptic hopes—the anticipation that God would choose that moment to intervene in world affairs and restore Israel's glory.[7] So Josephus, in trying to heal Jewish-Roman relations, was not in a position to develop apocalyptic themes. Accordingly, when he is explaining Daniel to his readers, he abruptly stops short of explaining the final outcome of history, evidently because he thinks that Daniel foretold the fall of the Roman empire to a new kingdom of God:

> And Daniel also revealed to the king the meaning of the stone [that would smash the final kingdom], but I have not thought it proper to relate this, since I am expected to write of what is past and done and not of what is to be (*Ant.* 10.210, LCL).

So in this case it is the Gospels that provide important background for understanding Josephus. From their fuller account of John's preaching, we are able to distill a plausible apocalyptic core:

> Whereas I am immersing you in water for repentance, the coming one will immerse you in fire. His winnowing fork is in his hand, to clear his threshing floor and to gather the wheat into his storehouse, but the chaff he will burn up with inextinguishable fire (cf. Matt 3:11–12).

If we have correctly recreated the original flavor of John's preaching, it corresponds well to another text from first-century Jewish baptist circles:

> Ah, wretched mortals, change these things, and do not
> lead the great God to all sorts of anger, but abandon
> daggers and groanings, murders and outrages,
> and wash your whole bodies in perennial rivers.
> Stretch out your hands to heaven and ask forgiveness. . . .
>   God will grant repentance
> and will not destroy. He will stop his wrath again if you all
> practice honorable piety in your hearts.
> But if you do not obey me, evil-minded ones, but love
> impiety, and receive all these things with evil ears,
> there will be fire throughout the whole world. . . .
> He will burn the whole earth, and will destroy
>   the whole race of men
> and all cities and rivers at once, and the sea.
> He will destroy everything by fire, and it will be smoking dust
>   (*Sybilline Oracles* 4.162–178).[8]

The case of John the Baptist underscores the point that we ought not to treat Josephus as a kind of "fact book" for the background of the NT. He too has a perspective, with its own limitations. His elaborate work often stimulates us to ask new questions of the NT; but, in turn, the NT can occasionally shed light on his narratives.

JESUS, A WISE MAN

We come now to Josephus' much-debated paragraph on Jesus, the so-called *testimonium flavianum* or "witness of Flavius [Josephus, to Jesus]." That this short paragraph has come to have its own Latin title reflects its vast and unique importance in the Christian tradition. Because Josephus talks about John the Baptist's death only in a flashback, while discussing the defeat of Antipas, his passage on John (*Ant.* 18.116–119) comes after his description of Jesus (*Ant.* 18.63–64). It seems clear from various independent statements within the NT, however, that John's arrest and execution preceded Jesus' trial.

Josephus mentions Jesus while relating some events during the governorship of Pontius Pilate (AD 26–36/37).[9] We have discussed most of these events in the previous chapter and may now summarize them as follows:

- Pilate arrives in Judea   18.35
- First incident: Pilate's introduction of imperial images into Jerusalem by night   18.55–59
- Second incident: Pilate's expropriation of temple funds for aqueduct   18.60–62
- *Third incident: Jesus and his followers*   18.63–64
- Fourth incident (contemporary, in Rome): seduction of a chaste, aristocratic follower of Isis in Rome, resulting in the crucifixion of priests and destruction of the temple of Isis   18.65–80
- Fifth incident (contemporary, in Rome): four Jewish scoundrels conspire to de-

fraud an aristocratic convert to Judaism of
money sent to the Jewish temple, resulting
in the expulsion of Jews from Rome

- Sixth incident (back in Palestine): Pilate   18.85–87
  quashes popular Samaritan movement

- Pilate's removal from office   18.88–89

This overview highlights several key points. (a) To fill out his
narrative of Pilate's governorship, Josephus has strung together
an assortment of episodes, probably from different sources.
The fourth and fifth incidents occur in Rome and have nothing
to do with Pilate directly. It seems that they are out of order
chronologically, for the expulsion of Jews and Egyptians (the
cult of Isis) from Rome probably occurred in AD 19, before
Pilate's arrival in Judea. (b) All of the episodes, except perhaps
the Jesus affair, are described as "outrages" or "uprisings" or
"tumults." Josephus is trying to paint a picture of escalating
tension for Jews around the world. (c) These episodes also
serve Josephus' larger literary aims in *Antiquities,* for example:
(i) the first, second, and sixth incidents illustrate the cruelty
and insensitivity of the Roman governors; (ii) the sixth incident reflects the gullibility of the masses (here Samaritan)
toward false prophets; and (iii) the parallel Egyptian and Jewish incidents at Rome show both that the Jews are no worse
than other national groups and, more importantly, that Jews
share the morals of the Romans. Josephus plainly expresses
his own abhorrence of the scoundrels' activities; they were led
by a man who only "pretended to interpret the wisdom of the
laws of Moses" (18.81). The entire Jewish community suffered
then (as now, after the war) for the actions of a few reprobates
(18.84).

In the midst of these stories of outrage and tumult, Josephus mentions Jesus and his followers. As we have it, the text
in Josephus reads:

> About this time comes Jesus, a wise man, if indeed it is proper
> to call him a man. For he was a worker of incredible deeds, a
> teacher of those who accept the truth with pleasure, and he
> attracted many Jews as well as many of the Greek [way]. This
> man was Christ. And when, in view of [his] denunciation by the
> leading men among us, Pilate had sentenced him to a cross,

those who had loved him at the beginning did not cease [to do so]. He appeared to them on the third day alive again, for the divine prophets had announced these and countless other marvels concerning him. And even now the tribe of the "Christians"—named after him—has not yet disappeared (*Ant.* 18.63–64, author's translation).

I say "the text as we have it" because this brief passage is brimming with problems. Scholars first noticed them in the sixteenth century. By 1863, when a German scholar wrote an entire book on this paragraph, he had to begin by justifying his study, since the question had already been so thoroughly debated. That was 1863! His own analysis was by no means the final word. During the period 1937–1980, one bibliographer counts eighty-seven more studies of the subject. The passage continues to attract scholarly interest in current journal articles (see "For Further Reading").

So, what is the problem? 1. To begin with the most obvious point: the passage does not fit well with its context in *Antiquities* 18. Like the tourist negotiating a bustling, raucous middle-eastern market who accidently walks through the door of a monastery, suffused with light and peace, the reader of Josephus is struck by this sublime portrait. Josephus is speaking of upheavals, but there is no upheaval here. He is pointing out the folly of Jewish rebels, governors, and troublemakers in general, but this passage is completely supportive of both Jesus and his followers. Logically, what should appear in this context ought to imply some criticism of the Jewish leaders and/or Pilate, but Josephus does not make any such criticism explicit. He says only that those who denounced Jesus were "the leading men among us." So, unlike the other episodes, this one has no moral, no lesson. Although Josephus begins the next paragraph by speaking of "another outrage" that caused an uproar among the Jews at the same time (18.65), there is nothing in this paragraph that depicts any sort of outrage.

2.A. Most problematic of all is the terse sentence concerning Jesus: "This man was Christ." This affirmation is difficult for several reasons. First, the word "Christ" (Greek *christos*) would have special meaning only for a Jewish audience. In Greek it means simply "wetted" or "anointed." Within the Jewish world, this was an extremely significant term because anointing was the means by which the kings and high priests of Israel had been installed. The pouring of oil over their heads represented their assumption of God-given authority (Exod 29:9; 1 Sam 10:1). The Hebrew word for "anointed" was *mashiach,* which we know usually as the noun Messiah, "the anointed [one]." Although used in the OT of reigning kings and high priests, many Jews of Jesus' day looked forward to an end-time prophet, priest, king, or someone else who would be duly anointed.

But for someone who did not know the Jewish tradition, the adjective "wetted" would sound most peculiar. Why would Josephus say that this man Jesus was "the Wetted"? We can see the puzzlement of Greek-speaking readers over this term in their descriptions of Christianity: Jesus' name is sometimes altered to "Chrestus" (Suetonius, *Claudius* 25.4), a common slave name that would make better sense, and the Christians are sometimes called "Chrestians."

Since Josephus is usually sensitive to his audience and pauses to explain unfamiliar terms or aspects of Jewish life, it is very strange that he would make the bald assertion, without explanation, that Jesus was "Christ." He has not used this term before and will only use it again when he calls James the "brother of Jesus, the one called Christ" (*Ant.* 20.200). That formulation, "the one called Christ," makes much better sense because it sounds like a nick-name. Nick-names were necessary among first-century Jews because there was a relatively small number of proper names in circulation. We have already met several people with the name Jesus (=Joshua), and the index to Josephus' writings lists some twenty-one individuals with this name. So it would make sense for Josephus to say, "This man had the nickname Christos," and he could do so without further explanation. But simply to say that Jesus *was* Christ, or Messiah, is a peculiar formulation. It is doubly suspicious, of course, because we know that Josephus' writings were preserved and recopied by Christians, for whom Jesus was indeed the Christ.

2.B. A second problem with the statement "This man was Christ" is that its solemn phrasing makes it seem to represent Josephus' own confession of faith: he believed Jesus to be Messiah. In addition to that direct statement, the passage says things that only a Christian could have written, it seems, about Jesus' appearances after death, his being more than just a man, and the many ancient prophecies concerning him. Indeed, William Whiston, who translated Josephus' writings in 1737, thought on the basis of this passage that Josephus must have been a Christian. But that seems impossible. As we have seen, he writes as a passionate advocate of Judaism. Everywhere he praises the excellent constitution of the Jews, codified by Moses, and declares its peerless, comprehensive quality. (Yet even Moses, who was as close as possible to God, is never credited with being more than a man.) Josephus rejoices over converts to Judaism. In all of this there is not the slightest hint of any belief in Jesus. Whiston thought that this omission was because Josephus was a *Jewish* Christian. But from everything we know of Jewish Christians in the first century (James, Peter, those mentioned in Acts), the figure of Jesus was still central to their faith. That is obviously not the case with Josephus. His total commitment to the sufficiency of Judaism seems to preclude any Christian affiliation.

2.C. The strongest evidence that Josephus did not declare Jesus' messiahship is that the passage under discussion does not seem to have been present in the texts of *Antiquities* known before the fourth century. Recall that we do not possess the original Greek text that Josephus wrote; we have only copies, the earliest of which (known as P and A) date from the ninth and tenth centuries. These relatively late copies provide the basis for our current Greek editions and English translations of Josephus. But we know of about a dozen Christian authors from the second and third centuries who were familiar with Josephus' writings. Since many of them were writing to help legitimize the young church, drawing upon every available means of support, it is noteworthy that *none* of them mentions Josephus' belief in Jesus. If the famous, imperially sponsored Jewish historian had declared Jesus to be Messiah, it would presumably have helped their cause to mention the fact, but they do not.

Most significant, the renowned Christian teacher Origen (185–254) flatly states, in two different contexts, that Josephus did not believe in Jesus' messiahship. Commenting on Josephus' (allegedly favorable) description of James, the "brother of the one called Christ," Origen expresses his wonder that the Jewish historian "did not accept that our Jesus is Christ" (*Commentary on Matthew* to Matt 10.17). Similarly, in his apologetic work, *Against Celsus,* he directs the reader to Josephus' own defense of Judaism, but then laments that he "did not believe in Jesus as Christ" (1.47). Origen knew Josephus' writings quite well: he cites accurately from *War, Antiquities,* and *Against Apion.* But it is hard to see how he could have made these statements about Josephus' unbelief if he had known of the *testimonium* that we find in our copies of Josephus. Evidently, his copy of *Antiquities,* like those of his predecessors, did not contain it.

The first author to mention the *testimonium* is Eusebius, the church historian who wrote in the early 300s. In the opening volume of his *Ecclesiastical History,* Eusebius cites Josephus extensively as an independent witness to the Gospels' statements about Jesus, John the Baptist, and the political events of the period. Following his quotation of the passage on John, he cites the *testimonium* just as it appears in our Greek manuscripts of Josephus (*Eccl hist* 1.11; quoted above). Another of his works, the *Theophany,* which exists only in Syriac, also includes Josephus' "witness to Jesus." Interestingly, a third work includes it, but with several variations of language (*Proof of the Gospel* 3.5). These minor variants seem to indicate that even at Eusebius' time the form of the *testimonium* was not yet fixed. Furthermore, Eusebius erroneously places it *after* Josephus' discussion of John the Baptist.

Long after Eusebius, in fact, the text of the *testimonium* remained fluid. Jerome (342–420), the great scholar who translated the Bible and some of Eusebius into Latin, gives a version that agrees closely with the standard text, except that the crucial phrase says of Jesus, "he was *believed to be* the Messiah."[10] In the tenth century, the Christian author Agapius wrote a history of the world in Arabic, in which he reproduced Josephus' statement about Jesus as follows:

> At this time there was a wise man who was called Jesus. His conduct was good, and [he] was known to be virtuous. And many people from among the Jews and the other nations became his disciples. Pilate condemned him to be crucified and to die. But those who had become his disciples did not abandon his discipleship. They reported that he had appeared to them three days after his crucifixion, and that he was alive; accordingly he was perhaps the Messiah, concerning whom the prophets have recounted wonders.[11]

And at the end of the twelfth century, Michael, the Patriarch of Antioch, quotes Josephus as saying that Jesus "was thought to be the Messiah. But not according to the principal [men] of [our] nation. . . ."[12]

Where did such equivocal versions of Josephus' account come from? Who had an interest in altering Josephus' enthusiastic statement so as to introduce doubt about Jesus' messiahship? The Christian dignitaries who innocently report these versions as if they came from Josephus had no motive, it seems, to weaken their testimony to Jesus. On the one hand, everything that we know of Christian scribal tendencies (for example, in the transmission of the NT texts) points the other way: they tend to heighten Jesus' grandeur and status. On the other hand, these accounts are not obviously *anti*-Christian, and so do not seem to have arisen from Jewish or pagan polemical corruptions of Josephus. Anti-Christian writers would presumably have left some trace of their disdain for Jesus in such corruptions. It seems probable, therefore, that the versions of Josephus' statement given by Jerome, Agapius, and Michael reflect alternative textual traditions of Josephus, which did not contain the emphatic statements that we find in the standard (medieval) manuscripts of *Antiquities* or in Eusebius.

3. A third kind of problem with the *testimonium* as it stands in Josephus concerns its vocabulary and style. It uses some words in ways that are not characteristic of Josephus. For example, the word translated "worker" in the phrase "worker of incredible deeds" is *poiētēs* in Greek, from which we get "poet." Etymologically, it means "one who does" and so it can refer to any sort of "doer." But in Josephus' day it had already come to have a special reference to literary poets, and that is how he consistently uses it elsewhere (nine times)—to speak of Greek poets like Homer.

Notice further that the phrase "they did not cease" has to be completed by the translator, for it is left incomplete in the text; the action from which his followers ceased must be inferred from the preceding phrase. This is as peculiar in Greek as it is in English, and such a construction is not found elsewhere in Josephus' writing.

Again, the phrase "the tribe of the Christians" is peculiar. Josephus uses the word "tribe" (*phylē*) eleven other times.

Once it denotes "gender," and once a "swarm" of locusts, but it usually signifies distinct peoples, races, or nationalities: the Jews are a "tribe" (*War* 3.354; 7.327) as are the Taurians (*War* 2.366) and Parthians (*War* 2.379). It is very strange that Josephus should speak of the Christians as a distinct racial group, since he has just said that Jesus was a Jew condemned by the Jewish leaders. (Notice, however, that some *Christian* authors of a later period came to speak of Christianity as a "third race.")

These examples, along with the use of "Christ" and other peculiarities, illustrate the stylistic difficulties of the *testimonium*. Stylistic arguments are notoriously dicey, because writers are quite capable of using words in unusual ways, on a whim. If a writer uses a high concentration of peculiar words within a short space, however, and if other factors cast doubt on the authenticity of a passage, the stylistic features may become significant.

Taking all of these problems into consideration, a few scholars have argued that the entire passage as it stands in Josephus is a Christian forgery. The Christian scribes who copied the Jewish historian's writings thought it intolerable that he should have said nothing about Jesus and spliced the paragraph in where it might logically have stood, in Josephus' account of Pilate's tenure. Some scholars have suggested that Eusebius himself was the forger, since he was the first to produce the passage.

Most critics, however, have been reluctant to go so far. They have noted that, in general, Christian copyists were quite conservative in transmitting texts. Nowhere else in all of Josephus' voluminous writings is there strong suspicion of scribal tampering. Christian copyists also transmitted the works of Philo, who said many things that might be elaborated in a Christian direction, but there is no evidence that in hundreds of years of transmission, the scribes inserted their own remarks into Philo's text. To be sure, many of the "pseudepigrapha" that exist now only in Christian form are thought to stem from Jewish originals, but in this instance it may reflect the thorough Christian rewriting of Jewish models, rather than scribal insertions. That discussion is ongoing among scholars. But in the cases of Philo and Josephus, whose writings are preserved in their original language and form, one is hard pressed to find a single example of serious scribal alteration.

To have created the *testimonium* out of whole cloth would be an act of unparalleled scribal audacity.

Second, if Christians had written the paragraph from scratch, they might have been expected to give Jesus a little more space than John, and to use language that was more emphatically Christian. Rather than merely doubting that Jesus could adequately be called a man, for example, they might have said something more positive, unless they were very clever. As it stands, the reticence to call Jesus a man seems like a rejoinder to the previous, already flattering statement that he *was* a wise man. It seems more like a qualification of an existing statement than part of a free creation.

Third, if some of the vocabulary and phrasing sound peculiar for Josephus, much of the rest is perfectly normal. The opening phrase "about this time" is characteristic of his language in this part of *Antiquities*, where he is weaving together distinct episodes into a coherent narrative (cf. *Ant.* 17.19; 18.39, 65, 80; 19.278). He uses the designation "wise man" sparingly, but as a term of considerable praise. King Solomon was such a wise man (Ant. 8.53), and so was Daniel (10.237). Interestingly, both men had what we might call occult powers—abilities to perform cures and interpret dreams— of the sort that Jesus is credited with in the *testimonium*. So to call Jesus a "wise man" here presents no special difficulties. If Josephus said it, it was a term of high praise. Moreover, Josephus often speaks of "marvels" and "incredible" things in the same breath, as the *testimonium* does. He even uses the phrase rendered "incredible deeds" in two other places, once of the prophet Elisha (*Ant.* 9.182; cf. 12.63). Josephus often speaks of the "leading men" among the Jews with the phrase used in the *testimonium*, especially in book 18 of *Antiquities* (17.81; 18.7, 99, 121, 376). Although the phrase "divine prophets" sounds peculiar at first, there is a close parallel in Josephus' description of Isaiah (*Ant.* 10.35). Even the word used for what the prophets "announced" is commonly used by Josephus in conjunction with prophecy. Consequently, although some of the language in the *testimonium* is odd, we have no linguistic basis for dismissing the whole paragraph.

These linguistic considerations have led many scholars to think that Josephus must have said something about Jesus, even if it is not what we currently have. Moreover, his later reference to James (*Ant.* 20.200) seems to presuppose some earlier reference to Jesus. James is introduced, rather oddly, as "the brother of Jesus who is called Christ, James by name." Josephus' primary identification of James as Jesus' brother, and his inclusion of James' own name as an incidental detail, suggests that this "Jesus who is called Christ" is already known to his readers. That expectation is easiest to explain if Josephus had mentioned Jesus in the foregoing narrative.

Finally, the existence of alternative versions of the *testimonium* has encouraged many scholars to think that Josephus must have written something close to what we find in them, which was later edited by Christian hands. If the laudatory version in Eusebius and our text of Josephus were the free creation of Christian scribes, who then created the more restrained versions found in Jerome, Agapius, and Michael? The version of Agapius is especially noteworthy because it eliminates, though perhaps too neatly, all of the major difficulties in the standard text of Josephus. (a) It is not reluctant to call Jesus a man. (b) It contains no reference to Jesus' miracles. (c) It has Pilate execute Jesus at his own discretion. (d) It presents Jesus' appearance after death as merely reported by the disciples, not as fact. (e) It has Josephus wonder about Jesus' messiahship, without explicit affirmation. And (f) it claims only that the prophets spoke about "the Messiah," whoever he might be, not that they spoke about Jesus. That shift also explains sufficiently the otherwise puzzling term "Messiah" for Josephus' readers. In short, Agapius' version of the *testimonium* sounds like something that a Jewish observer of the late first century could have written about Jesus and his followers.

We cannot resolve the problem of Josephus' "testimony" about Jesus here. Among the hundreds of books and articles on the subject, every conceivable position has been taken between two opposite poles. On the one side, as we have seen, some scholars are convinced that Josephus said nothing whatsoever about Jesus, and that is why no one before Eusebius mentions the *testimonium*. On the other extreme, a few influential scholars have held the passage to be entirely authentic. Some reconcile it with the rest of Josephus' writings by suggesting that Josephus saw Jesus' death as the end of messianic hope: Jesus did indeed fulfill Israel's hope, but his horrible execution shows the futility of persisting in such belief.

Others propose that Josephus included the passage so as to curry favor with the Christians, because he was in trouble with his own Jewish compatriots. Still others interpret the passage as intended sarcasm, though the argument for that view is too convoluted to summarize here. Note: even those who accept the authenticity of the *testimonium* do not share Whiston's belief that Josephus was a Christian. That theory seems highly improbable.

The vast majority of commentators hold a middle position between authenticity and inauthenticity, claiming that Josephus wrote *something* about Jesus that was subsequently edited by Christian copyists. Such a view has the best of both worlds, for it recognizes all of the problems with the passage as well as the factors that support its authenticity. Of the many scholars who take this position, a significant number have tried their hand at reconstructing the hypothetical original by removing Christian glosses. Their assessments of Christian influence vary greatly. The copyist might merely have changed the sentence "This man was believed to be Christ" to "This man was Christ." Or he might have practically rewritten the piece, inserting and omitting freely. The following two examples will give the reader an idea of the possibilities. Robert Eisler (1929), relying heavily on hypothetical alterations suggested by the Slavonic version of Josephus *see note 12) and on consistently unfavorable translations of the Greek, proposed:

> Now about this time arose (an occasion for new disturbances) a certain Jesus, a wizard of a man, if indeed he may be called a man (who was the most monstrous of all men, whom his disciples called a son of God, as having done wonders such as no man hath ever done).... He was in fact a teacher of astonishing tricks to such men as accept the abnormal with delight.... And he seduced many Jews and many also of the Greek nation, and (was regarded by them as) the Messiah.... And when, on the indictment of the principal men among us, Pilate had sentenced him to the cross, still those who before had admired him did not cease (to rave). For it seemed to them that having been dead for three days, he had appeared to them alive again, as the divinely-inspired prophets had foretold—these and ten thousand other wonderful things—concerning him. And even now the race of those who are called "Messianists" after him is not extinct.[13]

A recent journal article by John P. Meier (1991) offers a somewhat milder restoration. In Meier's view, the three most obvious Christian insertions can be easily removed to leave a
perfectly acceptable sense:

> At this time there appeared Jesus, a wise man. For he was a doer
> of startling deeds, a teacher of people who receive the truth
> with pleasure. And he gained a following both among many
> Jews and among many of Greek origin. And when Pilate, be-
> cause of an accusation made by the leading men among us,
> condemned him to the cross, those who loved him previously
> did not cease to do so. And up until this very day the tribe of
> Christians, named after him, has not died out.[14]

The problem with any such restoration, of course, is that we
simply have no copies of Josephus dating from the time before
Eusebius. Once it is granted that the standard text is corrupt,
a wide variety of hypothetical reconstructions must remain
equally plausible.

What, then, is the value of the *testimonium flavianum* for
the reader of the NT? Limited. Paradoxically, the intense effort
to reconstruct the "original" reading, in order to make it historically useful, itself diminishes the value of the passage, for
each new reading has to share plausibility, so to speak, with all
other proposals on the table. No matter how convincing a
restoration may seem to any given interpreter, he or she will
not be able to put much weight on it in the course of scholarly
argumentation, in the knowledge that few others will accept
it. Unless one of the many proposals manages to win the
allegiance of a significant majority, this situation will continue
indefinitely. But consensus is likely to come only with a major
new insight into the state of Josephus' text before the fourth
century, likely as the result of some new discovery.

It would be unwise, therefore, to lean heavily on Josephus' statements about Jesus' healing and teaching activity, or
the circumstances of his trial. Nevertheless, since most of
those who know the evidence agree that he said something
about Jesus, one is probably entitled to cite him as independent evidence that Jesus actually lived, if such evidence
were needed. But that much is already given in Josephus'
reference to James (*Ant.* 20.200) and most historians agree that

Jesus' existence is the only adequate explanation of the many independent traditions among the NT writings.

JAMES, THE BROTHER OF JESUS

The only other figure from the early Christian tradition mentioned by Josephus is James, the brother of Jesus. He says very little about this man, but the fact that he mentions him incidentally is strong support for the authenticity of the passage. No copyist has tried to turn this passage into a religious confession of any sort.

Josephus mentions James near the end of *Antiquities*, while discussing the political events in Judea of the mid-60s. The governor Porcius Festus has died in office (AD 62), and the emperor Nero sends Albinus to replace him (AD 62–64). At the same time, King Agrippa II, who has been granted control over the high priesthood, bestows it on Ananus II. Although Josephus had praised this man's virtues in *War*, here he wants to expose the lawlessness of many Jewish leaders before the revolt, to explain the cause of the catastrophe. So he introduces Ananus II as a rash and impertinent fellow. He "followed the school of the Sadducees, who, when it comes to judgments, are savage beyond all [other] Jews, as I have already explained" (*Ant.* 20.199, author's translation; cf. 13.294). To illustrate Ananus' impetuous cruelty, Josephus relates the following story:

> Ananus, supposing that he had an opportune moment with Festus having died and Albinus still on the way, convened the judges of the council [or Sanhedrin] and arraigned before them the brother of Jesus who was called Christ, James by name, and some others. Having brought the charge that they had violated the law, he handed them over to be stoned. Now those in the city who were regarded as the most reasonable and as precise with respect to the laws were burdened with grief over this. So they secretly send [messengers] to the king [Agrippa II], pleading with him to order Ananus to stop doing such things. For he had not acted properly from the outset. Some of them also go to meet Albinus as he makes his way from Alexandria, and inform him that it was not up to Ananus to convene the council without his consent (*Ant.* 20.200–202, author's translation).

Convinced by this delegation, Albinus angrily writes to Ananus, threatening punishment for this affront to his power. The diplomatic King Agrippa steps in, however, and deposes Ananus from the high priesthood after only three months in office (20.203).

What was Ananus' fault? The way that Josephus tells the story, his main defect was his savagery. It was this that offended the leading citizens. Their subsequent concern about correct procedure in convening the Sanhedrin appears as an afterthought, a technicality that would be sure to raise the ire of the new governor and so remove Ananus from office. But it was the removal of Ananus that they were after, because they were "reasonable" (or possibly "gentle," "considerate," "mild") and precise in observing the laws, whereas he was not.

Interestingly enough, these reasonable citizens look for all the world like Pharisees. Elsewhere, Josephus consistently describes the Pharisees as the school considered most precise in interpreting the laws (*War* 1.110; 2.162; *Ant.* 17.41; *Life* 191). In the passage above, he refers the reader back to an earlier discussion of Sadducean harshness. But the only passage in which he has raised this issue before is *Antiquities* 13.294, which describes John Hyrcanus' break with the Pharisees. There, the emphasis is not on Sadducean cruelty, but rather on Pharisaic "mildness": because the Pharisees were mild in punishment, they were reluctant to execute the man who had merely challenged Hyrcanus' high priesthood. The word used there of the Pharisees' "mildness" is the same as that used here for the "reasonableness" of the citizens. So the dispute that we see here over severity of punishment, involving a Sadducee on the rigorist side, is one that we saw elsewhere as an issue between Sadducees and Pharisees. Granted also that, in Josephus' view, the Pharisees are powerful enough to make Sadducean officeholders follow their principles (*Ant.* 18.17), it seems that we have here a case in point. This Sadducean leader is unwilling to submit to the Pharisees' way, so they use their considerable influence to remove him from office.

But the striking fact is that Josephus does not label these eminent citizens, with whom he obviously sympathizes, as Pharisees. The reader who had not made a study of the matter could not be expected to infer that they were Pharisees. We can only speculate as to why Josephus does not name them. Perhaps there were also non-Pharisees involved. But the parallels with what he says about the Pharisees elsewhere are compelling. Whatever his motive may have been, the net effect of this omission is to strengthen his negative portrayal of the Pharisees, for whenever he says good things about the group, he does not explain that he is speaking of Pharisees. We have seen this in the case of Samaias, who is not identified as a Pharisee when his virtues are being praised. Josephus seems intent on associating the Pharisees with improper actions only.

His main purpose here, however, is to expose the heartless character of a particular Sadducean leader. He implies that the actions of James and the others were not worthy of death in the view of those who knew the law best. He does not explain which laws were alleged to have been broken, only that these people were accused generally of being "lawbreakers." Nor does he clarify whether the "others" condemned with James were also Christians; the word used for "others" (*heteroi*) *might* suggest that they were others "of a different kind." That would fit with Josephus' point, which is not so much to support James as it is to condemn Ananus.

This passage is quite significant for the NT reader. First, it offers independent confirmation that Jesus' brother James was a leading figure through the church's first generation of existence (ca. AD 30–65). In the NT itself, James is an intriguing, somewhat shadowy character. He was not one of Jesus' original disciples, but is mentioned quite incidentally in the Gospels as one of Jesus' brothers (Mark 6:3; 15:40). According to Mark, Jesus' sanity is doubted by his family, at least early in his ministry (3:21).[15]

Strangely, however, James then appears without explanation as a prominent leader in the early church. Paul simply assumes that he is one of those "reputed to be a pillar" in the Jerusalem church (Gal 1:19; 2:9), even though James is not one of "the twelve" (cf. 1 Cor 15:7). Most surprisingly, Acts, which lays down stringent qualification for apostles (Acts 1:21–22)— qualifications that would exclude James—nevertheless quietly assumes that James is a leader, perhaps even *the* leader. When Peter escapes from prison, he sends word first "to James and the brothers" (Acts 12:17). James is the keynote speaker, apparently the president, of the apostolic council on the Gentile question (Acts 15:13–22), and it is James whom Paul first greets as head of the "elders" when he makes his final trip to Jerusalem (Acts 21:18).

The failure of the NT writers to explain how James came to prominence in the church is more than compensated for by the authors of later apocryphal writings. They tell, fittingly, of his miraculous conversion in response to a special appearance of the risen Jesus. But it is noteworthy that the NT writers themselves do not make a lot of Jesus' own brother. If we did not read between the lines, we would miss the fact that he held such a prominent position. Josephus' notice is valuable because it confirms our reading between the lines.

Second, Josephus' phrasing is significant. He introduces James first as the "brother of Jesus who was called Christ," and only secondarily supplies the name James. Within Josephus' narrative, this phrasing is best explained by his wish to recall his earlier reference to Jesus (*Ant.* 18.63–64), thus: "this man was the brother of the one I mentioned before." It might also be that Josephus means to indicate something of the accusations brought against James: just as his brother was condemned by some Jewish leaders, so also James ran afoul of Ananus. But if Josephus did not think James' actions worthy of death, that might support the view that the original form of the *testimonium* was similarly mild. Further, Josephus' phrasing seems to reflect James' usual nickname. Paul calls him "the Lord's brother" (Gal 1:19), from a Christian perspective, and this title distinguished him from the many others with the same name. But it also served to explain James' status as a "pillar": he was, after all, Jesus' brother.[16]

Third, the charge brought against James, however vague, is fascinating. He is accused of having violated the law. This is peculiar because in the NT James consistently appears as the most insistent *advocate* of Jewish law-observance, over against those like Paul, who understood the law to be supplanted by Christ (Gal 3:19–29). When Peter lapses into eating with Gentiles, the arrival of certain "men from James" frightens him back into strict observance of the dietary laws. In the same passage, the men from James are also called "the circumcision" (Gal 2:12). So James appears to represent fidelity to the law. Likewise in Acts, James is anxious to dispel the rumors about Paul, that he teaches departure from the laws. Consequently, James devises a plan that will publicly declare Paul's commitment to Judaism (Acts 21:20–24). It is no coincidence, in view of these passages, that later Jewish Christians tended to adopt James as their spokesman, against Paul and the mainstream church.

Notice that in Gal 6:12, Paul asserts that those who demand circumcision do so "only in order that they will not be persecuted for the cross of Christ." As always, we would like to hear the "judaizers' " own account of their motives. But this statement of Paul's fits with the story in Acts 21 about James' concern to be *seen* to be upholding the law. It also makes sense, I would suggest, of Josephus' claim that James was executed on the charge of violating the law. Since James was personally concerned to *keep* the church law-observant, he must have suffered for the actions of others. If some Christians not only abandoned law-observance themselves but also taught against it, as Paul was rumored to have done, the leaders of the movement in Jerusalem would naturally be held accountable.

Even if the Christians had remained fully law-observant, the fact that they exalted as Lord someone who had recently been crucified by the Romans would have made them troublesome to those Jewish leaders who were trying to maintain good relations with Rome (cf. Acts 4:18). Radical departure from the laws would only exacerbate the problem and extend to even wider Jewish circles.

A fourth significant point is Josephus' implication that the Sadducees, such as Ananus, were the ones most deeply offended by the early Christians. Although the Gospels generally portray the Pharisees as Jesus' opponents, the book of Acts claims that it was the Sadducees who arrested the apostles (Acts 4:1; 5:17) and wanted to kill them (5:33). By contrast, the Pharisee Gamaliel takes what might be called a "mild" approach: he advises the council to let the Christians alone and to see what comes of their movement (5:34–39). This story in Acts fits perfectly with the episode recounted by Josephus: the Sadducees consider the Christians worthy of death; the Pharisees, even if they do not especially like the Christians, take a milder view.

Finally, Josephus' account of James' death raises the whole question of the Sanhedrin's power over capital punishment. This issue has been much debated, and we cannot discuss it in detail. Briefly, the problem is this. John 18:31 claims that the

Jewish council of Jesus' day did not have the power to execute anyone; that is why they took Jesus to Pilate, since only he could carry out their sentence. None of the other Gospels explains why, given that the Jews were responsible for Jesus' death, he was crucified by Pilate's sentence. But John's notice agrees with the general tendency of the Romans to reserve the power of life and death for their governors.[17]

Nevertheless, the Jews had unusual rights of self-government in the early empire, and there is considerable evidence that the Jewish court in Jerusalem did inflict capital punishment in some cases. A prominent sign on the temple walls, permitted by the Romans, threatened Gentile trespassers with summary execution. We have several accounts of other deaths, including that of Stephen (Acts 7). If it could be shown that the Jewish court did have the power to execute offenders, of course, that would confirm the Gospel writers' tendency to downplay Roman involvement in Jesus' death: the Romans would not have needed to be involved unless they too had some charge against Jesus. So Pilate would have been a significant player in Jesus' death and not merely a pawn in the Jewish leaders' hands.[18]

The issue is passionately debated by scholars because of its potential significance for understanding Jesus' death, and one of the passages usually cited is the one that we are discussing. But it is cited by both sides. On the one hand, we have here a sentence and execution plainly conducted by the Jewish court. That seems to prove that the Sanhedrin had the power to execute. On the other hand, Josephus notes that the action was improper, because the court should only have been convened with the Roman governor's approval. So those who deny the Sanhedrin's authority to execute treat this episode as an aberration, not typical of the court's power. They argue that Ananus' impropriety included the use of the death penalty itself, which was reserved for the governor.

We cannot decide the larger question of the Sanhedrin's power here. But as far as this passage goes, our reading makes that a side issue. This episode has to do rather with a difference of opinion between the Sadducean high priest and more moderate leaders about the severity of punishments. The arrogant high priest was quickly removed from office because he practiced undue harshness, such as most law-observant Jews would not condone. So we have an internal Jewish dispute about legal interpretation. To accomplish his removal, the more lenient citizens advise the new governor that it is his right to approve all meetings of the court. But this seems to be a technicality calculated to get action from the governor. It is not clear that the moderates would have objected to a council meeting if it had not led to severe punishments. Their goal is to remove this high priest who flouts the accepted Jewish tradition. Nevertheless, Josephus' note that Ananus took advantage of an "opportune moment" does suggest that he could not have executed his enemies as easily if a governor had been present. Whether that was because the court had no authority to pass death sentences is another question, unanswered by this text.

SUMMARY

In this chapter, we have looked at Josephus' discussions of three people who played prominent roles in the origins of Christianity: John the Baptist, Jesus, and Jesus' brother James. Our analysis of these passages has produced a wide variety of results. In the case of John, Josephus and the NT authors are mutually illuminating. Incidental clues in the Gospels help us to reconstruct John's original preaching, which Josephus has adapted for his own ends; and Josephus' independent perspective allows us to trace the Gospel writers' adoption of John as one of their own. Josephus' account of Jesus provides little direct help because the version that we find in our manuscripts is almost certainly corrupt. Nevertheless, the exercise of analyzing that passage is useful for making us aware of the many stages through which all ancient texts have passed before reaching us. Finally, Josephus' reference to James, brief though it is, throws valuable light from outside the Christian tradition on one of the early church's most significant but little-known figures.

FOR FURTHER READING

On apocalypticism in ancient Jewish circles, see (among many fine studies):

- John J. Collins, *The Apocalyptic Imagination: An Intro-duction to the Jewish Matrix of Christianity* (New York: Crossroad, 1987).

See also the introduction with selected Jewish and Christian texts in:

- Mitchell G. Reddish, ed., *Apocalyptic Literature: A Reader* (Nashville: Abingdon, 1990).

A comprehensive collection of available texts in English trans-lation is:

- James H. Charlesworth, ed., *The Old Testament Pseud-epigrapha*, vol. 1: *Apocalyptic Literature and Testaments* (Garden City: Doubleday, 1983).

The intriguing figure of John the Baptist has stimulated much research. The most important works in English are:

- C. H. Kraeling, *John the Baptist* (New York: Charles Scrib-ner's Sons, 1951).

- Charles H. H. Scobie, *John the Baptist* (London: SCM, 1964).

- Walter Wink, *John the Baptist in the Gospel Tradition* (Cambridge: Cambridge University Press, 1968).

- Robert L. Webb, *John the Baptizer and Prophet: A Socio-Historical Study* (Sheffield: Sheffield Academic Press, 1991).

One might also consult:

- Steve Mason, "Fire, Water, and Spirit: John the Baptist and the Tyranny of Canon," forthcoming in *Studies in Religion/Sciences Religieuses.*

There is a huge bibliography on Josephus' paragraph on Jesus. Of the numerous recent discussions, some of the most acces-sible and/or comprehensive are:

- Shlomo Pines, *An Arabic Version of the Testimonium Flavianum and its Implications* (Jerusalem: Israel Acad-emy of Sciences and Humanities, 1971).

- Emil Schürer, *The Jewish People in the Age of Jesus Christ (175 B.C.—A.D. 135)* (Edinburgh: T. & T. Clark, 1973), vol. 1, 428–41.

- J. Neville Birdsall, "The Continuing Enigma of Josephus' Testimony About Jesus," *BJRL* 67 (1985), 609–22.

- John P. Meier, "The Testimonium: Evidence for Jesus Outside the Bible," *Bible Review* 7/3 (June, 1991), 20–25, 45.

- John P. Meier, "Jesus in Josephus: A Modest Proposal," *CBQ* 52 (1990), 76–103.

Most of the interest in Josephus' reference to James' death has focused on the implications of that episode for our assessment of the Sanhedrin's powers and, consequently, of the trial of Jesus. The section in Schürer mentioned above includes a discussion of Josephus and James, as well as some bibliography.

NOTES

1. Cf. Steve Mason, *Flavius Josephus on the Pharisees* (Leiden: E. J. Brill, 1991), 85–89.

2. Cf. Mason, *Josephus*, 184–86.

3. Cf. 1 Thess 1:1, 3; 1 Cor 1:2–3, 7–8, passim; 1 Pet 1:3; James 1:1; Acts 2:36; 4:26, 33; 7:59. In Isa 40:3 itself, the LXX expression "Lord" stands in obvious synonymous parallelism with "God" (*theos/elohim*).

4. To the original readers of Acts, the Greek word *mathētēs* did not have the aura that we have come to associate with "disciple." So I prefer to translate with the more neutral "student."

5. Matthew already deals with this problem by having John protest that he ought not to be immersing Jesus (Matt 3:14–15). The second-century *Gospel of the Nazaraeans* tells the story of Jesus' family's trip to be baptized: "Behold, the mother of the Lord and his brethren said to him: John the Baptist baptizes unto the remission of sins, let us go and be baptized by him. But he said to them: Wherein have I sinned that I should go and be baptized by him? Unless what I have said is a (sin of ignorance)." In Edgar Hennecke, *New Testament Apocrypha* (ed. Wilhelm Schneemelcher; 2 vols., trans. R. McL. Wilson; Philadelphia: Westminster, 1963), 1.146–47. Cf. also the *Gospel of the Ebionites* as reconstructed by Hennecke (vol. 1, 157–58). Ultimately, the church had to understand Jesus' immersion as a unique event, indicating some special moment in his mission, not as an immersion for repentance.

6. Trans. E. Isaac, in James H. Charlesworth, ed., *The Old Testament Pseudepigrapha. Apocalyptic Literature and Testaments* (2 vols., Garden City: Doubleday, 1983), vol. 1, 71.

7. Cf. *War* 2.390–394.

8. Trans. J. J. Collins, in Charlesworth, *Pseudepigrapha* vol. 1, 388–89.

9. The dates of Pilate's governorship, like virtually all historical questions, have been debated. One can only reach probable hypotheses after carefully considering all of the relevant literary sources, coins, inscriptions, and other factors. I give here the dates commonly accepted by those who know the evidence.

10. *Of Illustrious Men* 13.

11. This passage was brought to light by Shlomo Pines in his book, *An Arabic Version of the Testimonium Flavianum and its Implications* (Jerusalem: Israel Academy of Sciences and Humanities, 1971). His translation of the Arabic passage is on pp. 9–10. He compares it to the standard text of Josephus on p. 16.

12. The relevant portion of the text is given by Pines, *Arabic Version*, 26. Mention should also be made here of the "Slavonic Josephus," an old Russian translation of *War* (not *Ant.*) that contains a good deal of extra material on both John the Baptist and Jesus, not found in the standard text. Although this version has contributed to much of the scholarly debate this century, it is generally viewed as a late Christian embellishment of Josephus' text. One can read the "Slavonic additions" in the appendix to vol. 3 of the Loeb Classical Library edition of Josephus, edited by H. St. J. Thackeray.

13. So Robert Eisler, *The Messiah Jesus and John the Baptist* (trans. A. H. Krappe; London: Methuen & Co., 1931), 62.

14. From John P. Meier, "The Testimonium: Evidence for Jesus Outside the Bible," *Bible Review* 7/3 (June, 1991), 23. This restoration agrees almost exactly (independently, it seems), with that offered by Paul Winter in the revised E. Schürer, *A History of the Jewish People*, vol. 1, 437.

15. The Greek reads "they were saying 'He is beside himself.' " Some translations take this "they" to mean "[other] people" but in context there is no good reason to divorce it from the plural subject of the sentence, "his family." That this is one of the very few sentences in Mark omitted by Matthew and Luke may also indicate that the verse struck them as problematic.

16. Later church theology found it troublesome that Jesus should have had a physical brother, because it held that Mary remained a virgin. So James was understood to be a step-brother of Jesus (by Joseph, but not by Mary). We note only that Josephus' phrasing is even more pointed than Paul's in making James Jesus' brother.

17. Cf. A. N. Sherwin-White, *Roman Society and Roman Law in the New Testament* (Grand Rapids: Baker, 1978 [1963]), 24–47.

18. Cf. Paul Winter, *On the Trial of Jesus*, 2d ed. (Berlin: Walter de Gruyter, 1974), 110–30.

6 Josephus and Luke–Acts

At various points in this study, we have noticed especially close parallels between Josephus' narratives and the two NT volumes known as Luke and Acts. For example: Luke omits Mark's story of John the Baptist's death, which is rather kind to Herod Antipas, in agreement with Josephus' hostile portrayal of the tetrarch; the story of King Agrippa's death in Acts 12:20–23 is quite similar to Josephus' account; Josephus' characterizations of Agrippa II and the governor Felix shed indispensable light on Acts' presentation of these men; and Acts agrees with Josephus that it was the Sadducees, the harshest judges on the Jewish court, who most violently opposed the early Christians.

We cannot conclude our analysis of Josephus and the NT without discussing as a separate issue the many affinities between Josephus and Luke–Acts. They have been the subject of much debate. In 1894, one German scholar published a detailed study arguing that the author of Luke–Acts used Josephus as a main source. In the following year, another argued that Josephus used Luke–Acts.[1] Neither position has much of a following today, because of the significant differences between the two works in their accounts of the same events. A third position, that the two writers shared common oral and written sources, has more adherents because it allows some flexibility: Josephus and "Luke" could have merely heard similar stories and read the same material.

However the question of the Josephan/Lukan parallels is resolved, it is illuminating to review them in their own right. Usually, scholars investigating the question have isolated and compared the common episodes in the two accounts. Some have also looked at shared vocabulary. For our purposes, however, it will be useful to place those particular affinities within a larger context. We shall begin by looking at the general similarities between Josephus and Luke–Acts in literary type, or "generic" parallels; we shall then consider the incidents recounted by both authors; finally, we shall examine specific agreements in aim, themes, and vocabulary. As to whether one author used the other as a source, the generic parallels can say nothing, for many other works of the period shared similar features. Nor can the commonly reported incidents prove dependence, in the absence of extended verbal agreement. The third kind of coincidence, however—of aim, themes, and vocabulary—seems to suggest that Luke–Acts is building its case on the foundation of Josephus' defense of Judaism.

GENERIC PARALLELS

Josephus' work is of the same broad literary type or "genre" as Luke–Acts: they are both histories, written in Greek according to the conventions of their period, which we may loosely call Hellenistic.[2] Although we usually lump the four "Gospels" together in the NT, Luke is really quite different from the others on this point. It is the only one that self-consciously presents itself as a volume of history, along with Acts. In addition to being histories, both Josephus and Luke write from an apologetic stance, using their histories to support a thesis. Both of them also come from the "Jewish" world: whether or not the author of Luke–Acts was a Jew, he and Josephus were both heavily influenced by Jewish scripture (OT) and tradition.

By the time of Josephus and Luke–Acts, the writing of history had become a lively and refined art. Herodotus (ca. 484–420 BC) is often called "the father of history" for his pioneering research into the war between the Greeks and Persians. He was the first to conceive of the study of the past as scientific research (the original meaning of "history"), not as the mere repetition of old stories. He made a conscious distinction between the *accounts* of various interested parties and historical truth, identifying the latter with what he could personally verify. But it was Thucydides (ca. 460–400 BC), author of a

History of the Peloponnesian War, who formulated the prin-ciples and *standards* of evidence for the accurate portrayal of the past. He insisted that the historian seek out living wit-nesses, where possible, and rigorously compare differing accounts to get at the truth. Centuries later, Polybius (ca. 200–115 BC) wrote a so-called *Universal History* (actually a recent history of Roman power) in which he reflected at length on the principles enunciated by Herodotus and Thucydides. These three Greek-speaking historians were acknowledged masters by Josephus' time. Meanwhile, the study of rhetoric had pro-gressed steadily for hundreds of years and had helped to for-malize conventions for writing history. By the first century AD, therefore, anyone who took up the task could draw on a vast reservoir of familiar devices.

As we saw in chapter 3, an indispensable feature of any Hellenistic history book was the preface. The Greek sense of order required that written treatises have a clear beginning, middle, and end. In contrast to the Hebrew scriptures, which tend to jump right into the narration of events, Greek historians were required to begin with an introductory prospectus. This opening statement had to accomplish several things at once. It had to state clearly the aim, scope, and thesis of the work. Even more crucial to the writer's success, it had to convince the reader that the subject was of the utmost significance, and that the writer was singularly qualified to deal with it.

To achieve all of this tactfully and within a short space was a tall order. Inevitably, the more that historians tried to outdo each other, the more they began to sound the same. If we compare a large number of prefaces from the period, we see numerous commonplaces or *topoi.* Typically, a preface included remarks on: (a) the subject and its importance; (b) the inadequacy of previous histories of this period; (c) the author's circumstances and reasons for writing; (d) the au-thor's complete impartiality and concern for the truth; (d) the author's strenuous research efforts and access to eyewit-ness testimony (the original meaning of "aut-opsy"); (e) the author's thesis, including the writer's view of the causes of the events in question; and (f) a brief outline of the work's contents.

Because everyone ended up making much the same kind of appeal, the trick for the successful historian was to use the conventions in an original way. The historian had to make a convincing case that his history really was superior to all of the others. Josephus' preface to *War* is an admirable example. Although all of the conventions are there in spades, the reader hardly recognizes them as conventions because Josephus weaves them into an original, compelling statement. The Jewish war was the most important ever, he says, because the eastern part of the empire was in danger (1.1, 4–6). Previous accounts of it are defective because they were written either to flatter the Romans or denigrate the Jews, and many of the authors were not even eyewitnesses (1.2). Josephus is in a unique position to tell the truth, however, because he is intimately acquainted with both the Jewish and the Roman sides of the campaign: he is an extremely rare kind of eyewitness (1.3). So he is determined to give the world, at last, a perfectly accurate account of the revolt (1.6–8). His thesis is that revolt was caused by an aberrant, untypical handful of power-seeking rebels (1.10). So Josephus makes the conventions come alive in a plausible way: he tells readers what to expect and also entices them to read on.

Although the preface to Luke is much briefer than *War*'s, in keeping with the book's brevity, the author manages to work in all of the crucial points:

> Since many have taken it upon themselves to reconstruct an account of the deeds that have been accomplished among us, just as they were passed down to us by those who from the beginning were eyewitnesses and servants of the word, it seemed right that I, who have followed everything from the beginning with precision, should write an orderly account for you, noblest Theophilus, so that you might know the secure basis of the things about which you have been instructed (Luke 1:1–4).

"Luke" was not competing for readers in the marketplace with Josephus. Christianity was still relatively unknown in elite Roman circles at the end of the first century, and Luke seems to have had a much smaller, already well-disposed audience in mind. Nevertheless, the key ingredients of the historical preface are all here. The importance of the subject is indicated by the phrase, not fully captured in English, "the deeds that have been accomplished among us." The word "accomplished" really means "carried out in full" which conveys a sense of awe with respect to the remarkable actions that have occurred. The writer implies, however, that previous accounts of these actions have been less than satisfactory. That is why a new account is needed. Previous writers, the "many" (usually a term of disdain among the literate), did not succeed in writing orderly accounts. This writer, however, is in a position to offer an orderly account because of his precise research. Notice that he does not claim to be an eyewitness himself (unlike Josephus) but only that he will rely on eyewitness evidence. If the many could try their hand at such a critical undertaking, he can hardly fail to supply the superior information that he has discovered.

This author's thesis is that Christian teaching has a solid basis. He uses the word *asphaleia,* which is related to our word "asphalt." It is one of several words like "truth" and "precision" that ancient historians typically used to make their cases. Luke also mentions that he has followed events "precisely." But *asphaleia* also serves here as the writer's major theme: his two books will be geared to demonstrating the "sure foundation" on which Christianity rests, just as Josephus set out to give the unvarnished, precise truth about the course of the Jewish revolt.

Interestingly, both Josephus and Luke wrote sequels to their original compositions, with prefaces to match. In Josephus' *Antiquities,* he first reflects on his motives for writing *War* (*Ant.* 1.1–4) and then slides into the preface for *Antiquities* itself. Once again he explains why his work is necessary and how it improves on other treatments of Jewish history (1.5–13). Then he spells out the "lesson" to be learned: those who observe the Jewish laws prosper, whereas those who do not come to grief. All of this shows, in turn, the nobility of the Jewish laws.

The writer of Acts likewise begins with a glance back at his previous work:

> Formerly I discoursed, O Theophilus, on all that Jesus did and taught from the beginning until the day on which, having given his orders to the apostles, whom he chose through the holy spirit, he was taken up. To them he presented himself alive after his suffering with many sure proofs, through a period of forty days being seen by them and speaking with them about the reign of God (Acts 1:1–3).

Like Josephus, Luke moves imperceptibly from a summary of his earlier work to his present book. Whereas the former history had dealt with Jesus' actions and teachings, this one will recount the actions and teachings of his apostles. These men had already been introduced in the first volume (Luke 6:13–16). Now they are presented as Jesus' chosen representatives who carry on his mission. In particular, they are credible witnesses to his resurrection from the dead (cf. 1:22; 2:32; 3:15). Continuing his demonstration of the sure foundation of Christian teaching, Luke insists in this preface that Jesus' resurrection, the basis of the apostles' preaching, was witnessed during a forty-day period—it wasn't an illusion—and was confirmed with many "sure proofs" (*tekmēria*, a technical term in rhetoric for proof).

Luke's reference to Theophilus in both of his prefaces provides another significant parallel to Josephus, who dedicates his later works—*Antiquities, Life*, and *Against Apion*—to one Epaphroditus. Josephus introduces this figure in the preface to *Antiquities*, where he records his admiration and gratitude, for it was Epaphroditus who encouraged him to complete the laborious work. Josephus describes him as a statesman, one familiar with "large affairs and varying turns of fortune" (1.8). He goes on to say that Epaphroditus is "an enthusiastic supporter of persons with ability to produce some useful or beautiful work" (1.9). Most important, he calls him by the same form of address that Luke uses for Theophilus, "noblest" or "most excellent" (*Life* 430; *Ag. Ap.* 1.1), and just as Luke writes to demonstrate the truth of Christian teaching, Josephus concludes his *Against Apion*:

> To you, Epaphroditus, who excel in devotion to the truth, and on your account to those who likewise desire to know about our race, I beg to dedicate this and the preceding volume (2.296, author's translation).

So both Josephus and Luke write for dignitaries of some kind to explain and defend traditions that are not widely understood.

We have here two clear examples of literary "patronage." Patronage was an essential social feature of many ancient Mediterranean cultures, though our terminology comes from Rome itself. In traditional Roman society, only a tiny fraction of citizens held any real financial and political power. Known as "patricians," they came from the few noble families who could trace their lineage to the remote past. There was no real middle class, only the small fraction of wealthy power-holders and the masses of poor in varying degrees. But Roman ideals required that, just as the all-powerful father (*patēr*) of a family must exercise his power benevolently toward those dependent upon him (wife and children), so also the patricians should behave generously toward those of humble rank. Aristocrats or "patrons" were expected to offer legal help and protection to their inferiors, in return for whatever practical and political support these "clients" could provide. In the time of Josephus and Luke, such systems of patronage were deeply established throughout the Mediterranean. In Roman society, it was no longer only patricians but also other successful individuals who could assume the role of patron.

In literary circles, patrons were necessary for writers who were not independently wealthy. In the absence of government-run arts councils or private publishing houses such as we have today, hopeful writers might approach a wealthy benefactor who was known for being interested in appropriate kinds of literature and ask the patron to sponsor a project. Josephus' first major work, the *War*, hardly needed such sponsorship, for he was fully supported by an imperial pension. It is not clear what has changed in the later works. He claims that the honors given him by Vespasian were maintained and even increased by subsequent emperors (*Life* 428–429). If we can take that claim at face value (it may be an exaggeration to enhance his image), then the sponsorship of Epaphroditus is something additional, perhaps driven by the latter's personal fascination with such exotic matters as Jewish history. This man was not part of the old Roman aristocracy, however. His name appears commonly among "freedmen"—former slaves who often had the opportunity to rise dramatically with the help of former masters (cf. the Epaphroditus who visited Paul, Phil 2:25–30).

We seem to be in much the same situation with the Theophilus of Luke–Acts. Although Luke addresses him as if he were the book's sole recipient, we should probably assume that Luke is also writing for all who, like Theophilus, are interested in the truth about Christianity. The title "noblest" more literally means "strongest, mightiest, most powerful." It identifies both Theophilus and Epaphroditus as citizens of rank, perhaps as knights; note the use of the same title in Acts 23:26; 24:3; and 26:25 of the governors Felix (a freedman) and Festus. Just as Josephus was encouraged by a wealthy patron interested in Jewish history, so the author of Luke–Acts seems to have found a patron intrigued with Christianity. The latter was a greater feat, since Judaism had been known for centuries, whereas many aristocrats knew little or nothing of Christianity well into the second century.[3] Nevertheless, it is plausible that by the end of the first century some wealthy citizens, perhaps in the Eastern Mediterranean rather than Rome itself, had a quiet interest in the new teaching.[4] In any case, the amount of real support necessary for such a modest work as Luke–Acts would have been minimal, and the author may even be playing up the patronage angle for tactical reasons— to make his history seem part of the established social order.

A third standard feature of Hellenistic history shared by Josephus and Luke–Acts is the formulation of speeches for the leading characters. It was Thucydides who created a major role for the speech in history writing. In a famous passage in the introduction to his history, Thucydides observes that particular speeches could not be reconstructed as accurately as events. So he would try to give the general drift of what was said, being sure to make it fit the occasion and the speaker (*History* 1.22). But commentators have long since noted that, although Thucydides does give his characters speeches appropriate to the occasion—the arrogant speak arrogantly, statesmen speak like statesmen—the speeches are his own creations. Some may be based on recollection of what was actually said, but they are all ultimately Thucydides' own statements, a means of making his own points and advancing his narrative. A concordance shows that Thucydides does not allow the various characters true independence of vocabulary and style; they all convey his themes. Under the influence of rhetorical training, such speeches became even more essential vehicles for writers of Hellenistic history to put their own themes in the mouths of their characters.[5]

Josephus' *War* provides excellent examples of how such speeches could function. For example, Josephus gives a very long speech to Agrippa II, in which the king tries to dissuade the Jerusalemites from rebelling against Rome (2.345–404).

On the one hand, the general thrust of the speech accords well with what was clearly the king's political position. On the other hand, it is just as clearly Josephus' composition: it makes his own fully developed case for remaining at peace. In particular, it enunciates Josephus' themes that God is on the Roman's side at present (2.390), and that the temple must be spared at all cost (2.400). The vocabulary and style are typical of Josephus, and the content of the speech is closely paralleled by Josephus' later appeal to the rebels (5.375–419). In effect, then, he uses the speech as a convenient means of making a systematic argument, which would otherwise be out of place in a historical narrative.

A fascinating specimen of a crafted speech is the one attributed to the rebels at Masada before they take their own lives in the face of sure death from the advancing Roman army. Josephus had spoken vehemently against suicide when he was called upon to take his life rather than surrender (*War* 3.362–382). He argued there that suicide violated nature, that no other species voluntarily killed itself, and that only God could take life: soul and body were "fond companions" (3.362). In the mouth of the rebel leader Eleazar, however, he puts an equally philosophical discourse on life, according to which the soul is not at home in the body but always seeks release from it (7.323–387). He provides examples from sleep (in which the soul allegedly ranges freely from the body) and Indian self-sacrifice. This analysis of body and soul fits well with Josephus' language and outlook elsewhere, where he describes the afterlife (cf. *War* 2.154–158). Plainly, Josephus has composed both speeches, but he has cleverly adapted his arguments to suit the occasion. He does not impose a single theory of suicide, but allows Eleazar to speak in a manner appropriate to his role in the narrative.

Notice, however, that Josephus uses Eleazar's speech to convey his own main thesis about the war. The rebel leader ends up confessing that their miserable end is a sign of God's wrath "at the many wrongs which we madly dared to inflict upon our countrymen" (7.332). The rebel leader, in other words, serves as a mouthpiece for Josephus' interpretation of the revolt as the product of a few reckless tyrants. Eleazar's confession goes on: "For long since, so it seems, God passed this decree against the whole Jewish race in common, that we must

quit this life *if we would not use it aright*" (7.359, LCL). Thus
Josephus is not really commending suicide, even though he
wrote Eleazar's brilliant speech on the subject. Rather, he sees
the rebels' suicide as the fitting end for those who so flagrantly
violated Jewish tradition. The rebels die, not as heroes for the
Jewish cause, but as pathetic individuals who confess their
own folly before taking their lives. Yet Josephus had to come
up with a speech in defense of suicide that would suit Eleazar's
role, and so he did.

To summarize: the challenge of the Hellenistic historian
was to create speeches that, on the one hand, were appropriate to the speaker and occasion and, on the other hand, served
to advance the author's own narrative aims. Ancient readers
knew this, and were not expected to believe that such speeches
were merely reproductions of what was really said on a given
occasion.

The author of Acts follows the conventions of his day also
in the formulation of speeches. He includes at least thirteen
significant speeches in his relatively brief narrative:

1. Peter on the selection of an apostle to replace Judas
   (1:16–22)
2. Peter on the day of Pentecost (2:14–36)
3. Peter before the Jewish council (3:12–26)
4. The Pharisee Gamaliel in defense of Christianity
   (5:34–39)
5. Stephen facing martyrdom (7:1–53)
6. Peter to Cornelius (10:34–43)
7. Paul in Antioch of Pisidia (13:16–41)
8. James at the apostolic conference (15:13–21)
9. Paul at the Areopagus in Athens (17:22–31)
10. Paul to the Ephesian elders (20:17–35)
11. Paul to the Jews in Jerusalem (22:3–21)
12. Paul before Felix (24:10–21)
13. Paul before Agrippa II (26:2–23).

These speeches, along with many shorter ones, play a crucial
role in the development of the plot of Acts.

In keeping with the expectations placed on Hellenistic
authors, the writer of Acts has each of his characters speak in
an appropriate way. We have already seen that Paul's remarks
to Felix and Agrippa II are carefully chosen to make fun of

those rulers' personal lives. Similarly, when Paul is in Athens he quotes from Greek poets rather than from Jewish scriptures (17:28), which would have meant nothing to his audience. Again, Gamaliel's defense of Christianity is on the kind of pragmatic grounds that a Jewish councilor might have advocated; he does not personally confess belief in Jesus or even real enthusiasm for the Christian movement. As many studies of Acts have shown, the author satisfies one of the key criteria for Hellenistic history, for his writing is plausible; it has a realistic quality about it or "verisimilitude."

It is equally clear, however, that the speeches of Acts are the author's own and serve to advance his narrative aims.[6] To begin with, those addressed to Jewish outsiders share a remarkably similar structure, which includes: (a) direct address to the audience ("men of Israel," "men and brothers," etc.); (b) appeal for attention ("lend your ears," "let this be known to you," "hear me"); (c) a keynote quotation from scripture; (d) summary of the Christian preaching about Jesus; (e) scriptural proof; (f) final proclamation of salvation. But not only are the overall structures of the speeches similar; the specific content of each structural element is also consistent, no matter who the speaker is. For example, virtually everyone begins his address with the Greek word for "Men!" which is then qualified with "brothers," "Israelites," "Judeans," or whatever is appropriate (2:14; 3:12; 7:2; 13:16). Even the angels (1:11) and Gamaliel (5:35) speak this way.

Out of all the possible scriptures that one could cite as proof texts, according to Acts, Peter and Paul choose the same ones and use them in the same way.[7] Their summaries of Christian preaching are likewise similar, even though we know from Paul's letters that he, for one, had quite distinctive language for discussing Christ's work.[8] In his letters, because he writes as the apostle to the Gentiles, Paul spends no time at all proving that Jesus is the Messiah or recounting Israel's history in any connected way. Indeed, the absence of Jewish content in his gospel is what provoked a response from his Jewish-Christian opponents. Yet Acts depicts Paul, like Peter (2:14–31) and especially Stephen (7:2–50), as rooting his gospel in Israel's history (13:17–37). Like Peter in Acts (2:38; 5:31; 10:43), Paul even preaches "forgiveness of sins" (13:38; 26:18). But this phrase is part of the characteristic vocabulary of Luke–

Acts (cf. Luke 1:77; 24:47); it does not appear at all in Paul's undisputed letters, for he typically speaks of sin, in the singular, as a power.[9]

The result is that, in Acts, Paul sounds much like Stephen and Peter. As with Thucydides or Josephus, one does not find here the striking differences of style or personal spoken mannerisms that one would expect in an anthology of speeches from different individuals. Although the author has provided each character with a speech appropriate to the occasion and has even introduced *some* Pauline language into one of Paul's speeches (13:38–39), on the whole the speeches advance the author's own portrayal of Christian origins and belief. They are not meant to be mere reproductions of what was actually said.

The apparatus of the preface, the references to patrons, and the carefully crafted speeches are only a few of the most obvious features of Hellenistic history writing that are shared by Josephus and Luke–Acts. Historians of the period were also obligated to make their narratives exciting and "delightful." The story of Paul's shipwreck (Acts 27) is similar to an episode Josephus tells about himself (*Life* 14–16). Paul's encounter with the snake (Acts 27), in which he survives what should have been a fatal bite, was a common motif in the literature of the period. The immediate divine punishment of Ananias and Sapphira (Acts 5) and of Agrippa I (Acts 12) heightens the reader's sense of awe; Josephus tells of many similar episodes. "Poetic justice," immediate and fitting retribution for sin, was a standard feature of ancient Greek narrative. Further, like all Hellenistic historians, Josephus and Luke detail the human emotions of their characters—jealousy, envy, "fear and trembling," joy, and remorse. We have already noted that Luke's account of Jesus' genealogy and precocious youth (at age twelve) were common features of Greco-Roman biography also paralleled in Josephus. These and many other commonplaces situate Josephus and Luke–Acts squarely within the world of Hellenistic historiography.

Yet it is even more noteworthy that these two authors share a certain distance from that world—they are in it but not of it. Numerous other Hellenistic histories have survived, but most of them are products of the dominant Greco-Roman culture. They deal with the major political theme of the day:

the rise of Roman power and various conflicts along the way. But neither Josephus (in his later works) nor Luke writes political history in the same way. They write what might be called apologetic history, intended to publicize and legitimize their own subcultures within the larger world. Therefore, although they use the common conventions, they use them as "aliens" who are trying to help their own causes. Ironically, it was mainly Egyptian historians (who disparaged the Jews) who had developed this model of commending their traditions to the larger world.

Judea Capta coin, courtesy of the British Museum.

Both the Jewish and Christian communities faced massive image problems at the end of the first century. The reputation of the Jews, as we have seen, suffered serious injury from the recent revolt in Judea. It is clear from the Romans' production of commemorative coins after the war and from the prominent place given to the arch of Titus that they treated the conflict as a major event. Their victory was a symbolic triumph over a troublesome people. And post-war contempt for the Jews encouraged the revival of slanders about Jewish origins and customs.

To outsiders, the Christians were at first indistinguishable from Jews. But by the end of the century, many Christian communities were entirely non-Jewish, thanks largely to the missionary efforts of Paul. Almost nothing was known about them, and what was known was not good. They met at night, in secret, men and women together; they greeted each other with kisses, and shared a common meal of someone's "body and blood." By the middle of the second century, Christians were still widely associated with cannibalism and sexual promiscuity.[10] They were known to worship as "son of God" not a great hero but a man who had recently been crucified by a Roman governor—a punishment for murderers and other troublemakers—in the backwater province of Judea. Moreover, they had no history, no geographical center, no temple or sacrifice, no ancient constitution, and no ethnic base. So they were quite different from the many traditional religions that thrived in the Greco-Roman world. They resembled a "voluntary association," of which there were many; but whereas other associations were licensed by the central government (because of its fear of political agitation), Christians were newcomers whose real motives were unknown. Roman intellectuals tended to dismiss even the established foreign religions (including Judaism) as "superstitions," but Christianity was doubly disdained because it was a *new* superstition; it had all of Judaism's peculiar ways and "antisocial" behavior, but lacked even "the defense of antiquity."[11]

In the face of these image problems, both Josephus and "Luke" set out to demonstrate the truth about their group's origins and ideals. Each one found a patron who was already well disposed to hear his claims, but they both wrote for wider audiences as well. Josephus plainly says so (see above), and we may deduce the same from Luke–Acts. Both authors probably also wrote in part for internal consumption, to reassure their own members and to offer them a rationale for staying loyal to their tradition/faith in the face of a hostile world.

To legitimize their respective religions in the Roman world against current misinformation, Josephus and Luke must demonstrate both the *antiquity* and the *virtue* of those religions. "Virtue" in this context includes a high communal ethic, but also proven political respectability and cooperation with the Roman peace. We have seen how Josephus accomplishes these goals. He claims that only a small group of untypical Jews was responsible for the conflict in Judea (*War*); that Jewish tradition goes back to the remotest antiquity and is not a corruption of Egyptian religion (*Ant.*); and that Moses' constitution, which Jews scrupulously follow, reflects the highest standard of moral philosophy and human aspiration; it is the envy of the world (*Ant./Ag. Ap.*).

Luke seems to have an appreciably harder task, since Christian faith has not been around for more than a few decades at his time of writing. His strategy, which will be taken over by most of the young church's later spokespersons, is bold. He must plant Jesus' life and Christian origins deeply within the soil of Judaism. In his portrayal, Christianity is not in fact new but is the true descendant of the Jewish heritage.

First, unlike the other Gospel writers, he begins his story in Jerusalem, which was famous around the world as the national home of the Jews. The renowned Jewish temple is where the Christian story takes shape (Luke 1:8). Now Luke's sources tell him that Jesus spent most of his career away from Jerusalem, in the villages of Galilee, and came down to the great city only in the final days of his life (cf. Mark 11:1; Matt 21:1). But Luke gets around this problem by regularly introducing Jerusalem into the narrative before its time. He has Jesus' family visit the temple regularly (Luke 2:41–51), and he has Jesus "set his face toward Jerusalem" early in the narrative (9:51), long before Jesus actually goes there. Indeed Jesus remains in Galilee for most of the story, as in the other Gospels (cf. 19:28), but this author keeps reminding the reader that Jesus is on his way to Jerusalem all the while (9:51; 13:33; 17:11; 19:11).

After Jesus' resurrection, similarly, Luke departs from Mark and Matthew by insisting that the disciples stayed in Jerusalem for Jesus' appearances (Luke 24:13, 18, 33). They are explicitly told to remain in Jerusalem until the Spirit is given, for the gospel will go out from Jerusalem to the ends of the world (Luke 24:47, 52; Acts 1:8, 12). In Acts, Jerusalem is indeed the church's headquarters. The apostles who reside there, having been chosen by Jesus himself, oversee the church's affairs (Acts 8:1, 14; 9:26; 11:22; 15:2; 16:4; 21:17–18). Although Christianity might seem to observers in Rome or Asia Minor as a shadowy and secretive movement, Luke forthrightly claims that it has both a geographical center and an authorized leadership.

More than that, Jesus and the first Christians are solidly rooted in Jewish tradition. Luke's birth narrative is filled with quotations from and allusions to Jewish scripture. John the Baptist's parents obey all of the laws scrupulously (Luke 1:6), as do Jesus' parents (2:39–42). Jesus himself goes to the synagogue "as was his custom" (Luke 4:16). Only Luke has him eat dinner with a leader of the people who was a member of the

Pharisees, claimed by Josephus to be the dominant religious group in Jewish life (Luke 14:1). After his resurrection, Jesus opens the Jewish scriptures to demonstrate that Moses and the prophets all spoke of him (24:27, 44). The theme that Jesus fulfills Israel's ancient hope is equally strong in Acts (e.g., Acts 2:16, 25; 4:11, 25; 8:35).

Notice that even after Jesus has risen, the apostles continue to attend Jewish temple sacrifices (Acts 3:1).[12] A prominent Pharisaic "teacher of the law" defends the church (5:34–39), and Paul, who resoundingly removes himself from Torah observance in his letters (Phil 3:3–11; Gal 3:23–29; 4:21–31), appears in Acts regularly attending synagogue, "as was his custom" (17:2), and taking a Jewish vow (21:20–26). Clearly, Luke wants to impress his readers with the Jewish roots of Christianity. The mission to the Gentiles is for him an *extension* of this Jewish core, maintained by "thousands of Jews" (21:20), and so even Gentiles must observe a few basic Jewish laws (Acts 15:20, 29; contrast Paul, Gal 2:10).

It is this same theme of Jewish heritage that best explains why Stephen's speech prior to his martyrdom is mainly a review of Israel's history (Acts 7:2–53). Almost the entire speech (7:2–50) is a relatively detailed account of Abraham, the patriarchs, Moses, the exodus from Egypt, the giving of the law, and the conquest of Canaan. Only at the very end (7:51) does Stephen confront his hearers directly. Similarly, Paul's speech in Acts 13 begins with Israel's ancient history (13:16). The point seems clear enough: Jesus' coming is the most recent event in the unfolding of *Jewish* history.

An obvious problem with this claim is that Christianity has had considerable success among those with no Jewish background at all, in the provinces of the Eastern Mediterranean, whereas most Jews have not accepted the Christians' claims about Jesus. Luke must explain, then, how Christianity can be so thoroughly Jewish, when most Christians do not seem to be Jews and most Jews disavow it. His solution picks up a line of argumentation that Paul used in Romans: he notes that the Jewish scriptures themselves speak of the people's stubbornness and obstinacy toward God (cf. Rom 9:33; 11:1–12). So he takes these "in-house" prophetic criticisms and turns them against those Jews who do not believe in Jesus, in order to argue that both Jews and Gentiles who have believed in Jesus are the true heirs of the great Jewish tradition. The unbelievers, who may *claim* to be Jews, have in fact departed from their tradition by failing to see God's hand in the present. Jewish stubbornness is a powerful theme, introduced early in Acts and reiterated consistently throughout (2:23; 3:15; 13:45; 14:2). Its importance is indicated by the closing lines of the book, which cite Isa 6:9–10: "This people's heart has grown dull, and their ears are heavy of hearing, and their eyes they have closed" (28:27).

Like Josephus, Luke must also explain why his religion is not opposed to Roman order, though it seems to be from the outside. Whereas Josephus has to account for the Jewish revolt, Luke has to explain why Christians revere someone who was punished with death by a Roman governor. Luke's strategy is clear. He presents the Roman authorities as consistently friendly to the young church. In the trial of Jesus, Pilate insists three times on Jesus' innocence; he finds no "cause of death" in him (Luke 23:4, 14–15, 22). In the end, he merely capitulates to the clamor of the "chief priests and scribes," who vehemently accuse Jesus. Notice, however, that in the retelling of the story Pilate's role all but drops out. In Acts, the writer flatly claims that the Jews crucified Jesus (2:23; 3:15; 4:10). He goes as far as claiming that the Jewish leaders killed Jesus "by hanging him on a tree" (5:30). Thus the Roman crucifixion has quickly become a Jewish lynching, the effect of which is to remove the Roman authorities from the scene altogether. Similarly, in Paul's case, it is the Jews who relentlessly oppose him, but the Roman officials who spirit him to safety (Acts 17:12–17; 22:22–29; 23:10, 16–35).

An interesting case in point is Paul's trip to Cyprus in Acts 13:6–12. There he is welcomed by the Roman proconsul, a "man of intelligence," who wants to hear the word of God (13:7). But Paul's mission faces interference from a Jewish magician named Elymas. Paul has to confront this man, a "son of the devil, enemy of all righteousness, full of all deceit and villainy," and have him struck blind (13:10). This Jew anticipates the many others who will meddle in the gospel to the Gentiles later in the narrative (Acts 13:45, 50; 14:19; 17:5; 18:6; 19:9; 21:27).

So Luke's method of presenting Christianity as cooperative with Roman life and order is, on the one side, to portray Roman authorities as well-disposed to Jesus and the Christians. On the other side, to explain how the Christians ran into trouble with the authorities, he consistently blames the Jewish leaders (notwithstanding the friendly position of Gamaliel). Although the theme of Jewish obstinacy was present in Christian writings from the beginning (cf. 1 Thess 2:14–16), it must have taken on special significance after the revolt. When charges of Jewish "hatred of humanity" and resistance to legitimate authority were in the air, Luke's presentation would presumably have been expected to resonate with non-Jewish readers' assumptions. Both Josephus and Luke must show how, in spite of appearances, their groups pose no threat to Roman order. Josephus tries to obliterate the equation of "Jew" with "rebel," whereas Luke depends on it for his appeal.

As far as Christian teaching goes, Luke knows full well that the central claim concerning Jesus' bodily resurrection is difficult for many readers to accept. We know this also from second- and third-century writers on Christianity.[13] But Luke faces the problem squarely and insists that the event is certain because of ample eyewitness evidence. That is the basis of the apostles' office: they are witnesses to the resurrection. As for moral teachings and lifestyle, the church appears very much like the Essene community of Josephus—sharing all things in common, expressing great love for one another, and living upright lives. Like the Essenes, they pose no political threat.

In arguing for the established and orderly character of their respective constituencies, both Josephus and Luke idealize the real situation. We have seen that one of Josephus' major themes is the "harmony" of Judaism: Moses delivered a comprehensive constitution; it has been carefully preserved by the priesthood, under the supervision of the high priests, whose succession can be traced all the way back to Aaron; all Jews study the laws with devotion, are ready to die for them if necessary, and refuse to change a word.

> Could God be more worthily honoured than by such a scheme, under which religion is the end and aim of the training of the entire community, the priests are entrusted with the special charge of it, and the whole administration of the state resembles some sacred ceremony (*Ag. Ap.* 2.188, LCL)?

Yet Jewish life was never so serene. From at least 200 BC, we see major divisions shaping up in the community over the question of who truly represents the Jewish tradition. The Maccabean revolt, which began in 167 BC, was apparently as much a civil war over the proper course of the Jewish state as it was a conflict with the Seleucid regime of Antiochus IV. Our impression of a broad spectrum of Jewish belief and behavior was beginning to emerge even from the traditional sources—1 and 2 Maccabees, Josephus himself, Philo, and others—but it has been placed beyond doubt by the publication of the Dead Sea Scrolls and of numerous archaeological finds. All of these attest to a wide variety of Jewish perspectives, which were often in conflict. But this means that Josephus has, in order to enhance his portrayal of Judaism's virtues, exaggerated and idealized.

We see the same phenomenon in Luke–Acts. Careful study of Paul's own letters reveals fundamental divisions among the first generation of Christians. He condemns Peter for perceived misconduct (Gal 2:11) and regularly denounces Christians who disagree with him, no matter what their status, as servants of Satan and workers of evil (2 Cor 11:4, 15). He even pronounces a solemn curse on some of them (Gal 1:8; 5:10). These rifts were deep, as Christians debated with each other what it really meant to be a follower of Jesus. A major division was between those who saw Christian faith as continuous with Judaism and those who did not. But Christians also debated whether Jesus' primary work was already completed, so that one could enjoy new life now, or whether new life lay mainly in the future, so that one should invest little in this present age, waiting rather for Jesus' return (1 Cor 4:8–11).

Little or no trace of these sharp divergences can be found in Acts. To be sure, the dispute over gentile Christianity is the subject of some discussion (Acts 11:2; 15:1) as is Paul's stance toward Judaism (21:21). But in keeping with Luke's portrayal of a central authority in Jerusalem, these disagreements are resolved amicably through the counsel of the universally respected elders. Paul dutifully receives instruction from Jerusalem, even if it means taking a Jewish vow (21:22–26). But the friendly relations pictured in Acts seem to minimize some of the conflicts that we see in Paul's own letters, in which he insists on his utter independence from Jerusalem (Gal 1:12, 17; 2:1) and his disregard for the reputation of the Jerusalem apostles (Gal 2:6). It seems therefore that Luke tends to idealize his portrayal of early Christian relations, just as Josephus does for Judaism. In both cases, the idealization arises from a concern to present the group in question as worthy of respect.

So far, we have seen that Josephus and Luke–Acts share the same broad literary type. To be sure, there are important differences between them. Luke's Greek style is much more consistent than Josephus': the Jewish historian reaches higher, in imitation of fashionable trends, but sometimes falls lower. Josephus has nothing really parallel to the Gospel of Luke, with its many short sayings and episodes from one person's life. Nevertheless, both writers consciously develop their accounts with the conventional tools of Hellenistic historiography. In this respect, they are like numerous other writers of the period.

Yet Josephus and Luke also stand out from all other Hellenistic historians because they are both aliens, pleading with selected insiders for recognition of their causes. For this purpose, the points that they need to make are similar: they must show that their groups are worthy of respect because, contrary to first impressions, they are well established in remotest antiquity, possess enviable moral codes, and pose no threat to Roman order. In the event, both writers will lay claim to the great heritage of Judaism. But to explain popular misconceptions, they must also drive a sharp wedge between true representatives of the tradition and the troublesome renegades who have created bad impressions. For Josephus, the troublemakers are those who rebelled against Rome: they betrayed the heritage of their nation. For Luke, and this is his boldest claim, it is those Jews who do not believe in Christ (the vast majority, whom Josephus was defending!) who have departed from the tradition.

COMMONLY REPORTED EVENTS

The main reason for scholars' speculation about the relation between Josephus and Luke–Acts is the remarkable number of incidents reported by Luke, in both the Gospel and Acts, that have parallels in Josephus. More than any other Gospel writer, Luke includes references to the non-Christian world of affairs. Almost every incident of this kind that he mentions turns up somewhere in Josephus' narratives. Yet Luke and Josephus differ significantly in their reporting of these common events. So, although the correspondences are tantalizing, the differences seem to preclude any direct use of one author's work by the other. Some scholars have proposed, nevertheless, that Luke knew Josephus' work but remembered it imperfectly or, in some cases, deliberately altered it to suit his story. In this chapter, we can discuss only the most significant points of intersection.

The Census Under Quirinius

We turn first to the whole complex of persons and events associated with the census under Quirinius. Recall that this census plays a crucial role in both *War* and *Antiquities*. Josephus relates that with the removal of Herod's incompetent son Archelaus as "ethnarch" of Judea in AD 6, the Romans incorporated the Jewish heartland as a small province. Whereas they had ruled it only indirectly as a client kingdom under Herod's family, they now sent their own governor to manage its affairs. But direct administration inevitably meant direct taxation, and for that purpose the new governor of neighboring Syria conducted a census of property, both in his own territory and in the newly acquired province. It was this census, and the submission to Rome which it symbolized, that led Judas the Galilean to call for the creation of an independent Jewish state (*War* 2.117–118; *Ant.* 18.1–5).

Josephus places great emphasis on this early rebellion as a prototype of the later revolt: "They sowed the seed from which sprang strife between factions and the slaughter of fellow citizens" (*Ant.* 18.8, LCL). Judas and his followers set in motion a disastrous freedom movement that ended with the destruction of the "very temple of God" two generations later (*Ant.* 18.8–9). Indeed, the sons of Judas will be crucified as rebels in the 40s, and Josephus notes that one of the key leaders of the final revolt (Menahem) was also a son of Judas, "that redoubtable doctor who in old days, under Quirinius, had upbraided the Jews for recognizing the Romans as masters" (*War* 2.433, LCL). His emphatic repudiation of this mindset leads Josephus in both *War* and *Antiquities* to include his famous descriptions of the three normal "philosophical schools" among the Jews, by way of contrast. Finally, Eleazar ben Yair, rebel leader at Masada, was from Judas' family (*War* 2.447). So the census is not mentioned in passing by Josephus; it is for him a watershed event in recent Jewish history.

Before returning to Luke, we should note briefly that this analysis seems to be part of Josephus' peculiar way of seeing things. Recent historical scholarship has cast serious doubt on the notion that there was anything like a unified "zealot" faction or "fourth philosophy" as Josephus calls it, in first-century Palestine. There seem to have been all sorts of peasant movements, perhaps also aristocratic ones, that were opposed to Roman rule for a variety of economic and political reasons.[14] It appears, therefore, that Josephus has exercised a strong hand in making his point about the rebels: he has welded them into a single, aberrant "school of thought," which he traces back to the census under Quirinius. But this means that it is Josephus who gives the census its crucial function, because of his own literary aims. A writer with a different viewpoint might not have seen so much significance in the census and its aftermath.

It is noteworthy, therefore, that the census under Quirinius also appears in Luke's Gospel as a watershed event. Luke knows about the kind of political significance attributed by Josephus, as we shall see, but he uses the census mainly as a means of explaining how "Jesus of Nazareth" came to be born in Bethlehem. Luke's account begins as follows:

> Now it happened in those days that a decree was issued by Caesar Augustus that the entire civilized world should be enrolled [for taxation]. This, the first census, occurred while Quirinius was governor of Syria. And everyone was traveling to be enrolled, each to his own city (Luke 2:1–3).

Because Joseph was a descendant of David, Luke continues, he had to leave Nazareth with the pregnant Mary and travel to Bethlehem, the city of David's origin. That is how Joseph and Mary came to be in Bethlehem when Jesus was born. Two weeks later, they would return to Nazareth along with the newborn Jesus (2:22, 39; cf. Lev 12:1–8). So the census is critical to Luke's story because it provides the context for Jesus' birth.

Yet Luke's portrayal offers numerous well-known difficulties. (a) Luke puts Mary's pregnancy under the reign of Herod the Great, who died in 4 BC (Luke 1:5), in agreement with Matthew (Matt 2:1). So he seems to think that Quirinius was governor of Syria while Herod was still alive. But according to Josephus, Quirinius only arrived in Syria in AD 6, after the deposition of Herod's son Archelaus. It is impossible to modify Josephus' dates by more than a year either way without pulling down his whole elaborate chronology of the period. Further, it is not clear how there could have been a census of Judea under Herod's rule, since the territory was not yet subject to direct Roman taxation. According to Josephus, it was the removal of Herod's family that brought about the need for a census and direct Roman rule.

(b) The census described by Josephus was conducted only in Syria and Judea, for taxation purposes. There is no record anywhere of a worldwide census such as Luke reports in this period. Yet such an event, as described by Luke, would have caused massive upheaval, with each person returning to his or her ancestral home. This would mean that all the Jews of the Diaspora—nearly one million in Egypt and tens of thousands in all the major cities of the empire—would have had to return to Judea. In the very mobile Roman empire, virtually everyone would have been in transit somewhere!

(c) According to Roman law, one was taxed on the basis of one's possessions, especially land and produce. Therefore it made no practical sense to have people return to their ancestral homelands, much less their ancestors' villages, where their possessions could not be verified. We have no record anywhere of such a displacement of people. Moreover, Joseph was separated from David by about one thousand years. Was everyone, then, supposed to figure out who his ancestor was a thousand years before and track down the ancestor's town, if it still existed? And how was this possible? Since both ancestors and descendants grow exponentially, it takes only twenty generations (5–600 years) for one to have one million direct ancestors from a given time period. Josephus was a descendant of most of David's contemporaries. Which ancestor and town should one choose? Given that David's son Solomon had one thousand wives and concubines, who was *not* a descendant of David after a thousand years?

Some scholars have tried to solve problem (a) by proposing that there was an earlier census, also by Quirinius, while
Herod was still alive—different from the one mentioned by
Josephus in AD 6. But Josephus and Luke both make it clear
that this census under Quirinius was the "first" census. That
point is indispensable to Josephus' whole portrayal of Judas'
campaign, for if there had been a census ten years earlier, the
rebels' complaints would have been poorly timed. In any case,
Luke himself later refers to "Judas the Galilean," who "arose in
the days of *the census*" (Acts 5:37). It is clear that he thinks of
one famous census under Quirinius, the one in which Judas
initiated a rebel movement. And however one resolves problem (a), the equally serious (b) and (c) remain.

Here, then, is the issue. In the few lines that he devotes to
the census, Luke manages to associate it with both Quirinius,
governor of Syria, and Judas the Galilean. These points agree
with Josephus' presentation in a conspicuous way. Because of
his literary aims, Josephus is the one who makes the point that
the census symbolized Roman occupation and so was opposed by the arch-rebel Judas the Galilean. We suspect that
other writers would not have given the census such prominence or made such connections with the rebel psychology.
These observations suggest that Luke was familiar with Josephus' work. Otherwise, it would be a remarkable coincidence
that he also chooses to feature the census and to mention its
connection with Judas the Galilean. Yet if Luke had known
Josephus, it is difficult to understand why he placed Quirinius'
census at the end of Herod's reign, flatly contradicting Josephus. Perhaps these circumstances are best explained if Luke
knew some highlights of Josephus' story but did not recall or
was not concerned with the details.

Judas the Galilean, Theudas, and the Egyptian Prophet

In support of this conclusion, we may note that Luke
knows about Josephus' three most important rebel figures from
the pre-war period: Judas the Galilean, Theudas, and the Egyptian prophet. We have seen that Josephus makes Judas a kind
of rebel patriarch: some of his sons are crucified by the governor Tiberius Julius Alexander (AD 46–48; *Ant.* 20.102), and an-

other becomes an early leader of the great revolt. Theudas appears in the period AD 44–46. Josephus describes him as an impostor, or perhaps wizard (*goēs*), who deceived "the majority of the masses" (*Ant.* 20.97). Claiming to be a prophet, he persuaded his followers to accompany him to the Jordan river, which he promised to part before their eyes (in imitation of Joshua). But the governor's soldiers killed or dispersed his followers, and Theudas himself was beheaded. Finally, under Felix (AD 52–59), the false prophet from Egypt, also called an impostor or wizard, appeared in Judea. In *War,* Josephus claims that he had a following of about 30,000, with which he proposed to force his way into Jerusalem and overcome the small Roman garrison. In the event, most of his followers were killed or captured, though he escaped (*War* 2.261–263). In *Antiquities,* by contrast, the Egyptian promises only that the walls of Jerusalem will fall miraculously; only four hundred of his followers are killed, and two hundred taken prisoner (*Ant.* 20.171). The smaller numbers implied may account for the expectation of a miracle rather than a seizure of Jerusalem by force.

Notice Josephus' repeated assertion that there were *numerous* impostors, false prophets, and wizards around in the period before the revolt. These unnamed popular leaders typically led the masses out into the desert, promising them miraculous signs of imminent salvation: "Deceivers and impostors, under the pretence of divine revelation fostering revolutionary changes, they persuaded the multitude to act like madmen, and led them out into the desert" (*War* 2.259; cf. 264; *Ant.* 20.160, 188, LCL). In both of his major works, he presents the Egyptian as but one example of the many anonymous troublemakers at the time (*War* 2.261; *Ant.* 20.167–169). Notice also that Josephus distinguishes between these false prophets, whom we might call religious impostors, and the more militant popular leaders who engaged in guerrilla warfare. In particular, a group known as the *sicarii* (si-KAR-i-ee) emerged in the time of Felix. These men would conceal short daggers (*sicae*) under their clothing, mingle in a dense crowd, then dispatch their enemies with impunity (*War* 2.254–257; *Ant.* 20.164–165). Their methods struck terror into the moderate and pro-Roman factions. Josephus abhors both the false prophets and the guerrillas, and only distinguishes them in order to say that, between them, the country was in chaos (*War* 2.264). Interesting for our purposes is that in both of his works, he introduces the (political) *sicarii* immediately before his discussion of the (prophetic-religious) Egyptian. This is apparently his own narrative arrangement.

When we turn to Luke–Acts, we are struck by two facts: (a) the author happens to mention the same three figures who are featured by Josephus, and (b) he associates them in ways reminiscent of Josephus' narratives. Judas and Theudas appear together in the speech of Gamaliel, in which he advises the Jewish council to leave the Christians alone:

> For before these days Theudas arose, professing to be somebody, and he was joined by men numbering about four hundred; he was killed, and all those who followed him were dispersed and came to nothing. After this man, Judas the Galilean arose in the days of the census and inspired rebellion in the people who followed him. That one too was destroyed and all those who followed him were scattered (Acts 5:36–37).

Taken individually, Luke's remarks about these two figures match Josephus' accounts fairly well. Admittedly, Theudas' following of four hundred hardly captures Josephus' claim that he persuaded the majority of the masses; and Josephus does not mention Judas' death as Luke does. But numbers are notoriously fluid in ancient texts (compare Josephus' own differences with himself on the size of the Egyptian's following!), and Luke's statement that Judas was "destroyed" is quite vague.

The most obvious difficulty is Luke's order: he asserts that Judas' revolt and the census, placed by Josephus in AD 6, took place *after* the Theudas incident, which Josephus dates to about AD 45. An easy solution is to suggest that there was another false prophet named Theudas before Judas, but we do not know of such a person from any other source, and the coincidence—that Luke would just happen to mention another rebel with the same name as one of Josephus' featured figures—would be uncanny. It seems more likely that Luke has reversed the order of the two characters. Indeed, if the author wanted to mention Josephus' Theudas, he would face the problem that the speech of Gamaliel (Acts 5) occurs before the conversion of Paul (Acts 9), and therefore in the early 30s, at least a decade before Josephus' Theudas was killed. So if Luke wanted Gamaliel to cite Theudas as an example of a failed popular leader, he would be forced to re-date this figure. But that raises the question: why would Luke have felt compelled to use Theudas, if there were so many other popular leaders around, as Josephus insists? It seems that Luke could not draw on other figures, and this means either that Josephus misrepresented things entirely—that there really were no other suitable characters—or that Luke's knowledge is limited to the individuals mentioned by Josephus.

Perhaps Luke simply did not have a clear idea of when Theudas lived: as with the census, he knew of a significant event that he could use in his narrative but did not know the details. Yet that possibility also suggests that he knew of these events from having read or heard Josephus at some time, for Josephus is the one who isolates Judas and Theudas from among the many popular leaders of the time. Moreover, Josephus links the two characters in his story. Immediately after describing the fate of Theudas under Cuspius Fadus (*Ant.* 20.97–99), he summarizes the governorship of Tiberius Julius Alexander. Alexander's main claim to fame was that he crucified the sons of Judas the Galilean (20.100–102). In describing this action, Josephus reminds the reader about Judas, who incited the people to revolt during the census of Quirinius. The description of Judas here ("incited the people to revolt") is very close to the construction in Acts 5:37, quoted above. As several scholars have suggested, therefore, it may be that Luke's order, Theudas then Judas, was suggested by his memory of this passage from Josephus. Since Josephus links Theudas and Judas in this order for his own narrative purposes, the reproduction of this connection in Acts is either another noteworthy coincidence or the result of Luke's knowledge of Josephus.

Luke's reference to the Egyptian false prophet also recalls Josephus' narrative. In Acts 21, Paul is rescued from a Jewish mob by the Roman tribune, who whisks him to safety in the military garrison. When Paul addresses the tribune in Greek, the latter responds:

> You know Greek? Aren't you, then, the Egyptian, who stirred up trouble some time ago and led the four thousand men of the *sicarii* out into the desert (Acts 21:38)?

Paradoxically, it is the differences between this remark and Josephus' account that suggest Luke's awareness of Josephus. The similarity is clear enough: Paul is arrested while Felix is governor, and that is also the period to which Josephus assigns the Egyptian. But Josephus stresses that the Egyptian was not a member of the *sicarii*; they were guerrillas, whereas he was a religious-prophetic figure (*War* 2.258). Acts has him leading the *sicarii*. Josephus also claims that the Egyptian led his men to the Mount of Olives to prepare for the seizure of Jerusalem, whereas Acts has him leading men out into the desert. And, given the *sicarii* mode of operation, mingling with crowds to dispose of enemies, it is not clear why they would head for the desert. Further, whereas Josephus gives the Egyptian about thirty thousand men in *War*, rather fewer in *Antiquities*, Acts has only four thousand.

Are these discrepancies best explained by Luke's knowledge of Josephus, or by his use of another source or oral tradition? Notice first that, although Josephus does not make the Egyptian's followers *sicarii*, he mentions both groups in the same breath. As we have seen, he discusses the Egyptian immediately after describing the dagger-men (*War* 2.261; *Ant.* 20.167–169). But this is clearly part of his literary artistry. How did Luke, then, come to associate the Egyptian, incorrectly, with the *sicarii*? If he did so independently of Josephus, the coincidence is remarkable. It is even more remarkable because *sicarii* is a Latin term for assassins. Josephus seems to have been the first to borrow this word and make it a technical term for the Jewish rebels in his Greek narrative. How, then, did Luke, who also writes in Greek, happen upon the word? That he derived it from a source is clear because he uses it casually, without betraying any knowledge of its significance. It is easiest to suppose that he had some knowledge of Josephus, and that he linked the Egyptian with the *sicarii* because Josephus' account had done so.

Similarly, although Josephus has the Egyptian leading his men to the Mount of Olives (*War* 2.261–262; *Ant.* 20.169), he introduces this figure with a more general statement about impostors of this kind, that they "persuaded the multitude to act like madmen, and *led them out into the desert* under the belief that God would there give them tokens of deliverance" (*War* 2.260; cf. *Ant.* 20.167). Once again, Luke's claim that the

Egyptian led his followers into the desert, though it does not match Josephus' exactly, seems easily explained on the hypothesis that he imperfectly remembered Josephus and so ran together Josephus' distinct statements. His placing of the Egyptian in the desert is harder to explain if Luke knew the story from another source, perhaps from an independent oral tradition, which would not have included Josephus' general statement about impostors in the desert.

Luke's placing of the *sicarii* in the desert indicates that he knows their name but is not clear about what they do. This confusion is best explained if he is relying on a source that led him to link the *sicarii* with the Egyptian, and the Egyptian with the desert. Luke's use of this group is symptomatic of his general relation to non-Christian affairs. Like Judas and the census, Theudas, and the Egyptian, the *sicarii* lend an air of realism to Luke's narrative—an important quality in Hellenistic history-writing. He does not agree with Josephus in details, but the particular ways in which he disagrees suggest that he knew a narrative much like that of Josephus. His references to political events in Judea are understandable if he had read portions of Josephus or had heard the Jewish historian recite,[15] then later recalled some of this material for his own story. If Luke did not know Josephus, we are faced with an astonishing number of coincidences: he links Judas and the census as a watershed event, connects Judas and Theudas, connects the Egyptian with the *sicarii,* connects the Egyptian with the desert, and selects these three figures out of all the anonymous guerrillas and impostors of the period.

Minor Parallels

Space does not permit a complete inventory of the parallels between Luke–Acts and Josephus. Some of these have been considered in earlier chapters. We have seen, for example, that Luke's portrayals of King Agrippa's death, of the governor Felix and Drusilla, and of Agrippa II and Berenice all dovetail with Josephus' account very well. This means that Luke must have had, in each case, an account *like* Josephus' in his memory. Many scholars have pointed out the clear differences between Luke and Josephus in relation to the episodes considered in this chapter and have concluded that

Luke could not have known Josephus' work. I would propose, however, that even these differences require that Luke knew a source like Josephus. Most of the differences are best understood as conflations of closely related elements of Josephus' narrative structure. It would be far more difficult to explain the differences if Luke did not know something like Josephus' work.

In addition to the parallels considered in this and earlier chapters, several less significant ones may be mentioned: (i) Luke's mention of "Lysanias, tetrarch of Abilene" (Luke 3:1; cf. *War* 2.215, 247; *Ant.* 19.275); (ii) Luke's parable of the man who traveled to another country to receive his kingship, but was hated by his own people, whom he punished with death, which seems like a thinly veiled reference to the family of Herod as described by Josephus (Luke 19:12–27; *War* 1.282–285); (iii) Luke's description of the siege and destruction of Jerusalem, including a reference to the slaughter of children (Luke 19:43–44; cf. *War* 6 in general); and (iv) Luke's reference to a famine during the reign of Claudius, in which Barnabas and Saul brought relief to Jerusalem from Antioch (Acts 11:28–29; cf. *Ant.* 3.320; 20.51–53, 101). Although they do not seem at first to describe the same incident, (v) Luke's reference to Pilate's attack on some Galileans (Luke 13:1) sounds somewhat like Josephus' account of Pilate's dealings with some Samaritans at Mt. Gerizim (*Ant.* 18.85–87). In my view, these parallels are too vague to establish a relationship between the texts.

Nevertheless, the affinities discussed above and in earlier chapters do indicate such a relationship. In any given case—say, the connection of the Egyptian with the *sicarii* or with the desert—one might be content to dismiss the affinity with Josephus as a coincidence. But a series of half a dozen such coincidences of narrative detail, combined with the coincidence that Luke happened to include some key features of Josephus' story (the census, the three rebel figures), makes the hypothesis that Luke had some knowledge of Josephus more likely than not.

AGREEMENTS OF THEME AND VOCABULARY

In assessing the relationship between Josephus and Luke–Acts, scholars have often neglected to compare the two authors' specific aims. Yet this may produce the most telling evidence of all. To be sure, the neglect results from understandable causes: the literary aims of Josephus have until recent years been largely ignored, while those of Luke have been hotly debated. Since I have already revealed my hand on both issues, I can have no qualms about going further, to point out specific thematic and verbal parallels.

We have seen (chapter 3) that a major part of Josephus' bid to the Greco-Roman world involves the presentation of Judaism as a national philosophy. Moses is the founding teacher, and his teachings have been handed down intact by a "succession" of high priests. Like other philosophies, Judaism offers "well being" (*eudaimonia*) to those who carefully observe the teachings of Moses. Like other philosophies it teaches virtue, which means piety toward God and justice toward one's fellows. Prominent figures from Israel's past, such as Abraham and Solomon, in addition to Moses, were philosophers as well as great leaders. And like Greco-Roman society, Jewish culture has traditional schools (*haireseis*, hi-RE-sase; singular *hairesis*, HI-re-sis), which debate philosophical issues like the immortality of the soul or the roles of fate and free will in human actions. Josephus explicitly compares the Pharisees to Stoics and the Essenes to Pythagoreans; he insinuates that the Sadducees are Jewish equivalents of the Epicureans. His bid to make Judaism a philosophy is already implicit in *War*, but is fully developed in *Antiquities* and *Against Apion*.

We also noted in chapter 3 that Judaism appeared as a philosophy to its earliest outside observers. One can speculate about the reasons for this. On the theoretical level, it had no images of God, unlike all other cults, but considered the Deity invisible and indescribable, just as the philosophers did. On the practical level, outside of Judea the Jews had no temples and performed no sacrifices, in contrast to other cults. Rather, they met to study revered books, hear moral exhortation, and pray. Converts to Judaism adopted an entirely new lifestyle in accord with a comprehensive code. To outsiders, this kind of activity might have seemed more typical of a philosophical school than of a religious group. Nevertheless, by the Roman period, most non-Jewish writers saw Judaism primarily as the religion or "superstition" of the Judeans, sometimes as a corruption of originally noble philosophical ideas. Several Jewish writers before Josephus had invoked current philosophical language to describe aspects of Jewish thought, but Josephus offers by far the most comprehensive attempt to interpret the whole of Jewish culture—its origins, history, leading figures, ethics, and religious groups—in philosophical terms.

It is another noteworthy coincidence, then, that Luke seems to present early Christianity as a philosophical school within the Jewish orbit. While he does not make the claim explicit, much of his language has philosophical overtones, and its cumulative effect is strong. His portrayal of Christianity thus intersects precisely with Josephus' portrayal of Judaism as a philosophy. It fits with Luke's goal of rooting Christianity in Jewish history that he should try to make it another "school" (*hairesis*)—one founded by Jesus—in addition to those mentioned by Josephus. Consider some of the evidence.

In the preface to his Gospel, Luke uses two standard terms from the vocabulary of philosophical schools. First, he speaks of a succession of teaching from the teacher. He will record the deeds of Jesus, "even as those who from the beginning were eyewitnesses and servants of the word *handed* them *down* to us" (Luke 1:2). This word is the same one that Josephus used to describe Moses' "handing down" of the laws to the succession of priests, and the Pharisees' tradition, which was "handed down" from the fathers. By Luke's time of writing, the deeds of the revered founder of Christianity have become a tradition that must be carefully guarded from error. This recalls the concern of the Greco-Roman philosophical schools to preserve their various traditions through successions of teachers.

Another interesting term in Luke's preface is *asphaleia*: Luke writes so that Theophilus might come to realize the "secure basis" of what he has been taught. Although this word is characteristic of historical prefaces, as we have seen, philosophers also used the term to describe their efforts. Their goal was to provide a sure basis for ethical action. The philosopher Plutarch (ca. AD 100) distinguishes philosophy from superstition on the ground that only philosophy offers a way of seeing the world that is "secure" (*On Superstition* 171E). Justin Martyr (mid-second century), having set out to find a "philosophy which is secure and profitable" (*Dialogue* 8.1), finally became a Christian. Although he uses a different Greek word, Justin's contemporary Lucian has one of his characters turn to philosophy in order to find a "plain, solid path in life" (*Menippus* 4). These words had numerous other applications, but their appearance in the preface to Luke fits the notion that he wanted to present the religion of Jesus as a philosophy.

Second, Luke–Acts devotes considerable space to a critique of wealth, luxury, and the hypocrisy of the powerful. Yet these themes were staples of Greco-Roman philosophy. Virtually all philosophical schools agreed that the simple life, perhaps even poverty, was most conducive to the purity of the soul. Thus Paul's contemporary Seneca, though wealthy himself, says: "Riches have shut off many a man from the attainment of wisdom; poverty is unburdened and free" (*Moral Epistles* 17.3). He summarizes the heart of his teaching:

> We talk much about despising money, and we give advice on this subject in the lengthiest of speeches, that mankind may believe true riches to exist in the mind and not in one's bank account, and that the man who adapts himself to his slender means and makes himself wealthy on a little sum, is the truly rich man (*Mor. Ep.* 108.11, LCL).

He claims that when the philosophers utter proverbs against greed, such as "The poor lack much; the greedy man lacks all" or "He needs but little who desires but little," the crowds break out in thunderous applause—even the wealthy and the greedy (*Mor. Ep.* 108.9, 11–12)! Another philosopher sounds very modern when he says of happiness: "It is not in possessions. If you doubt that, . . . look at the rich nowadays, the amount of lamentation with which their life is filled" (Epictetus, *Discourses* 3.22.27, LCL).

As for hypocrisy, Seneca devotes one of his moral epistles to the theme of "practicing what you preach." He says:

> Philosophy teaches us to act, not to speak; it exacts of every man that he should live according to his own standards, that his life should not be out of harmony with his words. . . . This, I say, is the highest duty and the highest proof of wisdom,— that deed and word should be in accord (*Mor. Ep.* 20.2, LCL).

Lucian scorns teachers who fail to live by their own principles (*Menippus* 5), and Epictetus mercilessly satirizes philosophers who spout lofty wisdom but do not put it into practice (*Discourses* 2.9.13–22). Ever since Socrates, the image of the philosopher as "gadfly," relentlessly challenging the established order and especially those in power, had been basic to the enterprise of philosophy.

If we now return to Luke–Acts we find that Jesus and his followers represent these standard features of moral philosophy. In Luke's narrative, Jesus is born in an animal's stable (2:7, 16). As his poor parents lack the influence to find more fitting accommodation, they also lack the resources to present a sacrificial lamb at the temple; they can give only a pair of birds (2:24). Jesus' keynote address promises especially good news for the poor (4:18), and Luke's version of the beatitudes bears this out: it is the truly poor, not the "poor in spirit," who receive the reign of God. Only Luke includes *bad news* for the rich and complacent (6:20–26; cf. Matt 5:3–11). In this story, even John the Baptist offers advice to the crowds about how to live simply (3:10–14).

Much of the material found only in Luke underscores Jesus' concern for the poor and disdain for the rich. Only Luke's Jesus tells the story of the foolish man whose prosperity drove him to tear down his barns and build bigger ones, to find security in his wealth (cf. Gos Thom 63). Like other philosophers, Jesus declares that a man's wealth does not consist in the amount of his possessions (12:13–21). Only Luke has Jesus castigate the well-to-do host of a banquet for inviting only friends and rich neighbors, not the poor and destitute (14:1–14). It is in Luke that we find the poignant story of the rich man who dies and then longs for relief from his torment, while poor Lazarus, who had lived in abject suffering and poverty, is consoled in Abraham's bosom (16:19–31). Only Luke tells of the self-critical and repentant tax-collector, who is justified ahead of the complacent religious authority (18:9–14). Luke's Jesus sides with the defenseless widow who makes a nuisance of herself pleading for justice from a callous judge (18:1–8).

In Luke, then, Jesus is pitted against a smug, privileged establishment, whose representatives are "lovers of money" (16:14). Although highly trained in intellectual matters, like the logic-choppers and rhetoricians denounced by Seneca and Epictetus, they are incapable of offering real help to those in need. Jesus appears as a gadfly, to use Socrates' image, castigating these leaders for their misplaced values. Accordingly, as one scholar has recently shown, Luke portrays Jesus' death in a way that recalls the death of Socrates in Plato's *Phaedo*.[16] In keeping with his portrayal of Jesus, Luke goes on to claim that Jesus' followers shared all of their goods in common. They "sold their property and possessions and distributed the proceeds to everyone, according to a person's need" (Acts 2:44–45; 4:32–35). This idyllic portrayal of the Christian community recalls both the legendary followers of Pythagoras and Josephus' Essenes—a Jewish philosophical school.

Third, in his famous Areopagite scene at Athens (Acts 17:16–34), Luke deliberately places Paul in dialogue with Stoics and Epicureans (17:18) as a competitor in the philosophical marketplace. In keeping with his obligation to craft plausible speeches, Luke does not have Paul appeal to scripture to support his claims, for that would mean nothing to his Greek audience. Rather, Paul begins in a philosophical tone by arguing that there is one God behind all of the religious aspirations of different nations. In support of his assertion that God is "not far from each one of us," he cites two noted Greek authors to the effect that "In him we live and move and have our being" and "We are all God's offspring" (Epimenides and Aratus, respectively). But these slogans were precisely what the Stoics believed—that there was one divine spirit animating all of life. Luke's Paul here anticipates Christian apologists like Justin Martyr. Justin will connect Christian teaching with the best of Greco-Roman philosophy on the ground that the one principle of truth (*logos*), though most clearly embodied in Christ, was already given to those of all times and places who "lived reasonably" (*Apology* 1.46). Thus Paul's Areopagite address strengthens Luke's presentation of Christianity as a philosophy.

Fourth, one of the goals of philosophers in the first century was bold, fearless, frank speech (*parrhēsia*, par-rhay-SEE-uh). This frequently got them into trouble, especially if their audience included a humorless emperor. Several famous philosophers in the later first century, especially under Nero and the Flavian dynasty, faced death or exile for their endless moral prattling. One reporter complains that the offenders behaved "as if it were the function of philosophy to insult those in power, to stir up the multitudes, to overthrow the established order of things" (Dio Cassius, *Roman History* 65.12.2). As Epictetus said before he was exiled by Domitian, "Tyranny hates wisdom" (*Discourses* 1.29.10). The mark of a true philosopher therefore was a determination to speak with *parrhēsia* without regard for the consequences. This is exactly what we find among the early Christian preachers, according to Luke.

The word occurs only five times in Acts, but at strategic places. In his opening address, Peter sets the tone by claiming to confront the Jews on the issue of Jesus' resurrection with *parrhēsia* (2:29). In the repeated conflicts of chapter 4 between the apostles and the Sanhedrin, the word appears three times: first, the judges are amazed at the *parrhēsia* of these unschooled men; then the disciples pray for the ability to continue their *bold* manner of confrontation (4:29); and finally, their prayer answered so that they once again speak with *boldness* (4:31). The importance of this theme is clear from the fact that Acts closes with the statement that Paul, though under house arrest in Rome, was "preaching the kingdom of God and teaching about the Lord Jesus with all *parrhēsia*, unhindered (28.31)." Just as Jesus appeared in the Gospel of Luke as a tenacious critic of the wealthy and powerful, so his followers now appear as a fearless but persecuted, truth-loving minority.

It is truly remarkable that Acts takes over Josephus' classification of the Pharisees and Sadducees as "philosophical schools" (*haireseis*; 5:17; 15:5; 26:5), as if this terminology were self-evidently appropriate. The powerful "school of the Sadducees" opposes Jesus' followers (Acts 5:17), and some believers who belong to the "school of the Pharisees" insist on circumcising Gentile converts (Acts 15:5). Luke's Paul even calls the Pharisaic group the "most precise school" among the Jews (Acts 26:5). This is a triple coincidence because: the school language is part of Josephus' presentation; "precision" is also one of Josephus' key terms; and Josephus routinely claims that the Pharisees are reputed to be the most precise of the schools (*War* 1;110; 2.162; *Ant.* 17.41; *Life* 189). We do not know of any author but Josephus who called the Pharisees and Sadducees "philosophical schools" or the Pharisees the most precise school, yet we do know that this presentation fits with Josephus' carefully developed defense of Judaism. If Luke did

not know of Josephus' work, how did this language suggest
itself to him?

Still more interesting is that Acts presents the Christian
faith as yet another Jewish school (*hairesis*). The Jews who
accuse Paul claim that he is a ringleader of the "school of the
Nazarenes" (24:5). In his defense, Paul prefers to call Christianity the "way," but admits that *they* call it a "school" (24:14).
When Paul speaks with the leaders of the Jewish community
in Rome, they too have heard of this "school," and that it is
spoken against by everyone (28:22). By applying the title
"school" to Christianity, Acts implicitly places it within the
world of Judaism, alongside the Pharisees and Sadducees.

It has been objected, against this interpretation, that the
designation of the church as a school is rejected by Luke's Paul
(24:15) and elsewhere appears only on the lips of Jews (24:5;
28:22). But this objection misses the point. Luke's Paul dis-
dains the title of "school" not because he wants to dissociate
Christianity from the established Jewish system, but rather
because he thinks that the Christian "way" is for *all* Jews. He
does not want the Christian truth claims to be seen as matters of dispute like the mundane issues that divide the
other schools. Nevertheless, although Luke would prefer
that all Jews recognized Jesus as Messiah and Lord, he is
quite happy to concede that, until then, they do at least
recognize the church as one school within the Jewish community. By placing this acknowledgement matter-of-factly on the
lips of the Jewish leadership, he cleverly avoids the impression
that it is *he* who is bidding to bring the church under the
socio-political shelter of Judaism. He can have his cake and
eat it too.

In the interest of the church's social survival, then, Luke
will tolerate the status of "Jewish philosophical school" until
a better alternative comes along. This option will not be so
readily available to later Christian apologists, because of the
obvious distance between Judaism and Christianity by the
mid-second century. But Luke is keenly aware of the charges
of "novelty" that plague the church. His only recourse at the
end of the first century is to ground the Way solidly in Jewish
history. He wants to show that the young church, though
viewed by established Judaism (he claims) as merely one of its

several schools, is really a victim of the Jews' legendary intran-
sigence—from the Roman perspective, after 70.

Now we must ask how Luke came to settle on the approach of presenting Christianity as a philosophical school,
founded by Jesus, but solidly within Judaism. It is possible, of
course, that many of the factors that led Josephus to present
Judaism as a philosophy independently led Luke to the same
strategy. Like Judaism, Christianity differed markedly from the
ordinary religions of the Greco-Roman world. It was an inter-
national body that had no ethnic base, no temple, no images
of its God, and no sacrifice. Instruction and moral exhortation
formed a large part of its communal life, in addition to rituals
of a non-sacrificial nature. Conversion to Christianity required
a radical change of lifestyle.

These factors might indeed account for Luke's decision
to portray Christianity as a philosophy, as his second-century
successors—Justin Martyr and Athenagoras—would later do
even more forcefully. But these general social conditions do
not explain the marked similarities of language to Josephus'
narrative, especially the description of Pharisees and Sadducees as philosophical schools and the insinuation of Christianity as their partner within Judaism. It seems more likely
that Luke is building directly on Josephus' portrayal of Judaism as a philosophy by firmly embedding the church within
that context. Thus, the Christians, though scarcely mentioned by Josephus, constitute yet another school within Judaism. Their denigration by the Jews results only from their
fearless "gadfly" activity, confronting the complacent majority
with their truth and superior "way."

This hypothesis also explains why Luke, if he is drawing
details of Jewish life from Josephus, makes no mention of the
Essenes, whom Josephus admires so greatly. The obvious explanation for this omission is that in Luke's portrayal the
Christians take the place of the Essenes. Recall that Josephus
had depicted that group as the most philosophical of all Jews,
sharing everything in common, living peaceful and disciplined
lives, and accordingly having powers of healing and prophecy.
In Acts, it is the school of the Nazarenes, or Christians, that
fulfills this role. They share their goods, live in peace, practice
healing, exorcism, and prophecy, and shame all other Jews
with their love of the truth. To include the Essenes in his

narrative would have caused needless problems for the author of Acts, for that group would have been in direct competition with the Christians!

So it seems that the author of Luke–Acts does for Christianity what Josephus does for Judaism, except that he is able to include the additional theme of the persecuted philosophers. He completes Josephus' picture of an idyllic philosophical nation, with three recognized schools, by making Jesus and the Christians the most sincere philosophers of all: they challenge the complacent establishment, which explains why the Jews dislike them.

SUMMARY AND CONCLUSION

In this chapter we have seen that Luke–Acts is unique among the NT writings in the extent of its affinities with Josephus' narratives. To begin with, both authors employ the same genre or literary type to convey their message: they both consciously adopt the forms of Hellenistic history. They have good reason to do so, since they want to make their groups seem part of the established order. Yet that very goal sets them apart from other Hellenistic histories, for they both write as outsiders, trying to commend their causes to the world. In attempting to legitimate their respective faiths, both writers had one eye on their own membership; Luke may even have had new Christians as his primary intended audience, in spite of the formal address to Theophilus.

These similarities of literary type do not require that "Luke" knew Josephus' work. It is true that they resort to similar techniques. They go to great lengths to demonstrate that their communities are friendly to Rome, have ancient traditions, and espouse the highest moral ideals. Both authors obviously minimize internal conflicts in their desire to portray unified, centrally administered, disciplined bodies. But these generic agreements may result only from the similar pressures that they faced: the Jew and the Christian had to show that their constituencies, which seemed troublesome to the Romans in view of the revolt, Jesus' crucifixion, and withdrawal from normal civic-religious life, were in fact respectable and politically harmless components of the empire.

More suggestive of a relationship between the works is the striking number of incidents reported in common. In several cases—Agrippa I's death, Felix and Drusilla, Agrippa II and Berenice—Luke's narrative seems to depend squarely on such information as Josephus presents. In other cases—the complex of events associated with the census and ensuing rebel movements—Luke regularly disagrees with Josephus. But his disagreements can be readily understood as conflations of Josephus' narrative, resulting from imperfect memory or deliberate schematization. Since the conflated elements lie together only in the narrative that Josephus constructed, as far as we know, Luke's product is much more difficult to explain if he had no knowledge of Josephus.

Most telling, however, is Luke's presentation of Christianity as a "philosophical school" within Judaism, alongside the other schools but based on the teachings of its founder Jesus. To our knowledge, Josephus is the only Jewish writer who undertook a systematic account of Jewish history and tradition as philosophy, of the Pharisees, Sadducees, and Essenes as "schools," and of the Pharisees as reputedly the "most precise school." Although Luke might have been moved to adopt the theme "Christianity as philosophy" independently, by the same conditions that led other Jewish and Christian writers to adopt this apologetic device, his agreement with peculiar features of Josephus' narrative suggest that he was building directly on the more famous work of the Jewish historian. He was saying, in effect: You know what Josephus said about the nobility of history and tradition. Well, we Christians are part of the same culture; we are another school, alongside the Pharisees and Sadducees. We agree in many respects with the Pharisees (cf. Acts 23:6–9), but the obstinate Jewish leadership (witness the recent war) finds us troublesome because of our devotion to truth.

In short, we cannot prove beyond doubt that Luke knew the writings of Josephus. If he did not, however, we have a nearly incredible series of coincidences, which require that Luke knew something that closely approximated Josephus' narrative in several distinct ways. This source (or these sources) spoke of: Agrippa's death after his robes shone; the extramarital affairs of both Felix and Agrippa II; the harshness of the Sadducees toward Christianity; the census under Quirinius as a watershed event in Palestine; Judas the Galilean as an arch-rebel at the time of the census; Judas, Theudas, and the Egyptian as three rebels in the Jerusalem area worthy of special mention among a host of others; Theudas and Judas in the same piece of narrative; the Egyptian, the desert, and the *sicarii* in close proximity; Judaism as a philosophical system; the Pharisees and Sadducees as philosophical schools; and the Pharisees as the most precise of the schools. We know of no other work that even remotely approximated Josephus' presentation on such a wide range of issues. I find it easier to believe that Luke knew something of Josephus' work than that he independently arrived at these points of agreement. Nevertheless, we await a thorough study of the matter.

Of course, if Luke did know Josephus, then we can fix the date of Luke in the mid-90s or later, for Josephus finished *Antiquities*, the major work in question, in 93/94. Luke may have heard an earlier version or only a part of the work recited, perhaps in 90 or so. But a date of 95 or later for Luke would seem most plausible if he knew *Antiquities* 18–20. Although such a late date may seem troubling at first, I see no cause for concern. Even without the hypothesis that Luke knew Josephus, most scholars date Luke–Acts to the 80s or 90s (or later), on entirely different grounds. Recall that the author does not identify himself at all; the name "Luke" became established only in the mid-second century as far as we know. He implies that he is not an eyewitness of Jesus' life (Luke 1:2). He takes Paul's career up to the mid-60s (Acts 28), and seems to know about the destruction of the temple in AD 70 (Luke 19:41–44). Most important, he reflects a period when the era of the apostles was seen as a bygone "golden age" of serenity; the sharp intramural conflicts of Paul's letters appear only as mild disputes, resolved with good will. Furthermore, the author assumes that a high degree of church structure is normal. So the acceptance of Luke's knowledge of Josephus would not have radical implications for dating Luke–Acts.

FOR FURTHER READING

One can gain a vivid sense of the conventions of Hellenistic historiography by looking at a manual produced on the subject by a second-century author:

- Lucian of Samosata, *How to Write History,* in vol. 6 of the Loeb Classical Library edition of Lucian's works (trans. K. Kilburn; London: W. Heinemann; Cambridge Mass.: Harvard University Press, 1959).

Classic introductions to ancient historiography are:

- J. B. Bury, *The Ancient Greek Historians* (New York: Dover, 1958 [1909]).

- Arnold J. Toynbee, *Greek Historical Thought: From Homer to the Age of Heraclitus* (New York: New American Library, 1952).

Toynbee includes numerous prefaces for comparison.

On the relationship between Josephus and Luke–Acts as apologetic histories, see:

- Gregory E. Sterling, *Historiography and Self-Definition: Josephos, Luke–Acts and Apologetic Historiography* (Leiden; New York: Brill, 1992).

A more recent study of the preface is:

- Donald Earl, "Prologue-Form in Ancient Historiography," *ANRW* (Berlin–New York: W. de Gruyter, 1972), vol. 1, 2, 842–56.

Among the current general introductions, note especially:

- Michael Grant, *The Ancient Historians* (London: George Weidenfeld & Nicolson, 1970).

- Charles W. Fornara, *The Nature of History in Ancient Greece and Rome* (Berkeley: University of California, 1983).

The relationship between Josephus and Luke–Acts has not been much discussed in recent English-language scholarship. A monumental discussion of both works, in terms of ancient literary conventions, with attention to prologues, speeches, and numerous other features, can be found in:

- Frederick J. Foakes Jackson, Kirsopp Lake, and Henry J. Cadbury, *The Beginnings of Christianity* (5 vols.; London: Macmillan, 1922).

For a current summary of Luke–Acts within its literary context, one can hardly improve upon the concise presentation and carefully selected bibliography in:

- David E. Aune, *The New Testament in its Literary Environment* (Philadelphia: Westminster, 1987), 77–157.

Almost any commentary on Acts discusses the parallels with Josephus. For two quite different perspectives, see the commentaries by:

- Ernst Haenchen, *The Acts of the Apostles: A Commentary* (Philadelphia: Westminster, 1971).

- F. F. Bruce, *The Acts of the Apostles. The Greek Text with Introduction and Commentary* (Grand Rapids: Eerdmans, 1951).

Since we do not have a recent study in English of the specific parallels between Josephus and Luke–Acts, special mention should be made of an important German article:

- Heinz Schreckenberg, "Flavius Josephus und die lukanischen Schriften," in *Wort in der Zeit: Neutestamentliche Studien. Festgabe für Karl Heinrich Rengstorf zum 75. Geburtstag* (ed. W. Haubeck and M. Bachmann; Leiden: E. J. Brill, 1980), 179–209.

NOTES

1. Max Krenkel, *Josephus und Lukas* (Leipzig: H. Haessel, 1894); J. E. Belser, "Lukas und Josephus," *ThQ* 77 (1895), 634–62. Cited with full discussion by H. Schreckenberg (see his article listed in "For Further Reading").

2. As a historical era, the "Hellenistic period" ended in 31/30 BC, with the end of Egyptian autonomy under Cleopatra, and thus the collapse of the last kingdom remaining from Alexander the Great's

conquest. In literary terms, however, the "Hellenistic" style of writing continued for several centuries.

3. This is clear from the fact that the earliest Roman writers on Christianity, from AD 110 to 120, either have to find out for themselves what Christians believe (Pliny the Younger) or explain basic Christian beliefs to their readers (Tacitus).

4. There is a famous story in Dio Cassius about the emperor Domitian's punishment (90s of the first century) of his own relatives—a high-ranking official and his wife—for their "atheism, a charge under which many were condemned who had drifted into Jewish practices" (in Whittaker, *Jews and Christians*, 90). Since the woman involved was later remembered by Christians from the fourth century as a convert to Christianity, many scholars have thought that Dio confused Judaism and Christianity in this case. This now seems unlikely, but it remains plausible that some aristocrats were actively interested in Christianity at the time.

5. On speeches in Greco-Roman historiography, see most conveniently David E. Aune, *The New Testament in its Literary Environment* (Philadelphia: Westminster, 1987), 91–93, and bibliography on 113–14.

6. The summary in this paragraph is partly adapted from Eduard Schweizer, "Concerning the Speeches in Acts," in *Studies in Luke–Acts* (ed. Leander E. Keck and J. Louis Martyn; Philadelphia: Fortress, 1980), 208–16.

7. Note especially the use of Ps 16:10 in Acts 2:27; 13:35. Both Peter and Paul understand the line "Thou wilt not let thy holy one see corruption" as a proof text for Jesus' resurrection, identifying Jesus as the "holy one." But the designation of Jesus as the holy one or child of God is part of Acts' special vocabulary (cf. 3:14; 4:27, 30). So the interpretation of this verse by Peter and Paul fits with the author's own perspective.

8. Almost entirely absent from Paul's speeches in Acts are his distinctive themes, especially being "in Christ," dying and rising with Christ, Paul's sharp distinction between this present evil age and the one about to break in with the return of Jesus, or his flesh/spirit dichotomy. Only in 13:38–39 do references to "freedom from the law of Moses" and righteousness through faith in Christ approach one of Paul's major themes. This parallel reflects the author's effort to make each of his speeches fit the speaker and situation.

9. Col 1:14 does have a similar phrase, but many scholars doubt that Paul wrote Colossians. In any case, the phrase in Greek there is not exactly the same as the one used in Luke–Acts, which has no definite article. On the question of Colossians, see Steve Mason and Tom Robinson, *An Early Christian Reader* (Toronto: Canadian Scholars Press, 1990), 364–66.

10. See Robert L. Wilken, *The Christians as the Romans Saw Them* (New Haven: Yale University Press, 1984).

11. This phrase is from Tacitus, *Histories* 5.5. He uses it to distinguish between those customs of the Jews that are merely quaint,

but deserve respect on account of their age (sabbath rest and food laws), from those that are "evil and disgusting" (misanthropy, lust, circumcision, and mean-spirited behavior).

12. That is, the disciples are said to go up to the temple "at the hour of prayer, the ninth hour." This was the time of the daily afternoon sacrifice.

13. In particular, Celsus (second century) and Porphyry (third century). See Wilken, *Christians*, 94–163.

14. See Richard A. Horsley with John S. Hanson, *Bandits, Prophets, and Messiahs: Popular Movements at the Time of Jesus* (San Francisco: Harper & Row, 1985), xi–xxviii.

15. Recitation by the author was the common mode of publishing a new work.

16. See John S. Kloppenborg, "*Exitus clari viri:* The Death of Jesus in Luke," in *Scriptures and Cultural Conversations: Essays for Heinz Guenther at Sixty-Five, Toronto Journal of Theology* 8/1 (1992), forthcoming.

Conclusion: The Significance of Josephus for New Testament Study

I wrote this book in order to introduce the NT reader to the most significant non-biblical writer for NT interpretation. Although Josephus' name is widely known, his writings seem bewildering and impenetrable on a first approach. My goal therefore was to sketch out a map of this territory, to indicate some highlights and features "not to be missed." If successful, this tour guide will have left more questions than answers, along with a desire to explore the territory for oneself. As the reader probes more deeply, even the information offered here may seem not to be "information" at all, but only my faulty interpretation of the data. Some may ultimately decide that Josephus had no sincere interest in defending his nation, that John the Baptist consciously declared Jesus to be Messiah, or that Luke could not possibly have known Josephus' writings. I am willing to take that risk. All history is, at bottom, someone's formulation of the past. It usually happens that we find the first maps offered to us defective: as we experience the territory in question, we see things that were not on the map and routes that are no longer open. But none of this diminishes the need for a map in the first place.

Before summarizing the results and implications of this book, it may be helpful to recall what we did not set out to do. This study was not intended to be an exhaustive analysis of the relationship between Josephus and the NT. The areas that were not discussed far outnumber those that were. We said almost nothing, for example, about the versions of the Bible used by

Josephus, about Josephus on the historical geography of Palestine, the temple and its service, the economic and social conditions of Jerusalem, Galilean history and geography, the Samaritans, the Jewish communities of the diaspora, or about numerous other topics that are pertinent to the study of the NT. The fact is that virtually every line of Josephus' copious work is relevant in some way or other to NT interpretation. We have merely sighted and described the proverbial tip of the iceberg.

Our procedure has been straightforward. We have looked first at Josephus on his own terms (chapters 1–3). That phrase, "on his own terms," is admittedly deceptive, because we do not have immediate or objective access to his life; we can only *interpret* what he has left behind. Nevertheless, we can resolve to avoid some of the most obvious errors of the past. We can at least make it our goal to understand him *in his world*, recognizing that he did not write some kind of "fact book" from which we can cut and paste, and that he did not intend to be a witness to the truth of Christianity. He was a man of at least moderate intelligence who wrote because he had important stories to tell. So our questions were: Who was this man? What did he do? and, What are his writings about?

Pursuing these questions, we found an apparently sharp conflict between his personal biography and his major writings. His biography, on the one hand, especially the period from his assumption of "command" in the Galilee to his surrender to the Romans, is filled with contradictions and unanswered questions. It seems clear that he has a great deal to hide. Moreover, the rest of his life story is told in such thoroughly rhetorical terms that we can learn little about it. His major writings, on the other hand, are bold attempts to defend and even commend Jewish culture in the Greco-Roman world. In the face of anti-Jewish government policies, widespread popular resentment, and violence after the failed Judean revolt, he goes to incredible lengths to argue that Jews are typically cooperative with those in power (*War*), that they have an ancient and respectable history, and that their influence on the world is thoroughly beneficial (*Antiquities, Against Apion*).

Although we might wish to make a final decision about Josephus' character, on the basis of his career, I have argued that several factors prevent us from doing that responsibly. (a) Any account of his personal life must be hypothetically reconstructed, and no reconstruction has yet won widespread acceptance. By contrast, we know what he wrote in defense of Judaism. (b) He seems deliberately to play up his own duplicity and deviousness, for rhetorical effect. (c) Like any political figure, especially an aristocrat involved in a war in the Middle East, Josephus must have had all sorts of genuinely divided loyalties; we cannot assume that he always had a clear direction of any sort. And (d) even if he did fail morally, people cannot be so easily separated into the good and the bad. If we removed all moral failures from the ranks of the great, those ranks would be sorely depleted.

Armed with some initial awareness of (my interpretation of) Josephus' life and writings, we proceeded to consider his direct relevance for the study of the NT. We looked first at his accounts of some key figures in the background of the NT—the family of King Herod, the Roman governors of Judea, the high priesthood, and the religious groups in Palestine. In each case, our goal was to understand these groups as they function in Josephus' own narratives. What this showed was that everyone who recounts the past necessarily interprets it. This means that the historical questions "What really happened? What were these people *really* like?" so far remain largely unanswered. To answer them would require further investigation, which would develop hypotheses to explain the accounts in Josephus and the NT as well as other written sources and, in some cases, archaeological evidence. Our goal was much more limited, namely, to understand how an important author of the period integrated these figures of interest to the NT reader into his writings, which are quite different in outlook from the NT texts.

Chapter 5 examined what Josephus has to say about figures from the Christian tradition. He mentions only three—John the Baptist, Jesus, and James—and these very briefly. In the case of John the Baptist, Josephus provides a crucial perspective from outside the NT. In that single case, I made bold to proceed to a historical hypothesis about the real Baptist, to illustrate how Josephus' accounts might be used in historical reconstruction. But that exercise also highlighted the degree to which Josephus, as much as any other writer, interprets the past and does not simply report it. His account of Jesus is filled with textual problems, and the investigation of those was a welcome reminder of the distance between ancient texts and our modern English translations. Finally, his note about the death of Jesus' brother James, in spite of its brevity, provided a valuable supplement to the NT's few references to this crucial but little-known figure.

It seemed advisable to devote a separate chapter (6) to the relationship between Josephus and Luke–Acts. Regardless of how one settles this famous problem, the parallels of genre between the two works illuminate the interpretation of Luke–Acts. We see here a two-volume history written according to current conventions, which shares with Josephus' works the goal of explaining and defending what seemed troublesome to many in the Roman world. But it seems that we can go further. Close inspection of the many affinities between Josephus and Luke–Acts indicates that Luke probably knew the writings of his famous Jewish contemporary. He appears to build his case for Christianity squarely on the foundation of Josephus' case for Judaism. If he is not doing so, the coincidences are remarkable.

What, then, is the significance of Josephus for NT interpretation? On the one hand, a few particular points emerge from this study. (a) Josephus wrote to defend Judaism against the Roman suspicion that this antisocial superstition had finally proven impotent in the face of Rome's Fortune. (b) Therefore, although Josephus is the most valuable non-biblical source for understanding the NT, his outlook was fundamentally at odds with that of Paul and most other NT writers, who believed that Judaism per se had been made obsolete with the coming of Christ. (c) His aim was ignored by later Christians, who used him as a witness against Judaism. (d) To understand any given passage in Josephus, one must recognize that it is part of a larger story, and attempt to understand the passage within the terms of that story. The NT reader in particular must resist the temptation to assimilate Josephus too quickly to the NT environment. (e) Nevertheless, since he often includes significant accounts of people, places, and events that intersect with the NT world, his portrayal offers us an invaluable "outside" perspective.

On the other hand, our analysis of Josephus and the NT has direct implications for the relationship between faith and history: What role can history play in Christian (or other) faith? History is commonly seen as a given, as a set of known events written down somewhere. With this view in mind, many NT readers have professed an interest in "the history of the period," by which they have meant the background of the NT, the manners and customs of first-century Jews, the religious, social, political, and economic world in which Christianity was born. The NT stood by itself as a serene island of divine revelation, while "history" swirled around it.

But we have seen that such history, comprising pure facts about the past, does not exist anywhere. By definition, the past—Vespasian's campaign against the Jews, the career of Josephus in Galilee, or the aims of John the Baptist—no longer exists. So it is not immediately accessible to us. We have only traces of the past: occasional physical remnants, like a piece of pottery or papyrus, and literary interpretations of certain periods by people like Thucydides, Josephus, and "Luke." And these people did not write about their times merely to generate chronicles of facts; they carefully selected episodes that would help them make their points. Their accounts are thoroughly conditioned by: (a) the limited information available to them; (b) their assumptions and values; (c) their habits of thought and speech; and (d) their conscious literary purposes. Indeed these same factors affect our evening news. It is also a product of someone's conscious and unconscious perspective—decisions about what *is* news, limitations of camera angles, choice of how much context to supply, commentators' choice of vocabulary. If perspective is unavoidable even where we have video cameras and satellite relays, how much more does it figure in any text from the Greco-Roman world?

History, therefore, is not simply a matter of reading whatever portrayals of the past happened to survive. It is a much more active enterprise, requiring the interpreter to try to re-create the past. Such a re-creation can only be hypothetical: the historian sets out to develop the hypothesis that will best explain all of the available evidence. Strictly speaking, then, there are no "historical facts," but only hypotheses that range from highly probable to scarcely conceivable. We have one portrait of John the Baptist in Mark, another in Josephus, another in John, and perhaps another in Q. Which one does the historian "accept"? He or she appreciates all of them, but must then go on to develop a hypothesis that will explain all of them. This activity produces still another interpretation, but one that will be more plausible because it explains more of the surviving evidence. So the historian is a detective who listens carefully to each surviving witness, but then proceeds to create a new and independent hypothesis on a given question.

Once we read Josephus historically, we are compelled to read the NT, written by his contemporaries, in the same way. When we become sensitive to his perspectives, we want to know those of the NT authors. When we see how the census under Quirinius functions in his narrative, we want to know how it serves Luke's story. When we see how he chooses Pontius Pilate to mark a shift toward unbearable and incompetent Roman rule in Judea, we become more aware of the Gospel writers' perspectives. Similarly, his discussions of the Pharisees and Sadducees, the high priesthood, or any other element of Jewish culture, force us to ask how the NT writers present them. This heightened sensitivity to the NT writers' perspectives enriches our reading of the NT.

Index of Subjects

NB: References to the notes are given according to the page on which the note number appears (in the body of the text). The notes themselves appear at the end of each chapter.

Index of Ancient Sources

246 JOSEPHUS AND THE NEW TESTAMENT